C Pointers and Dynamic Memory Management

Computer Books from QED

Systems Development

The Complete Guide to Software Testing
Developing Client/Server Applications
Quality Assurance for Information Systems
User-Interface Screen Design
On Time, Within Budget: Software Project Management
    Practices and Techniques
Managing Software Projects: Selecting and Using PC-
    Based Project Management Systems
From Mainframe to Workstations: Offloading Application
    Development
A Structured Approach to Systems Testing
Rapid Application Prototyping: The Storyboard Approach
    to User Requirements Analysis
Software Engineering with Formal Metrics
Testing Client/Server Applications
Making Software Measurement Work: Building an
    Effective Measurement Program

Information Engineering/CASE

Practical Model Management Using CASE Tools
Building the Data Warehouse
Information Systems Architecture:
    Development in the 90's
Enterprise Architecture Planning: Developing a Blueprint
    for Data, Applications, and Technology
Data Architecture: The Information Paradigm

IBM Systems Software

REXX in the TSO Environment
REXX Tools and Techniques
The MVS Primer
Cross System Product Application Development
TSO/E CLISTS: The Complete Tutorial and Reference
    Guide
MVS/JCL: Mastering Job Control Language
MVS/VSAM for the Application Programmer
Introduction to Cross System Product
CICS: A How-To for COBOL Programmers
CICS: A Guide to Performance Tuning
CICS Application and System Programming:
    Tools and Techniques
CICS: A Guide to Application Debugging

OS/2

Thinking Person's Guide to Using OS/2 2.1
OS/2 Presentation Manager Programming for COBOL
    Programmers
OS/2 C Programming

Programming – Micro Focus

Micro Focus COBOL Workbench for the Application
    Developer
Micro Focus CICS Option 3.0

Programming – C

Learn C and Save Your Job: C Language for COBOL
    Programmers
C Pointers and Dynamic Memory Management
Developing Portable System Call Libraries Using C

AS/400

AS/400: A Practical Guide for Programming
    and Operations
AS/400 Architecture and Applications:
    The Database Machine

UNIX

UNIX C Shell Desk Reference
The UNIX Industry and Open Systems in Transition

Management and Operations

Total Quality Management in Information Services
The Disaster Recovery Plan
Controlling the Future: Managing
    Technology-Driven Change
How to Automate Your Computer Center
Mind Your Business: Managing the Impact of
    End-User Computing
Understanding Data Pattern Processing: The
    Key to Competitive Advantage
The Software Factory: Managing Software
    Development and Maintenance
Ethical Conflicts in Information and Computer
    Sciences, Technology, and Business
Strategic and Operational Planning for Information
    Services
Object Technology and Distributed Computing

VAX/VMS

Rdb/VMS: Developing the Data Warehouse
Network Programming Under DECNet
    Phases IV and V
VAX/VMS: Mastering DCL Commands and Utilities

Database

Client/Server and Distributed Database Design
Third-Wave Processing: Database Machines and
    Decision Support Systems
Database Management Systems: Understanding
    and Applying Database Technology

Database — DB2

QMF: How to Use Query Management Facility
    with DB2 and SQL/DS
SQL for DB2 and SQL/DS Application Developers
DB2: the Complete Guide to Implementation
    and Use
Embedded SQL for DB2: Application Design and
    Development
DB2: Maximizing Performance in Online
    Production Systems

C Pointers and Dynamic Memory Management

Michael C. Daconta

QED Publishing Group
Boston • London • Toronto

This book is available at a special discount when you order multiple copies. For information, contact QED Publishing Group, POB 812070, Wellesley, MA 02181-0013 or phone 617-237-5656.

© 1993 QED Publishing Group
P.O. Box 812070
Wellesley, MA 02181-0013

QED Publishing Group is a division of QED Information Sciences, Inc.

Library of Congress Catalog Number: 0-89435-473-6
International Standard Book Number: 93-25628

Printed in the United States of America
93 94 95 10 9 8 7 6 5 4 3 2 1

Library of Congress Cataloging-In-Publication Data

Daconta, Michael C.
    C pointers and dynamic memory management / Michael C.
    Daconta.
        p.   cm.
    includes index.
    ISBN 0-89435-473-6
    1. C (Computer program language)   2. Memory
management (Computer science)   I. Title.
QA76.73.C15D33   1993
005.13'3—dc20   93-25628
                                                         CIP

Contents

List of Illustrations

List of Tables

List of Source Codes

Note: Due to typographical restrictions, a few lines of source code in the book have been broken where they would normally continue on the same line. These have been marked with a black bar in the margin.

Foreword

Pointers are probably the most difficult aspect of the C language for programmers to understand and use. While training C and C++ programmers, and in my columns for the C User Journal, the most frequently asked questions concern pointers. Manipulating addresses of variables and functions gives C functionality that is either inherent or infeasible in other languages.

Programmers in many other high-level languages do not have to deal with pointers as much as C programmers do. Subprogram parameters are usually passed using "call by reference", so that the address passing is implicit. In PASCAL, call by reference is provided as a keyword. In C, you must deal with pointers to obtain the same feature.

However, many of these same languages do not permit allocating dynamic memory, which is storage not needed during the entire execution of a program. Nor do they permit using addresses of functions to create device drivers, or allow using a pointer to access array elements for faster code than using an index.

All these uses can create the potential for erroneous code, as well as possible programmer confusion. In this book, Michael Daconta has covered pointers in a number of different ways to help prevent both these possibilities. For the novice programmer, he has pictures of memory to show how pointers work. For the intermediate programmer, he shows standard data structures, such as stacks, constructed with pointers. For the advanced programmer, he offers an elaborate C language parser. For all, he offers the solutions to several common pointer traps.

Data pointers, pointers to pointers, and function pointers are all covered in detail with numerous programming examples. To lighten the subject, he introduces dialog between himself and the reader. His sense of humor enhances this book's readability and decreases the anxiety of learning and using pointers.

As I like to point out to students, pointers are like fire. If you don't know what you are doing with them, you are going to get burned. After reading this book, you may avoid the heat.

Kenneth Pugh
Durham, NC
Compuserve 70125, 1142
kpugh@allen.com

Preface

"What is confusing, though, is when a single system admits of two or more descriptions on different levels which nevertheless resemble each other in some way. Then we find it hard to avoid mixing levels when we think about the system, and can easily get totally lost."—*Godel, Escher, Bach: An Eternal Golden Braid*, Douglas Hofstadter

This book fills a gap not filled by the current scores of programming books on the market. I've read a lot of those programming manuals, and because they cover the whole C language, they only give a cursory treatment of pointers. They leave the hard experimentation to the dedicated programmer. That is dangerous because many beginning and intermediate programmers do not have hours to spend experimenting with pointers. They have to get those programs to work now, and if that means doing it without pointers, then they will use an inefficient and ugly method just to get the program to compile! I am dedicating this book to all those programmers on Prodigy® whose many pointer questions convinced me there was a gap to be filled. I hope that I am worthy of the task.

This book has been structured and written with many different programmers (of varying experience) in mind. Different people absorb information in different ways. This book provides three avenues of learning and experimentation:

1. **Concepts**—Explain the concepts of Pointers and Dynamic Memory Management in detail.

2. **Code Reviews**—Walk through working code examples (also use a "Paper Computer" to illustrate code execution).
3. **Libraries**—Provide generic code libraries to protect and enhance your own applications.

Note: Due to typographical restrictions, a few lines of source code in the book have been broken where they would normally continue on the same line. These have been marked with a black bar in the margin.

Acknowledgments

Thank you, Lynne, my wife, for struggling through this with me. Day by day. Page by page.

Thank you, Ed Kerr, president of QED Publishing Group, for helping me through my first book with patience and wise counsel.

Thank you, Everett Nelson, my friend, for proofing this, printing drafts, and always being there.

Thank you, my other friends and co-workers at Mystech Associates, Inc., who reviewed pieces of the manuscript.

Thank you, computer friends on Prodigy, Compuserve, and AppleLink for you inspiration and assistance.

Introduction

If you cringed when you saw the title of this book, this book is for you! So many programmers are downright petrified of pointers that any mention of them will send novice programmers diving beneath their desks and grabbing for crosses! BACK! BACK, I SAY! Some programmers use pointers only when they are backed into a corner and forced to dig out their data structure textbooks. If you are one of those people, let me show you how simple pointers really are so you can unlock their power and take on challenging programming tasks! If you are already familiar with pointers, this book will hone your skills to the point of mastery! If you already use pointers, let me show you advanced techniques on pointer manipulation and memory management!

Why should I learn pointers? Pointers are a defining issue in the growth of a programmer. Until you vault the "pointer obstacle" you cannot move forward and grow further in your programming skills. Pointers are a defining issue because they are the keys to real data manipulation within a computer. Most advanced applications use data structures involving pointers. Pointers allow you to store data in an infinite variety of ways. The C language provides open access (and an open challenge) to the full scope and breadth of pointers. This book will guide you through each step of the way to vault the "pointer obstacle."

Why should I learn pointers through C? Why not learn Pascal pointers? Most languages protect both programs and programmers from the dangers of pointer errors by tightly controlling manipulation of pointers and by hiding operations only accomplished through pointers. On the other hand, C both encourages and sometimes forces programmers to pass and manipulate data through pointers! If you want to retrieve arguments from the command line, you must use pointers. If you want to pass an argument into a function and have that function change its value, you must pass a pointer to the variable. If you want to pass a variable number of arguments to a function, you must use pointers. The bottom line is that to program effectively in C you must love pointers!

Love pointers? Not in the romantic sense, but pointers have to thrill you! You should get excited when you see

```
char **dynamic_string_array;
dynamic_string_array = (char **) malloc(sizeof(char *) * 10);
```

Don't be afraid of the symbols! Get used to (**) and (&) and (->) and even (array[*myvar]->yourvar)! After a few practice exercises in the following chapters you will see that those symbols are just funny shapes for (hammer) and (saw) and (screwdriver)—just funny symbols for programming tools! In the chapters ahead you will learn hundreds of reasons why pointers are the fastest and most efficient method of manipulating data!

What do I already need to know to understand this book? The only prerequisite for this book is a basic understanding of the C programming language. If you know how to write and compile simple C programs, then you can benefit from this book. Most everything else is explained in detail.

Source Code, Platforms and Compilers:

The over 150 source code functions in the book were developed on a Macintosh running THINK C. All the source has been ported and tested on an Intel 386 running Turbo C. All major pieces of code and the code libraries have been ported to SUN (UNIX) with the GCC compiler and also to a DEC VAX 3800 (VMS) with the DEC C compiler.

The Turbo C compiler had minor warnings that can be ignored. Filenames had to be truncated or changed when copying to DOS. The source disk provided is a DOS-formatted disk.

Questions and Comments:

This book is being written *by* a programmer *for* programmers. All comments, suggestions, questions, and advice from the entire computing community are greatly appreciated. My goal is to produce the best book possible, and therefore I am always willing to improve on my work. I can be reached on Prodigy (JFXV08A), Compu Serve (71664, 523), or you can write to

Michael Daconta
c/o QED Group Publishing
P.O. Box 812070
Wellesley, Massachusetts 02181-0013

An Intuitive Approach

**OBJECTIVE: An intuitive understanding of pointers through
an analogy to storage containers.**

A pointer can be defined as a *memory location* that stores the *address* of
another memory location; however, this definition is dependent upon
the reader knowing the meaning of memory location and address. Let's
first get an intuitive picture:

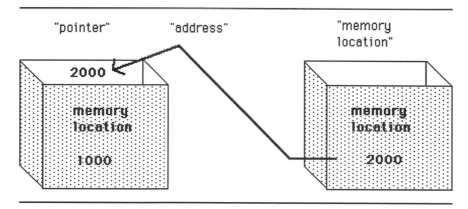

Figure 1.1.   A pointer as a container.

Visualization is a good method to remember concepts. That is just what we need with pointers—a good mental image of what is going on inside the computer! A simple way to visualize a memory location is as a container, and therefore a computer's entire memory would be a long row of containers. A container is a good analogy for a memory location because they both can *store things*. Each container has a unique number on it so that the computer can access any container in the same amount of time. This is why computer memory is called Random Access Memory, or RAM. The CPU can access all memory locations in the same amount of time by putting the address of the desired memory location on the address bus. Remember, the address is that unique number that identifies each piece of memory. Each memory location is numbered sequentially starting from 0. Another common analogy for computer memory is rows of houses. A house can store things, and you locate a specific house by its address.

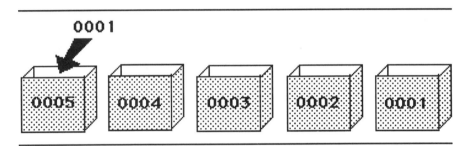

Figure 1.2.   Memory as a row of containers.

Continuing with our container analogy, another definition of a pointer would be a container that stores the unique number of another container! So, here we have nontechnical (but functional) definitions for memory location, address, and pointer:

Memory location—a container that can store a binary number.

Address—a unique binary number assigned to every memory location. The size of the addressable space depends on the number of data lines in the address bus.

Pointer—a memory location that stores an address.

The above intuitive explanation of pointers answers the question "What is a pointer?" but does NOT answer "How does a memory location store a binary number?" or "How can a computer use an address to access a memory location?" The answers to these questions are good for general knowledge but not critical to our discussions of pointers. The interested reader will find the two questions answered in Appendix A.

Let's look at a practical example of code that demonstrates our general concept:

```
/* pointer_intro.c */
#include <stdio.h>
#include <stdlib.h>
main()
{
  /* declare a pointer variable to hold an address of
  an integer. Do not worry about understanding the
  exact syntax, we will cover this in more detail in
  chapter 3. */
   int *integer_pointer;

  /* declare an integer variable. This is a container
  that holds an integer. */
  int myint;

  /* assign an integer to the variable "my_int" */
  myint = 10;

  /* print out the address of the integer. This is the
  unique memory location where the integer is stored. */
  printf("the address of myint is %p.\n",&myint);

  /* Remember that a pointer can store the address of
  another container. This means that we can put the
  address of the integer myint into out integer
  pointer. */
   integer_pointer = &myint;

  printf("the integer_pointer holds the address
  %p.\n",integer_pointer);
}
```

Source 1.1.   pointer_intro.c.

Here is a run of the above program:

```
the address of myint is 003E200E.
the integer_pointer holds the address 003E200E.
```

CHAPTER QUESTIONS

1. Why is a container a good analogy for a memory location?
2. Why is it necessary for each container to have a unique number on it?

2

Globals, the Stack, and Heap Space

OBJECTIVE: An understanding of the three different memory storage areas accessible to C programs with emphasis on the role of the stack. Also introduce the more accurate notion of "parameter copying."

There are three memory spaces the application programmer needs to be familiar with: application global space, the stack, and heap space. Although different microcomputers organize their memory in different ways, most are similar. Here is the organization of a typical personal computer's memory:

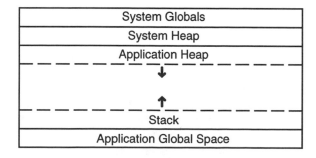

Figure 2.1.   A microcomputer's memory.

2.1. GLOBALS

Application global space is where all global variables are stored. These variables will be stored for the entire runtime of your program. The storage for global variables is allocated at compile time. In C programs, you store variables in global space by declaring them outside of any function.

```
/* globals.c */
#include <stdio.h>
#include <stdlib.h>

/* the next two variables will be stored in the global
application space. Any function within the file may
read or write to these variables. */
int global_int;
char global_char;

main()
{
  int local_int;
  printf("this program does nothing except show the ");
  printf(" declaration of global and local
  variables\n");
}
```

Source 2.1. globals.c.

2.2. THE STACK

The stack is critical to understanding argument passing between functions (especially in a mixed-language environment); however, most beginning programmers are usually only told that the stack is a place where function calls are pushed and popped during recursion (*recursion* is when a function calls itself until it hits an end condition). The stack stores all function calls, function arguments, function variables, and the state of the processor registers. Let's first examine what a stack data structure is and then discuss how the compiler uses this data structure.

The classic example to describe a stack is the spring-loaded dish bin in a cafeteria line.

A Classic STACK (of dishes)

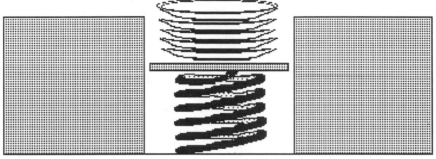

Figure 2.2.   A classic stack.

In the dish stack example, the dishwasher would be busily putting (pushing) plates onto the top of the dish stack while kids in the cafeteria line would be taking (popping) dishes off the top of the stack. As a data storage structure you can see how the stack is useful in keeping track of the order of stored items. The most recent items pushed on the stack are the first to be popped off, which is why it is a "Last In First Out" (LIFO) structure.

Top of Stack ⟶

newest item
2nd
3rd
4th
5th
oldest item

Figure 2.3.   Stack as a LIFO structure.

You can create a stack data structure in your application program to store data; but more important is the fact that the compiler uses a system stack to run your application program. All modern computers include a stack pointer as well as assembly language instructions to push and pop from the stack. So even though you may not use a stack in your application program, the compiler *is using a stack* to run your program.

2.3.   THE COMPILER AND THE APPLICATION STACK

The compiler uses the application stack for two purposes:

1. passing arguments
2. storing call frames (also called stack frames) and local variables

Good program design calls for tight, modular code. Modular code involves breaking down each function or task of an application into one simple *module* (in C a module is called a function). Each function of an application usually processes data input and produces data outputs. The input data to a function is called the function *parameters*. Introductory programming courses describe function parameters as being *passed into the function by the calling program*. This is absolutely not true, and in fact I believe that this line of thinking is dangerous because beginning programmers get the impression that the calling function's variables are actually being passed to the called function! This is not the case at all! What really happens in C is that the values entered into the function call are *copied* onto the stack! Then execution jumps to the called procedure, which refers to the parameter values as offset locations from the stack pointer (some computers store an argument pointer to the start of the functions arguments) !

There are two specific reasons why the notion of "passing arguments" is erroneous and confusing to beginning programmers:

1. The term "passing" gives a false impression that variables in one function are physically transferred into a second function. This follows from just using the term "passing." If I pass you a ball, I throw the ball to you, and I am left without a ball. There is only one ball! If we carry this analogy over to programming, if one function passes some of its variables to another function, the first function should no longer have those variables. This is obviously not what is going on inside the computer.

2. The notion of "passing arguments" supports an abstraction not used in the C language. The abstraction that "passing arguments" supports is that of representing a function as a black box. Here is an example of how many introductory programming courses discuss functions:

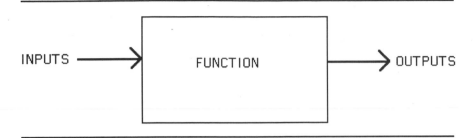

Figure 2.4.   Function as a black box.

In this high-level concept the definition of a function is a set of instructions that process inputs to produce outputs. This abstraction is useful in its similarity to a factory that makes it intuitive to grasp. This is why languages like Pascal and Fortran support this black box paradigm; however, the C language is more interested in assembly language power than ease of instruction! This is a great credit to the C language that it keeps us closer to the machine by design. Now we begin to understand students' confusion with passing addresses to a function (this will be discussed in the next section): they have been taught the black box analogy of functions and are now faced with a programming language that tears aside the abstraction and brings them right to the machine. Therefore, to understand pointers we need to lose the black box abstraction and understand copying arguments to the stack!

Let's examine function arguments being copied to the stack:

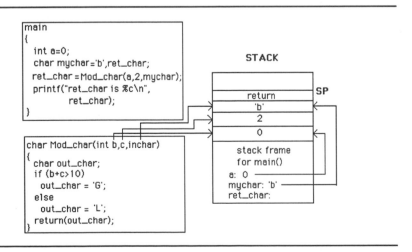

Figure 2.5.   Parameter copying.

Let's trace how the compiler executes the call to *Mod_char(a,2,mychar)*. Before jumping to the starting address of the function, the arguments must be copied onto the stack. C compilers always push the last argument on the stack first and the first argument last. This convention is used to allow a variable number of parameters to be passed (copied) to a function. This way the called procedure can always find the first parameter in a known place. After the function arguments are pushed onto the stack and execution jumps to the new function, the first job of the new function is to build its stack frame on the stack. The stack frame contains state information needed by the return instruction to restore the registers, clean up the stack, and return control. Essentially, the stack frame is simply all the data needed for the CPU to continue execution in the function that was "suspended" when the CPU jumped to the new function.

2.4.   THE HEAP

The heap is where all dynamic memory management is performed. By dynamic memory management, I mean the ability for an application to dynamically (during runtime) allocate and deallocate blocks of memory. (*Note*: on a machine with virtual memory the memory may not be actual physical RAM. Virtual memory is an operating system technique that allows a hard disk to be used as memory by swapping in to physical memory only data that is immediately needed for processing.).

There are two important points to keep in mind about the heap:

1. It grows toward the stack (on microcomputers): As shown in Figure 2.1, the memory map, the stack, and heap grow toward each other. Therefore you should know how much memory you have available at your application's disposal at all times (if you do not have virtual memory). All popular microcomputers will have a system function to allow you to check the amount of available memory.
2. You must manage the heap: Your application is in full control of allocation and deallocation, which means it is your responsibility to return all the memory that you use! If you do not, you may run out of dynamic memory.

CHAPTER QUESTIONS

1. When is the storage for global variables allocated?
2. What does LIFO stand for?
3. Are arguments actually passed to a function?
4. What other items besides function arguments are pushed onto the application stack?

5. Why is a heap necessary?

6. What would happen if you never returned any of the memory you allocated?

FURTHER READING

Levy, Henry M., and Richard H. Eckhouse, Jr. *Computer Programming and Architecture, The VAX-11,* © 1980, Digital Equipment Corporation.

Mak, Ronald. *Writing Compilers and Interpreters: An Applied Approach,* © 1991, John Wiley and Sons, Inc.

Tanenbaum, Andrew S. *Operating Systems: Design and Implementation,* © 1987, Prentice-Hall Inc.

Declaring, Assigning, and Dereferencing Pointers

OBJECTIVE: To learn what declaring a pointer means and how it differs from declaring a data type, how to assign values to a pointer, and finally how to "dereference" a pointer ("dereference" is a fancy word for "access the data the pointer points to").

Pointers are memory locations that store *addresses*. In fact, from this moment on, *any time I write "pointer," your mind should immediately translate it into "stores the address of."* For example, when I write

"my_ptr is a character *pointer*."

Your mind says, "Aha! You really mean:"

"my_ptr *stores the address of* a character."

A "data type" is a memory location that stores a *value* from a set of values. For example, an integer is the set of values that includes all whole numbers. The five C basic data types are character (char), integer (int), floating point (float), double floating point (double), and valueless. (Void, valueless? The need for a void data type may not be readily apparent, but it is really very useful because you can declare void pointers that allow the pointer to point to any data type. This flexibility is very valuable when you are creating generic tools. We will see this later in the generic linked list code.)

Pointers are not a data type even though you can retrieve the value a pointer variable holds in the same method that you retrieve the values in other data types like integers or characters. It is important to differentiate pointers from the basic data types (despite some of their similarities) because they clearly perform different functions. A good precedent for this differentiation is the Ada programming language that categorizes pointers as "access types." The crux of the difference between pointers and the basic data types lies in their purpose. Integer and character variables have the sole purpose of storing an integer or character value, while pointers have both the purpose of storing a pointer value (address) and the purpose of pointing to another data type (providing *access* to another object's stored data). This means that the programmer has access to both the stored address and the data type that the address "points to" (which is called dereferencing the pointer).

Let's declare some pointers:

```
/* declare.c */
/* Before we declare our header files, let me say that
when you use a lot of pointers in your programs you may
want to get into the habit of always including the
following four header files. */
#include <stdio.h> /* common input-output routines */
#include <stdlib.h> /* the dynamic memory management
routines */
#include <ctype.h> /* the isalpha, ispunct ...
character checking routines. */
#include <string.h> /* string manipulation routines */
/* on an IBM PC, use quotes " instead of <> and you
will also need malloc.h */
void main()
{
        /* first let's declare some basic data types. So
        you can compare basic data type declaration to
        pointer declaration */
        char mychar;
        int myint;

        /* now to declare a pointer, you specify the data
        type your variable will be pointing to and then
        put an asterisk (*) in front of your variable
        name */
```

Source 3.1.   declare.c.

```
        char *char_ptr;
        int *int_ptr;
        void *void_ptr;

        /* since we just wanted to learn how to declare
        pointers this program doesn't  need to do
        anything else. */
}
```

Source 3.1. *Continued.*

So the format for declaring pointers is

basic_data_type *variable_name;

For assigning values to pointers, there is only one rule you need to know:

ONLY ASSIGN ADDRESSES!

(amazing how this matches up with a pointer being synonymous with "address of"). How can you be sure that you are assigning addresses to pointers? Simple, because there are only two ways that your application program can get addresses:

1. Access an address of a global or local variable that is set aside memory space by the compiler using the address-of (&) operator.
2. Grab your own memory space with malloc, and the address of the memory space grabbed (from the heap) will be returned to you. (We will examine malloc in Chapter 13.)

Here is an example of the first method:

```
/* address_operator.c */
#include <stdio.h>
#include <stdlib.h>
#include <string.h>
#include <ctype.h>
void main()
{
        char mychar;
        int myint;
```

Source 3.2. address_operator.c.

```
char *char_ptr;
int *int_ptr;
void *void_ptr;

/* when you declare variables in a program
(pointers included) the compiler sets aside the
correct amount of memory for those variables.
Since the compiler has assigned memory locations
(and addresses) to the variables you can be sure
that declared variables have addresses. To assign
an address to a pointer variable you use an
assignment statement and the address operator
(&). */
mychar = 'm';
char_ptr = &mychar;
printf("mychar is %c.\n",mychar);
printf("the address of mychar is at %p.\n",
&mychar);
printf("char_ptr is also %p.\n",char_ptr);
printf("char_ptr points to %c.\n",*char_ptr);
}
```

Source 3.2. *Continued.*

The output of this program is

```
mychar is m
address of mychar is at 003E2009.
char_ptr is also 003E2009.
char_ptr points to m.
```

If you compile, link, and run this on your home computer, your addresses will differ based on the machine you have and the layout of your memory, but the rest of the output will be identical. You may be saying, "Hey, what did you do in the last statement of that program?"

You mean this one?
printf("char_ptr points to %c.\n",*char_ptr);
"That's the one! Did you declare another pointer called char_ptr?"

No. I dereferenced the pointer. I figured if I snuck that into the program I could easily slip into our next topic. Good tactic, huh?
"Great, laughing boy. Just start explaining."

Okay, I know it is confusing that the dereferencing operator (*) is the same as the asterisk used to declare a pointer, but I didn't write the language. Also, you will quickly learn the difference by the position of the asterisks in the program. The *asterisk in a declaration* tells the compiler to "make this a pointer variable," and the *asterisk used on the pointer variable in the body of the program* means "access what my pointer points to."

The best way to understand the dereferencing operator is to go through an example step by step and then simulate how the computer would run the program:

```
/* dereference.c */
#include <stdio.h>
#include <stdlib.h>
#include <string.h>
#include <ctype.h>
void main()
{
  int myint, yourint;
  int *int_ptr;

  /* step one: assign the value 10 to myint */
  myint = 10;

  /* step two: assign myint's address to int_ptr */
  int_ptr = &myint;

  /* step three: assign the value of myint to yourint
      by dereferencing int_ptr */
  yourint = *int_ptr;

  /* print out the results */
  printf("myint is %d.\n",myint);
  printf("yourint is %d.\n",yourint);
}
```

Source 3.3.   dereference.c.

Here's the simulation of the above program on my high-tech "paper-computer":

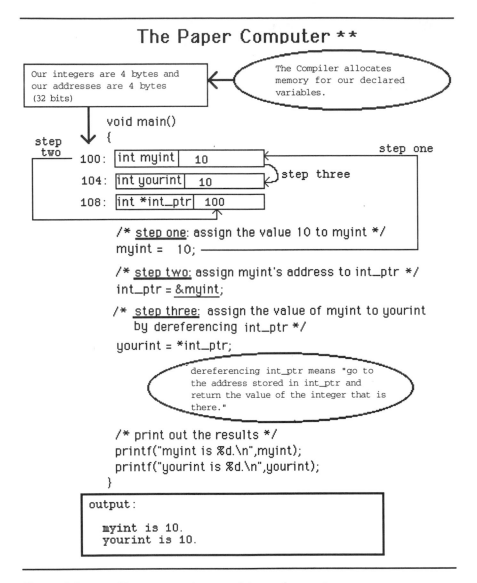

Figure 3.1. Paper computer on pointer assignment.

My paper computer clearly shows how dereferencing is just a fancy word for accessing the pointer's memory address and returning the value of the pointer's data type.

CHAPTER QUESTIONS

1. Why is it important to differentiate pointers from the basic data types?
2. What are the two methods for assigning addresses to a pointer?
3. What is dereferencing?
4. In the paper computer (Figure 3.1), why do we need to know how many bytes an integer is?

CHAPTER EXERCISES

1. Assign the integer value of mychar into myint using char_ptr.
2. Write a simpler way to assign myint to yourint in source 3.3.

FURTHER READING

Kernighan, Brian W., and Dennis M. Ritchie. *The C Programming Language,* © 1988, Prentice Hall Software Series.

Pass by Value versus Pass by Reference

OBJECTIVE: Learn the real meaning and utility of the techniques "pass by value" and "pass by reference." Understand the lvalue and rvalue of a variable. Examine in detail the process of passing arguments to functions using a paper computer.

Although I strongly disagree with using the words "pass" or "passing" to describe copying function arguments to the stack, the current computer literature often uses these terms. Since you are going to run into these terms in those manuals, we need to cover what they really mean. Also, you will learn how pass by reference is the method you use to have a function modify the contents of the calling function's variables.

A variable is a named memory location that can store a value of a certain data type. Also, since different variables are stored in different memory locations, there are actually two different types of values for each variable:

1. The variable's address in memory is called its lvalue.
2. The variable's content is called its rvalue.

The best way to understand this is again through our container analogy. The container's number (or address) is the lvalue, while the contents of the container (a binary number) is the rvalue.

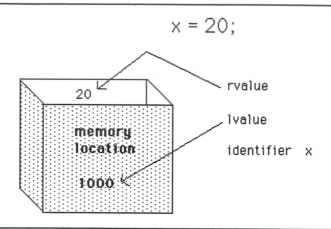

Figure 4.1.   lvalue and rvalue of a variable

Knowing the two different parts of a variable makes it simple to understand pass by value and pass by reference. Pass by value means copy the value of the function argument to the stack. If the function argument is a variable, it means to copy the rvalue to the function stack.

■   *Rule for default argument passing in C:* By default all argument-passing (copying) in C is pass by value.

Let's look at an example:

```
/* stack_copy.c */
#include <stdio.h>
#include <stdlib.h>
#include <ctype.h>
#include <string.h>

int add(int a, int b)
{
        int c;
        c = a + b;
        return(c);
}
```

Source 4.1.   stack_copy.c.

```
void main()
{
        int cc, aa;
        aa = 20;
        cc = add(aa,80);
        printf("cc is %d.\n",cc);
}
```

Source 4.1.   *Continued.*

What do you think gets copied to the stack for the add function? If you said the values 20 and 80, you are correct!

The output of the program would be

cc is 100.

If pass by value passes (copies) the rvalue to the stack, then it is evident that pass by reference copies the lvalue (address) to the stack.

"What good is that?"

Passing the address of a variable is the only way to have a function modify the contents (rvalue) of the variable.

If you studied Pascal in school, you were taught that there are two different types of parameters, a value-parameter and a variable parameter. The value parameter was explained as a self-initializing local variable (by self-initializing they mean it takes the value of the argument in the procedure call). The variable parameter was described as an alias for a global variable that allows you to change the contents of that global variable inside a procedure. In Pascal, you specify between the two different variables by placing the *var* keyword in front of variable parameters. Do you see the charade that is going on here? A Pascal value-parameter simply means that the argument rvalue is copied to the stack and the Pascal variable-parameter means that the lvalue is being copied to the stack! Essentially, the Pascal language is disguising what is really going on in the computer and replacing it with keywords and high-level abstractions!

Let's examine some code that uses pass by reference:

```
/* pass_address.c */
#include <stdio.h>
#include <stdlib.h>
```

Source 4.2.   pass_address.c.

```c
#include <string.h>
#include <ctype.h>
void swap(int *a, int *b)
{
    int temp;
    temp = *a;
    *a = *b;
    *b = temp;
}
void main()
{
    int shella=10, shellb = 20;
    printf("Before swap, shella holds %d and shellb holds %d.\n",
    shella, shellb);
    swap(&shella, &shellb);
    printf("After swap, shella holds %d and shellb holds %d.\n",
    shella, shellb);
}
```

Source 4.2.   *Continued.*

The results of the program are:

Before swap, shella holds 10 and shellb holds 20.
After swap, shella holds 20 and shellb holds 10.

It is very important to understand how the above program works. Let's watch it run on our "paper computer":

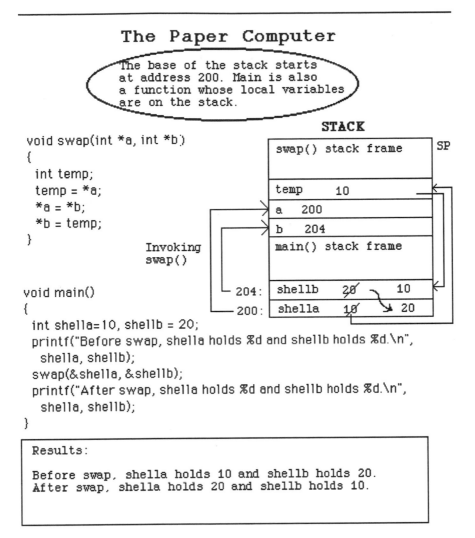

```
void swap(int *a, int *b)
{
  int temp;
  temp = *a;
  *a = *b;
  *b = temp;
}
```

Invoking
swap()

```
void main()
{
  int shella=10, shellb = 20;
  printf("Before swap, shella holds %d and shellb holds %d.\n",
    shella, shellb);
  swap(&shella, &shellb);
  printf("After swap, shella holds %d and shellb holds %d.\n",
    shella, shellb);
}
```

Results:

Before swap, shella holds 10 and shellb holds 20.
After swap, shella holds 20 and shellb holds 10.

Figure 4.2.   Paper computer on pass by reference.

CHAPTER QUESTIONS

1. What is the difference between an lvalue and an rvalue?
2. What is the default passing method for C?
3. How does Pascal language avoid teaching about the application stack?
4. Are the main() function values put on the stack?

CHAPTER EXERCISES

1. Describe what would occur if we removed all the asterisks from the swap() function.
2. Add printf() statements to Source 4.2 to examine the address of shella and shellb and the contents of a and b.

FURTHER READING

Schildt, Herbert. *C: The Complete Reference*, © 1988, Osborne McGraw-Hill.

5

Arrays and Pointers

OBJECTIVE: Learn how the C compiler treats arrays to understand their similarity to pointers.

This chapter will demonstrate how array declarations and pointers are intimately related. Once you understand the similarities you can then use a "pointer method" to access array elements instead of array indexes. You may be thinking, "I don't want to use a pointer method to access an array. The method I normally use is just fine." The goal of using a pointer method to access an array is not for you to adopt this method but for you to use the method to understand the underlying concept of WHAT AN ARRAY REALLY IS. An array is an artificial, invented, high-level construct that goes like this: "Let's let the programmer group like pieces of data and access that data by its position in the contiguous list." That is the high-level way of thinking about it, but how does the compiler (through assembly language instructions) implement that? Here we see the benefit of learning C because it forces us to think between two levels of computer understanding, between the high-level construct and the assembly language implementation. C reveals to us that pointers and arrays are related because arrays are implemented through pointer arithmetic at the assembly language level. Let's see how!

An array is simply a set of contiguous (one right after the other) variables of a single data type. For example, int int_array[5] would look like this:

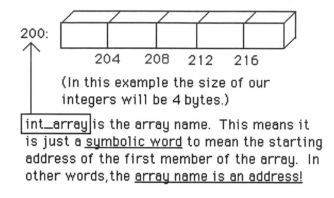

200:

204   208   212   216

(In this example the size of our
integers will be 4 bytes.)

int_array is the array name. This means it
is just a <u>symbolic word</u> to mean the starting
address of the first member of the array. In
other words, the <u>array name is an address!</u>

Figure 5.1.   An array as containers.

If you are saying, "Do you mean to tell me an array name is a pointer?"

No, No, NO! A pointer is a memory location (container) that can hold any address. A pointer is a variable. The important concept to understand about variables is that you can change their values as many times as you like (unlike constants whose values are fixed)! The best way to think of the actual word used for the array name is as an *address tag*. An address tag is *just a word that stands for an address*. After the compiler compiles your program, it never uses the word "int_array", it just uses the address 200. The word int_array is the symbolic name that you used to stand for an address, but no one ever tells you that you are creating an address tag! Instead they tell you that you are creating an array, and you can use the array name just like a pointer when you "pass" (really, copy) the array to a function. It is important to understand that *an array_name is NOT a pointer*!

"Okay. So how about giving us a definition for an address tag."

Address tag—a symbolic name for an address.

Now that we know what an address name really is, let's see what happens when you *"index into an array."*

Let's write a simple program and watch what happens on our paper computer.

```
/* index.c */
#include <stdio.h>
```

Source 5.1.   index.c.

```c
#include <stdlib.h>
#include <string.h>
#include <ctype.h>

void main()
{
    int int_array[5] = {1,2,3,4,5};
    int i=0;

    int *int_ptr;

    printf("the address of int_array is %p.\n",
    int_array);
    printf("the value of the 2nd member is %d.\n",
    int_array[1]);
    printf("the value of the 3rd member is %d.\n",
    *(int_array+2));

    int_ptr = int_array;

    printf("the value of int_ptr is now %p.\n",int_ptr);
    printf("the value of the 2nd member is %d.\n",
    *(int_ptr+ 1));
    printf("the value of the 3rd member is %d.\n",
    *(int_ptr+ 2));
}
```

Source 5.1.   *Continued.*

"If I am seeing straight, you are telling me that *indexing an array* is identical to *dereferencing a pointer plus an integer offset!*"

Correct. So now if I write int_array[4], you know that the compiler translates that into "add (4 * sizeof(int)) to the address int_array and returns the value the new address points to," which, since we know pointers, we can also write as *(int_array + 4) (since we declared int_array as an integer, the compiler automatically scales the new address for integers). In our paper computer, the compiler allocated int_array starting at address 200 so int_array is a tag for address 200. Our paper computer has four-byte integers, so if I say

x = int_array[4];
the compiler translates that into
x = *(200 + (4 *4))
which equals

x = *(216)
which means "get the integer value at address 216"
which assigns 5 to x.

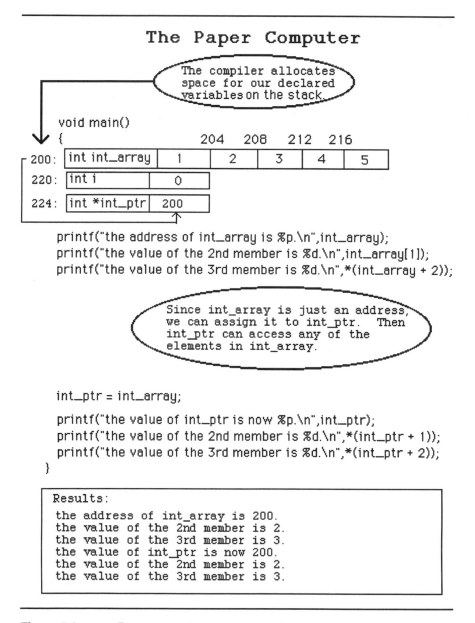

The Paper Computer

The compiler allocates space for our declared variables on the stack.

```
void main()
{                    204   208   212   216
200: | int int_array |  1  |  2  |  3  |  4  |  5  |
220: | int i         |  0  |
224: | int *int_ptr  | 200 |

    printf("the address of int_array is %p.\n",int_array);
    printf("the value of the 2nd member is %d.\n",int_array[1]);
    printf("the value of the 3rd member is %d.\n",*(int_array + 2));
```

Since int_array is just an address, we can assign it to int_ptr. Then int_ptr can access any of the elements in int_array.

```
    int_ptr = int_array;

    printf("the value of int_ptr is now %p.\n",int_ptr);
    printf("the value of the 2nd member is %d.\n",*(int_ptr + 1));
    printf("the value of the 3rd member is %d.\n",*(int_ptr + 2));
}
```

```
Results:
the address of int_array is 200.
the value of the 2nd member is 2.
the value of the 3rd member is 3.
the value of int_ptr is now 200.
the value of the 2nd member is 2.
the value of the 3rd member is 3.
```

Figure 5.2. Paper computer on array indexing.

5.1.   CODE REVIEW

Now that you have an understanding of the concepts behind arrays, it is important to "walk through" a nontrivial program to see the details of implementing those concepts.

```c
/* test_scores.c */
#include <stdio.h>
#include <stdlib.h>
#include <string.h>
#include <ctype.h>

void main()
{
  /* Here is another suggestion, keep all of your same
  data types grouped together. */
  double score_array[100];
  double entered_score=0.0, temp=0.0;
  double high=0.0, low=100.0, average=0.0, sum=0.0;

  int i=0,j=0,good_input=0, bad_input=0;
  int score_cnt=0;

  char user_input[256];

  /* explain to the user what the program will do. */
  printf("This program will allow you to enter up to
  100 test scores.\n");
  printf("Once scores are entered,
  I will sort the scores and \n");
  printf("calculate the average,
  high and low score.\n");

  /* we will loop until the user types a -1 or we have
  100 scores */
  while ( (entered_score != -1.0) && (score_cnt < 100) )
  {

    good_input = 0; /* set to false */

    /* it is a good practice to error check all user
    input. This will help prevent GIGO! One way to
```

Source 5.2.   test_scores.c.

```
error check user input is to allow him to enter
characters and then check the characters and
convert as necessary. */
 while (!good_input)
   {
     bad_input = 0;
     printf("\nEnter a score (-1 to stop): ");
     /* here we scan a character string into the
     character array user_input. */
     scanf("%s",user_input);

     /* I will check all the characters in the
        string for the occurence of any alpha or
        control char.
        **** Notice the end condition of the for loop,
        *(user_input + i). This is our pointer method
        for accessing array element i in the
        user_input array. */
     for (i = 0; *(user_input+i); i++)
     {
       /* if the character is a letter or cntrl
       character this is bad input */
       if ( (isalpha(*(user_input+i))) ||
            (iscntrl(*(user_input+i))) )
           bad_input = 1;
       if (bad_input) break;
     }

     if (!bad_input)
     {
       /* translate the string to a float */
       entered_score = atof(user_input);
       /* error check float */
       if ( ((entered_score>0) &&
             (entered_score<=100)) ||
             (entered_score == -1) )
           good_input = 1;
       else
           good_input = 0;
     }
     else
     {
       /* print an error and try again */
```

Source 5.2.   *Continued.*

```
        printf("Incorrect input. Try again (-1 to
        quit).\n");
        good_input = 0;
      }
   } /* while not good input */

   if (entered_score != -1)
   {
     /* now that we have good input, add it to our
     array. */
     score_array[score_cnt] = entered_score;
     score_cnt++;
   }
} /* while not -1 or a 100 scores entered */

if (score_cnt)
{
  /* before we sort lets calculate our average,
  high and low */
  for (i = 0; i < score_cnt; i++)
  {
    sum += *(score_array+i);
    if ( *(score_array+i) > high)
        high = *(score_array+i);
    if (*(score_array+i) < low)
        low = *(score_array+i);
  }
}

average = sum/score_cnt;

/* now lets sort the scores using the bubble sort */
/* bubble sort is the simplest and least efficient
sort; however, in our non-data intensive example we
won't have to worry about efficiency. */
for (i = 1; i < score_cnt; ++i)
{
  for (j = score_cnt - 1; j >= i; -j)
  {
    if ( *(score_array + j - 1) > *(score_array+j) )
    {
      temp = *(score_array + j - 1);
      *(score_array + j - 1) = *(score_array + j);
      *(score_array + j) = temp;
```

Source 5.2. *Continued.*

```
        } /* end if */
      } /* for */
    } /* for */

    /* print the results */
    printf("Number of scores entered was %d.\n",
    score_cnt);
    printf("The sorted list of scores:\n");
    for (i = 0; i < score_cnt; i++)
      printf("\t%f\n",*(score_array + i));

    printf("The high score was %f.\n",high);
    printf("The low score was %f.\n",low);
    printf("The average score was %f.\n",average);
  } /* if any scores */
  else
    printf("No scores entered. Bye.\n");
}
```

Source 5.2.   *Continued.*

The results of this program on some simple test data were

**This program will allow you to enter up to 100 test scores.
Once scores are entered, I will sort the scores and
calculate the average, high and low score.**

Enter a score (–1 to stop): 80

Enter a score (–1 to stop): 90

Enter a score (–1 to stop): 65

Enter a score (–1 to stop): 70

**Enter a score (–1 to stop): –1
Number of scores entered was 4.
The sorted list of scores:
65.000000
70.000000
80.000000
90.000000**

The high score was 90.000000.
The low score was 65.000000.
The average score was 76.250000.

CHAPTER QUESTIONS

1. Why would you want to use a "pointer method" to access arrays?
2. How does C, being a midlevel language, help us understand programming better?
3. What is the difference between an array name and a pointer?
4. Define dereferencing.
5. In source 5.1, why don't we let the while loop go until (score_cnt <= 100)?

CHAPTER EXERCISES

1. In Source 5.1, how would you assign int_ptr to be equivalent to a two-element integer array that starts at the fourth element of int_array?
2. Rewrite Source 5.2 to use subscripting instead of the pointer method to access the arrays.

FURTHER READING

Wortman, Leon A., and Thomas O. Sidebottom. *The C Programming Tutor*, © 1984, Brady Communications Company, Inc.

6

Structures and Pointers

OBJECTIVE: Learn about structures, structure pointers, and how to access members of structures with dereferencing or the arrow operator (->).

Structures are "aggregate data types," which means that they are a collection of one of more data types grouped together for easy handling. Pascal calls these "records," which is a good name considering that the purpose of a structure is to keep related data (even of different types) under one name and handled as a single unit of data.

Let's look at an example structure, and then we will examine how we access the structure members.

```
struct employee {
        char name[80];
        char street[80];
        char city[80];
        char state[3];
        char zip[11];
} mike;
```

We have a struct type of employee and have declared a variable of this type called "mike." To access the members of the structure "mike," we use the dot (.) operator. For example, to fill the name field of the structure we would write

gets(mike.name);

You always use the dot operator if the structure variable is in the scope of your function. This means you use the dot operator for either a locally declared structure variable or a global structure variable. When you declare a pointer to a structure (as when you want a function to modify the contents of your structure), you can use an arrow operator as a shortcut to always typing the dereference operator (*). For example,

struct employee *sptr;
sptr = &mike;
gets(sptr->name);
or
gets((*sptr).name);

The above examples show that you can use the dereferencing operator if you choose; however, if you use a lot of structures, it is quicker to use the shortcut arrow (->) operator.

Let's examine a short program that uses structures and pointers to structures:

```
/* struct_tst.c */
#include <stdio.h>
#include <stdlib.h>
#include <string.h>
#include <ctype.h>

struct employee {
   char name[80];
   int age;
   char address[256];
};

void func1(struct employee *employee_ptr)
{
   strcpy(employee_ptr->name,"harry houdini");
}

void func2(struct employee employee_copy)
{
   strcpy(employee_copy.name,"Theodore Roosevelt");
```

Source 6.1.   struct.c.

```
    printf("my employee has a new name %s.\n",
    employee_copy.name);
}

void main()
{
    struct employee joe = {"joe blow",32,"222 main street,
    nowhere, US"};

    struct employee *eptr;

    printf("the starting address of joe is %p.\n",&joe);
    eptr = &joe;
    printf("eptr holds %p.\n",eptr);
    printf("the full name of joe is %s.\n",joe.name);
    printf("the full name of joe is %s.\n",eptr->name);
    printf("the full name of joe is %s.\n",(*eptr).name);

    /* we can copy the address of the joe structure to the stack,
    for func1 */
    func1(&joe);

    /* func1 changed the name of our employee */
    printf("the full name of joe is now %s.\n",joe.name);
    printf("the full name of joe is now %s.\n",eptr->name);

    /* we can copy the entire structure to the stack for func2 */
    func2(joe);

    /* func2 DID NOT CHANGE the name of our employee */
    printf("the full name of joe is still %s.\n",joe.name);
    printf("the full name of joe is still %s.\n",eptr->name);
}
```

Source 6.1.   *Continued.*

Here is a run of this program:

```
the starting address of joe is 003E1C4A.
eptr holds 003E1C4A.
the full name of joe is joe blow.
the full name of joe is joe blow.
the full name of joe is joe blow.
the full name of joe is now harry houdini.
the full name of joe is now harry houdini.
my emloyee has a new name Theodore Roosevelt.
```

```
the full name of joe is still harry houdini.
the full name of joe is still harry houdini.
```

The important things to note about the above program are

1. Unlike the names of array variables (which we called address tags), a structure name is NOT the starting address of the structure. The structure name represents the entire structure, which lets us assign whole structures at a time. (You will see an example of this in tiny_dict.c at the end of this chapter.)
2. The arrow operator (->) is a shorthand method for dereferencing that can only be used with structures.
3. You copy the address of a structure to the stack if you want a function to modify the contents of your structure. This is shown in func1.
4. You can copy the entire structure to the stack by just putting the structure's name as the function argument. This is shown in func2.

6.1. CODE REVIEW

This chapter will finish with a nontrivial tiny-dictionary program that you should study and improve in the exercises.

Here is the header file:

```
/* tiny_dict.h */

#define SENTENCE_MAX 3
#define ENTRY_MAX 50

/* the following typedefs are just used to simplify
   how we refer to the structure. Just think of
   typedefs as aliases. The first typedef replaces
   the declaration struct dict_entry with
   dict_entry. The second makes it simpler to refer
   to a dict_entry pointer */
typedef struct dict_entry dict_entry;
typedef dict_entry *dict_entryp;
struct dict_entry {
        char keyword[80];
        char sentence[SENTENCE_MAX][80];
} dictionary[ENTRY_MAX];

int entry_count=0;
```

Here is the code:

```
#include <stdio.h>
#include <stdlib.h>
#include <string.h>
#include <ctype.h>
#include "tiny_dict.h"

/* tiny_dict.c - a fixed length dictionary */

/* **************************************************
   FUNCTION NAME: get_definition
   PURPOSE: uses gets to receive input of a definition
     from the user.
   INPUT: none.
   OUTPUT: a dict_entry structure.
   AUTHOR: MCD
************************************************** */
dict_entry get_definition()
{
  int i;
  dict_entry out_entry;

  printf("\n Enter keyword: ");

  /* since out_entry is a local structure variable and
  not a structure pointer we access
  its members using the dot operator. */
  gets(out_entry.keyword);
  printf("\n Enter definition of up to %d lines.",
  SENTENCE_MAX);
  for (i = 0; i < SENTENCE_MAX; i ++)
  {
    printf("\n Line %d: ",i+1);
    gets(out_entry.sentence[i]);
  }
  return(out_entry);
}
/* **************************************************
   FUNCTION NAME: display_entry
   PURPOSE: prints to stdout the members of the
     dictionary structure.
   INPUT: display_rec - a pointer to a dict_entry
     structure
```

Source 6.2.   tiny_dict.c.

```
     OUTPUT: none.
     AUTHOR: MCD
*************************************************** */
/* display_entry.
   NOTICE that display_rec is a structure pointer. This
   will change how we access the members of the
   structure. */
void display_entry(dict_entryp display_rec)
{
   int i;

   /* since display_rec is a structure pointer we use
   the arrow operator to access the members. */
   printf("Keyword: %s\n",display_rec->keyword);
   for (i = 0; i < SENTENCE_MAX; i++)
   {
      printf("%s\n",display_rec->sentence[i]);
   }
}

/*  ***************************************************
   FUNCTION NAME: list_entries
   PURPOSE: to print all the dictionary entries
     currently in the dictionary.
   INPUT: none.
   OUTPUT: none.
   AUTHOR: MCD
*************************************************** */
/* list_entries */
void list_entries()
{
   int i;

   printf("Dictionary Entries\n");

   /* dictionary is a global array of structures so we
   access it with the dot operator. */
   for (i=0; i < entry_count; i++)
      printf("%s\n",dictionary[i].keyword);
   printf("****** End of Entries ******\n");
}

/*  ***************************************************
   FUNCTION NAME: find_entry
```

Source 6.2.   *Continued.*

```
   PURPOSE: locates an entry in the dictionary array of
      structures that matches the keyword passed in.
   INPUT: keyword - a character string.
   OUTPUT: an integer which is the index of the matching
      entry in the array of dictionary structures.
   AUTHOR: MCD
*************************************************** */
int find_entry(char *keyword)
{
   int i;

   for (i=0; i < entry_count; i++)
   {
      if (!(strcmp(keyword,dictionary[i].keyword)))
             return(i);
   }
   return(-1);
}
/*   ***********************************************
   FUNCTION NAME: main for tiny_dict.c
   PURPOSE: present a menu of the available functions,
      retrieve the response from the user and call the
      appropriate function.
   INPUT: none.
   OUTPUT: none.
   AUTHOR: MCD
*************************************************** */
void main()
{
   int done=0;
   int choice=0,idx=0;
   char display_kw[80];

   while (!done)
   {
      printf("<<<< Your-Webster >>>>\n");
      printf("1) enter a definition.\n");
      printf("2) list all entries.\n");
      printf("3) display an entry.\n");
      printf("4) exit.\n");
      printf("choice: ");
      scanf("%d",&choice);
      fflush(stdin); /* this is so the \n gets flushed
                          out of the buffer */
```

Source 6.2.   *Continued.*

```
switch (choice) {
  case 1:
  if (entry_count < ENTRY_MAX)
  {
  dictionary[entry_count] = get_definition();
  entry_count++;
  }
  else
    printf("\n%d is Maximum number of entries!\n",
    ENTRY_MAX);
  break;
  case 2:
    list_entries();
  break;
  case 3:
    printf("\n Enter keyword to display: ");
    gets(display_kw);
    if ((idx = find_entry(display_kw)) >= 0)
        display_entry(&(dictionary[idx]));
    else
        printf("\n %s not found.\n",display_kw);
  break;
  case 4:
    done = 1;
  break;
  default:
  printf("\nInvalid choice - try again.\n");
  } /* switch */
} /* while not done */
}
```

Source 6.2. *Continued.*

Here is a run of the program:

<<<< Your-Webster >>>>
1) enter a definition.
2) list all entries.
3) display an entry.
4) exit.
choice: 1

Enter keyword: computer

Enter definition of up to 3 lines.
Line 1: a spectacular machine

Line 2: that unlocks the power of

Line 3: information.
<<<< Your-Webster >>>>
1) enter a definition.
2) list all entries.
3) display an entry.
4) exit.
choice:
choice: 2
Dictionary Entries
computer
****** End of Entries *******
<<<< Your-Webster >>>>
1) enter a definition.
2) list all entries.
3) display an entry.
4) exit.
choice: 3

Enter keyword to display: computer
Keyword: computer
a spectacular machine
that unlocks the power of
information.
<<<< Your-Webster >>>>
1) enter a definition.
2) list all entries.
3) display an entry.
4) exit.
choice:

CHAPTER QUESTIONS

1. What is the purpose of structures?
2. When do you use the dot operator versus the arrow operator?
3. Do you ever have to use the arrow operator?
4. How do the typedefs in tiny_dict.h make it simpler to declare a pointer to the dict_entry structure?

CHAPTER EXERCISES

1. In Source 6.1, declare a second employee structure and assign all of the data from joe to the second employee.
2. Create a remove_entry function that will remove a definition from the dictionary.

7

Strings and Pointers

OBJECTIVE: Learn the difference between arrays and strings. Also examine the power of string manipulation in C.

In C, a string is a null-terminated character array. Since you have already learned what arrays are and how to index into them, let's briefly examine the differences between strings and arrays. A *string* is a special *one-dimensional character array*. What is special about C strings is that they are *terminated (ended) with an ASCII NULL (represented by a \0)*. ASCII NULL is equivalent to a decimal 0.

"Why should I go through the extra trouble of tagging this NULL onto the end of all my character arrays?"

It is important to differentiate strings from arrays of characters. A string is a grouping of characters that are to be handled as one unit. Many functions have been written (in string.h and stdio.h) to work on strings. If a function is going to work on a group of characters, it has to know how many characters belong to this group called a "string." There are three common ways to denote how many characters are in a string:

1. The VMS operating system by Digital Equipment Corporation uses a special structure called a descriptor to store strings. This descriptor structure has separate fields for the string length and the address of the character array.
2. The Pascal programming language calls strings "packed arrays"

47

where they store the length of the string in the first byte. This is one reason Pascal strings have to start at 1 instead of 0. If you were programming in a mixed-language environment, and you assigned a character to string[0], you would overwrite the length of the Pascal string. How long do you think a packed array can be if Pascal uses one byte to store the length? If you said 255, you are correct! If you can live with being limited to 255 characters, Pascal does allow you to assign strings to other strings of the same length.

3. The C language's NULL-terminated strings. With the NULL terminator there is no reason to store the length. Although this means that you cannot assign strings to other strings, it is very easy to create numerous string manipulation functions. I will demonstrate several string manipulation functions in the next chapter on dynamic memory.

■ **Rule for strings:** Whenever you declare a character array, add one character for the NULL terminator.

Forgetting space for the NULL terminator is the *leading cause* of "smashing the stack."

smash the stack *[C programming] n.* On many C implementations it is possible to corrupt the execution stack by writing past the end of an array declared auto in a routine. Code that does this is said to smash the stack and can cause return from the routine to jump to a random address. This can produce some of the most insidious data-dependent bugs known to mankind.[1]

For example, let's say that I want to store my name in a character array:

char myname[12]; /* WRONG, no room for the NULL!!! */

Then I strcpy my name into this space.

strcpy(myname,"Mike Daconta");

Since strcpy automatically appends the NULL to the string, it writes the NULL at the thirteenth byte from address myname! You have no idea what memory strcpy just wrote a NULL over, which is why this simple error is so dangerous in C. We discuss this error in more detail (as well as provide a solution) in Chapter 14.

Now that I have stressed the importance of leaving space for the NULL, let's look at how that NULL terminator makes string manipulation easy. The majority of functions you write to work with strings will have one thing in common: The function traverses the characters of the string until it hits the NULL character. This allows great flexibility because your functions can be generic enough to work on strings of any size. Since most functions are written based on the assumption of a NULL-terminated string, you can see the havoc you cause by not terminating all your strings.

Here is a program that demonstrates four manipulation functions on strings:

```c
/* traverse.c */
#include <stdlib.h>
#include <stdio.h>
#include <string.h>
#include <ctype.h>

/*  ************************************************
   FUNCTION NAME: mycopy
   PURPOSE: copy the input string into the output
     string. A variation on strcpy.
   INPUT: instr - the input character string.
          outstr - the output character string.
   OUTPUT: outstr will be modified to be identical to
     instr.
   AUTHOR: MCD
************************************************ */
/* mycopy requires the caller to insure instr is NULL-
terminated and outstr has enough space to hold a copy of
instr. */
void mycopy(char *instr, char *outstr)
{
   while ( (*outstr++ = *instr++) != '\0');
}

/*  ************************************************
   FUNCTION NAME: slen
   PURPOSE: determine the length of the input string. A
     mimic of strlen.
   INPUT: a nul-terminated string.
   OUTPUT: an integer which represents the number of
     characters in the string.
   AUTHOR: MCD
************************************************ */
```

Source 7.1.   traverse.c.

```
int slen(char *instr)
{
  int i;

  for (i=0; *(instr+i); ++i);
  return(i);
}


/*  **************************************************
   FUNCTION NAME: search
   PURPOSE: the routine searches for a substring within
     a string and returns the index of the start of the
     substring in the string.
   INPUT:  searchstr - character string to seach.
           word - character string to search for.
   OUTPUT: an integer which is the index in the
     searchstr where the word starts.
   AUTHOR: MCD
**************************************************** */
int search(char *searchstr, char *word)
{
  int idx,i,j;

  for (i=0; searchstr[i]; i++)
  {
    if (searchstr[i] == word[j])
    {
      if (!j) idx = i;
      j++;
    }
    else
      j = 0;
    if (word[j] == '\0')
      break;
  }
  if (word[j] != '\0')
      return(-1);
  else
      return(idx);
}


/*  **************************************************
   FUNCTION NAME: reverse
   PURPOSE: reverse the characters in the input string.
```

Source 7.1.   *Continued.*

```
    INPUT:  instr - the character string to reverse.
            reverse - the character string to store the
            reversed characters.
    OUTPUT: none.
    AUTHOR: MCD
************************************************** */
void reverse(char *instr, char *reverse)
{
    int len,i=0;

    len = slen(instr);
    reverse[len] = '\0'; /* null terminate */
    while (instr[i] != '\0')
        reverse[--len] = instr[i++];
}

/*  **************************************************
    FUNCTION NAME: main for traverse.c
    PURPOSE: examples on the use of the above string
      functions.
    INPUT: none.
    OUTPUT: none.
    AUTHOR: MCD
************************************************** */
void main()
{
    char name[80];
    char quote[256];
    char name_copy[80];
    char reverse_name[80];

    int index;

    /* we will look at four types of string operations:
       copying, counting, searching, reversing. */
    /* first let's load some test data into our strings.  */
    strcpy(name,"Michael Daconta");
    strcpy(quote,"The C language has brought forth a new
    era in computing");

    /* now let's send name to our own string copy routine */
    printf("name is %s.\n",name);
    mycopy(name,name_copy);
    printf("name_copy is %s.\n",name_copy);
```

Source 7.1.   *Continued.*

```
/* let's also write our own string length routine */
printf("the length of :\n%s\n is %d.\n",
quote,slen(quote));
printf("the length of :\n%s\n is %d.\n",
name_copy,slen(name_copy));

/* let's rewrite strstr to return an the index of
a word in larger string. */
index = search(quote, "forth");

if (index != -1)
  printf("the index of \"%s\" in \n%s\n is %d.\n",
  "forth",quote,index);
else
  printf("%s is not in \n%s\n","forth",quote);

/* now let's write a function to reverse the
characters in a string */
reverse(name,reverse_name);
printf("my name is %s.\n",name);
printf("my reverse name is %s.\n",reverse_name);
}
```

Source 7.1. *Continued.*

Here is a run of this program:

name is Michael Daconta.
name_copy is Michael Daconta.
the length of :
The C language has brought forth a new era in computing
is 55.
the length of :
Michael Daconta
is 15.
the index of "forth" in
The C language has brought forth a new era in computing
is 27.
my name is Michael Daconta.
my reverse name is atnocaD leahciM.

There are five points of interest about the above program:

1. I was able to make the mycopy function extremely compact by using dereferencing and auto-increment. The algorithm for the function is as follows, "WHILE the character assigned to outstr is not a NULL

do: assign the character that instr 'dereferences to' to outstr. After the assignment, increment the addresses of both outstr and instr." Remember that instr and outstr are just local pointer variables on the stack that have the initial values of the address tag (name and name_copy) copied into them. Here is a diagram that illustrates this:

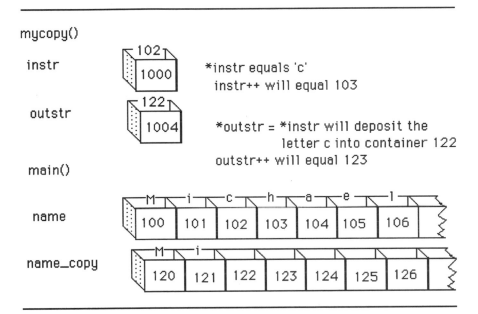

Figure 7.1.　Strings as containers.

2. The slen function uses dereferencing and pointer arithmetic instead of array indexing. It also uses a for loop to traverse the string instead of a while loop. You can also see how the NULL character is evaluated as a 0 and used to terminate the for loop.

3. The search function uses array indexing instead of pointer dereferencing just to show you that they are the same thing. The algorithm used for the search is a straightforward comparison of the first letter in word to each letter in searchstr. If a letter matches, the next letter in word is tried. If all the letters in word match so that we are at the NULL terminator in word, we end the program and return the index where the first letter matches. Any time we don't find a match we reset the word index to point to the 0th character. Even though this is an inefficient search, it is good enough for this example.

4. The function reverse has nothing new except some autodecrementing. The autodecrement is also done before the comparison because we don't want to write over our NULL terminator.
5. All the functions have one thing in common: They all work on the assumption that their loop will be ended when the function hits the NULL terminator in the string. It is evident the danger these functions could do if the string did not have a NULL terminator. To put it simply: They would waltz through memory until they hit an ASCII 0 (NULL)—the infamous "stomping on memory"!

7.1.   CODE REVIEW

Here is another program for your study and expansion through the exercises. This program performs the counting of characters, words, and paragraphs just like many of today's word processors.

Here is the header file:

```
/* count.h */

#define MAX_CHARS 5000

typedef struct score score;
typedef score *scorep;
struct score {
  int char_count;
  int word_count;
  int par_count;
};

typedef struct cursor cursor;
typedef cursor *cursorp;
struct cursor {
  int row;
  int col;
};

typedef struct count_pos count_pos;
typedef count_pos *count_posp;
struct count_pos {
  cursor char_pos;
  cursor word_pos;
  cursor par_pos;
};
```

Here is the code:

```
/* count.c - this program will read in a block of text (up
to 5000 characters) and count the number of characters,
words, and paragraphs in the text. */

#include <stdio.h>
#include <stdlib.h>
#include <string.h>
#include <ctype.h>
#include <console.h>
#include "count.h"

/* ****************************************************
   FUNCTION NAME: read_text
   PURPOSE: gets characters from standard input until
      either an end of file or 5000 characters have been
      entered.
   INPUT: storage - the character string to store the
      text.
   OUTPUT: an integer which is the number of
      characters read.
   AUTHOR: MCD
**************************************************** */
int read_text(char *storage)
{
   char inchar;
   int i=0;

   while ( ((inchar = getchar()) != EOF) && (i<MAX_CHARS) )
   {
      *storage++ = inchar;
      i++;
   }

   if (i == MAX_CHARS)
      printf("\nMaximum characters (%d) reached!\n",
      MAX_CHARS);

   return(i);
}

/* ****************************************************
   FUNCTION NAME: count
```

Source 7.2.   count.c.

```
     PURPOSE: counts characters, words and paragraphs in
       the input text.
     INPUT:    storage - the character string holding the
                          text.
               length -  the length of the string.
               coords -  a THINKC specific structure used to
                         go to a specific coordinate on the
                         screen.
     OUTPUT: counts are written to stdout. function
       returns nothing.
     AUTHOR: MCD
     *************************************************** */
/* count */
void count(char *storage, int length, count_posp coords)
{
   int i;
   score thescore= {0,0,0};
   short int char_flag=0;

   char last_char='~';

   /* we use cgotoxy to keep the cursor fixed at one
      spot so that the numbers will increment in the same
      position and not fill the entire screen. */
cgotoxy(coords->char_pos.col,coords->char_pos.row,
   stdout);
printf("%d",thescore.char_count);
cgotoxy(coords->word_pos.col,coords->word_pos.row,
   stdout);
printf("%d",thescore.word_count);
cgotoxy(coords->par_pos.col,coords->par_pos.row,
   stdout);
printf("%d",thescore.par_count);

/* the methodology for counting properly is to go
   through every character. Save the last character
   looked at and by using the two figure when you
   hit the end of a word or the beginning of a
   paragraph. */
   for (i=0; i<length; i++)
   {
      if ( (isalnum(storage[i])) || (ispunct(storage[i])) )
      {
```

Source 7.2. *Continued.*

```
      if (!thescore.par_count)
      {
        thescore.par_count++;
        cgotoxy(coords->par_pos.col, coords->par_pos.row,
          stdout);
        printf("%d",thescore.par_count);
      }

      if (i == length - 1)
      {
        /* last char is a non-whitespace,
          count last word. */
        thescore.word_count++;
        cgotoxy(coords->word_pos.col, coords->word_pos.row,
          stdout);
        printf("%d",thescore.word_count);
      }

      thescore.char_count++;
      cgotoxy(coords->char_pos.col,coords->char_pos.row,
        stdout);
      printf("%d",thescore.char_count);
      char_flag = 1;
    }
    else if ( (isspace(storage[i])) && (char_flag) )
    {
      thescore.word_count++;
      cgotoxy(coords->word_pos.col,coords->word_pos.row,
        stdout);
      printf("%d",thescore.word_count);
      char_flag = 0;
    }

    if ( ((storage[i] == '\n') && (last_char == '\n')) ||
         (storage[i] == '\t') )
    {
      thescore.par_count++;
      cgotoxy(coords->par_pos.col,coords->par_pos.row,stdout);
      printf("%d",thescore.par_count);
    }
    last_char = storage[i];
  } /* for */
}
```

Source 7.2.   *Continued.*

```
/*   **************************************************
   FUNCTION NAME: main for count.c
   PURPOSE: calls read_text, prints a header, then calls
      count to print the counts.
   INPUT: none.
   OUTPUT: none.
   AUTHOR: MCD
************************************************** */

void main()
{
   char text[MAX_CHARS];
   int txt_length = 0;
   int x,y;

   count_pos positions;

   /* set up console size. This is specific to THINK C.
   NON-ANSI.*/
   cshow(stdout);

   /* cgotoxy is similar to TURBO C's gotoxy */
   cgotoxy(1,1,stdout);

   printf("Type text and hit ctrl-D or command-D to stop.\n");
   txt_length = read_text(text);

   printf("+------------- COUNT ---------------+\n");
   /* now count the characters */
   /* cgetxy is similar to _gettextposition, it gets the
   current position of the cursor. NON-ANSI.*/
   cgetxy(&x,&y,stdout);

   positions.char_pos.row = y;
   positions.word_pos.row = y+1;
   positions.par_pos.row = y+2;
   positions.char_pos.col = 19;
   positions.word_pos.col = 19;
   positions.par_pos.col = 19;

   printf("# of characters : \n");
   printf("# of words : \n");
   printf("# of paragraphs : \n");

   count(text,txt_length,&positions);
}
```

Source 7.2.   *Continued.*

Here is a sample run of the program:

Type text and hit ctrl-D or command-D to stop.
    Mary had a little lamb whose fleece was white as
snow and wherever the mary went the lamb was
sure to go.

    Jack be nimble, jack be quick.

The end.

```
+————————— COUNT ——————————+
# of characters : 116
# of words : 30
# of paragraphs : 3
```

CHAPTER QUESTIONS

1. What is the purpose of attaching an ASCII NULL to a character array?
2. What are the three methods to denote a string?
3. What is the consequence of forgetting a NULL terminator?
4. Which has a higher precedence, * (dereference operator) or ++?

CHAPTER EXERCISES

1. Write mycopy and slen using array subscripting instead of the pointer access method.
2. Add the counting of sentences to count.c.

REFERENCES

[1]Raymond, Eric. *The New Hacker's Dictionary*, © 1991, MIT Press.

FURTHER READING

Plauger, P.J. *The Standard C Library*, © 1992, Prentice-Hall.

8

Pointers and Dynamic Memory

OBJECTIVE: An extensive examination of the increased flexibility and speed of using dynamic storage. Previous code examples rewritten in a more dynamic fashion.

The goal of this chapter is not just to instruct you on the proper procedures for using dynamic memory management functions like malloc and free, but to reveal powerful programming concepts that must be the cornerstone of all your future applications! With RAM continually getting cheaper and the time gap between memory access and disk access growing, if you want to improve the flexibility and speed of your applications, *you must shift your programming style to use more memory and less disk access*! So, the second goal of this chapter, in addition to detailed instruction, is an introduction to *"thinking dynamic."*

8.1. BASIC BUILDING BLOCKS

The malloc() function in "stdlib.h" allocates a requested number of bytes of storage from the heap for your applications to use. Here is the function definition:

void *malloc(size_t nbytes);

There are several important points to note about this function:

1. Size_t is a typedef (usually for an integer) representing the number of bytes to allocate. Here is a declaration of size_t:

   typedef int size_t;

2. Malloc returns a void pointer that must be cast to the data type of your pointer. For example, if I want to allocate 10 characters from the heap:

   char *char_ptr;
   char_ptr = (char *) malloc(sizeof(char) * 10);

   The (char *) is the cast operator that tells the compiler that the address returned by malloc points to characters (which in most implementations are one byte and not integers, which are four bytes). This is important because in order for pointer arithmetic to work, the compiler must know the size of the object that the pointer points to.

   You also see that I used the *sizeof* compile time operator to compute the number of bytes in a character. The use of sizeof aids the portability of the code and should always be used.

■ *Sizeof rule:* Always use the sizeof operator to compute the size of data types and structures to be malloced.

The free() function returns a previously allocated block of memory to the free list.

"What do you mean by free list? And what does it have to do with reserving storage off of the heap?"

Random access memory is a *computer system resource* that is not only used for your application, but is also used for the system programs and possibly other simultaneous system tasks like updating a clock or running other programs in the background (the term background is more applicable to multiuser computer systems like SPARC workstations or VAX minicomputers that support multiple users simultaneously; however, microcomputers are becoming fast enough to permit background processing of jobs. By "running in the background," we mean a program that does not require any user interaction, in contrast to the current foreground program, and runs simultaneously with foreground programs.) So, as a system resource, the system must control the fair distribution of RAM to fulfill all of the system's needs. Therefore, when your application program first calls malloc, malloc makes a request to the system (via a system service) for a portion of its system resource. Here is a diagram of how a computer system handles requests and provides services:

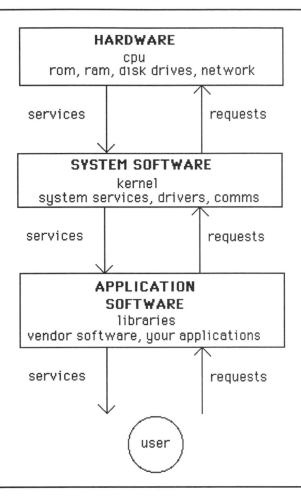

Figure 8.1.   Requesting a system resource.

The above diagram shows how your program has to "go outside of itself" to the system to request a system resource. By "go outside of itself" I mean that your program suspends execution and transfers control to a system service (which is just a system function), which in turn interacts with the hardware. The important thing to understand is that the more times you call system services (which you have no idea how many functions the system service calls in turn), the slower your program will run. Therefore, to limit calls to the system, C's dynamic memory management philosophy is to grab a large chunk of memory and slice off the correct size piece that your program currently needs. In a sense, the C language is making an assumption that you will probably ask for more memory later. Any memory it has not given you yet, it maintains on a list called the "free list." If you are finished with a block that you requested and you "free" it, the block is returned to the free list. If you ask for a block of memory and the free list does not have the exact size that you asked for, it cuts up a larger piece and gives you what you asked for. If the free list does not have any blocks that are large enough to satisfy your request, malloc goes back to the system and gets another large block, which it adds to the free list. Here is a diagram of a free list:

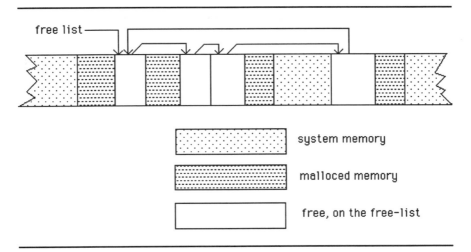

Figure 8.2.   The free list.

Here is the definition of the free() function:

void free(void *malloced_ptr);

The discussion above covered the basic operations of free; however, I still need to stress a critical rule for free:

■   *Rule for free():* Only free malloced or calloced pointers!

This rule has an exclamation point because the free function will except nonmalloced pointers; however, this can have grave side effects and consequences. We will discuss these in more detail in later chapters. Let's examine some code that uses malloc and free (the code is in two parts, the first is a source code file that will hold a collection of string manipulation routines, and the second is a main program that calls some of those functions):

Here are the utility routines:

```
/* strings.c */
#include <stdlib.h>
#include <stdio.h>
#include <string.h>
#include <ctype.h>

/*  **************************************************
   FUNCTION NAME: strdup
   PURPOSE: allocates space on the heap for a copy of the
      input string.
   INPUT: instr - the string to be copied.
   OUTPUT: a character pointer which points to the space on
      the heap where the string is copied.
   NOTE: this function MALLOC's memory. it is the
      responsibility of the calling routine to free this
      memory.
   AUTHOR: MCD
************************************************** */char
*strdup(char *instr)
{
  char *outstr=NULL;

  if (!instr)
  {
    fprintf(stderr, "strdup: FATAL - NULL argument!\n");
    return(NULL);
  }

  outstr = (char *) malloc(sizeof(char) * (strlen(instr) + 1) );
  if (!outstr)
  {
    fprintf(stderr, "strdup: FATAL - malloc failed!\n");
    return(NULL);
  }

  strcpy(outstr, instr);
```

Source 8.1.   strings.c.

```
   return(outstr);
}

/*  **************************************************
   FUNCTION NAME: substr
   PURPOSE: allocates space on the heap for a substring
     of a larger string.
   INPUT: string1 - a character string which contains
               the substring.
           start - an integer which is the character
               where the substring starts.
           numchars - an integer which holds the number
               of characters in the substring.
   OUTPUT: a character pointer which points to the start
     of the substring on the heap.
   NOTE1: start is the ith character in the string to
     start at (for example if you wanted to start at the
     first character you would put 1 and not 0.
   NOTE2: The substring may be terminated early by a
     string terminator in the input string or by a
     newline character.
   NOTE3: this function MALLOCs memory.
   AUTHOR: MCD
**************************************************
*/char *substr(char *string1, int start, int numchars)
{
   char *p;

   int cnt=0, slen=0;

   slen = strlen(string1);
   if ( (slen < 2) ||  /* is this a valid string? */
        (start< 1) ||  /* is start valid? */
        (start>slen) ) /* is the substring in the string? */
        return(NULL);

   p = (char *) malloc(sizeof(char) * (numchars + 1));
   if (!p)
   {
     fprintf(stderr,"substr: FATAL - malloc failed!\n");
     return(NULL);
   }

   start--; /* subtract one since C strings start at 0. */
```

Source 8.1. *Continued.*

```
  while (cnt < numchars)
  {
    if ((string1[start+cnt] == '\0') ||
        (string1[start+cnt] == '\n') ) break;
    p[cnt] = *(string1+start+cnt);
    ++cnt;
  } /* end of while */
  p[cnt] = '\0';
  return(p);
}
```

Source 8.1.   *Continued.*

Here is a test program for the above utilities:

```
/* string_tst.c */
#include <stdio.h>
#include <stdlib.h>
#include <string.h>
#include <ctype.h>

extern char *strdup();
extern char *substr();
/*  ************************************************
FUNCTION NAME: main for string_tst.c
PURPOSE: an example on the use of strdup and substr.
INPUT: none.
OUTPUT: none.
AUTHOR: MCD
************************************************** */
void main()
{
  char *dynamic_name=NULL;
  char *piece1=NULL, *piece2=NULL;

  char full_name[80];

  /* if you want to store a name in a character array.
     You are limited to either knowing the correct size
     or wasting space. Even if you know the correct size
```

Source 8.2.   string_tst.c.

```
you cannot put a larger name in the array if the need
arises. The best way to store data is in dynamic
structures! */

/* old, inflexible way */
strcpy(full_name,"Michael C. Daconta");

/* better way */
dynamic_name = strdup("Michael C. Daconta");

printf("My full_name is %s and %s.\n",
  full_name,dynamic_name);

/* if you want to change the name pointed to by full
name, it is easy. */
if (dynamic_name) free(dynamic_name);
dynamic_name = NULL;
dynamic_name = strdup("Frank Daconta");

printf("The new full name is %s.\n",dynamic_name);

/* let's just grab a piece of the string. */
piece1 = substr(full_name,9,10);
piece2 = substr(dynamic_name,1,5);

printf("The pieces of my name are: %s %s.\n",
  piece2,piece1);

/* cleanup */
if (piece1) free(piece1);
if (piece2) free(piece2);
if (dynamic_name) free(dynamic_name);
}
```

Source 8.2. *Continued.*

Here is a run of the program:

**My full_name is Michael C. Daconta and Michael C. Daconta.
The new full name is Frank Daconta.
The pieces of my name are: Frank C. Daconta.**

Points to note on strings.c and string_tst.c:

1. Strdup is a handy function to create a dynamic copy of a string. You will notice that the declaration of the character pointer outstr is

initialized to NULL. This is a good practice that will speed up debugging of errors because it assures that you know the value your pointer started at. This eliminates the possibility that you used a pointer with garbage in it to start with.

■ *Initialize pointers rule:* Initialize pointers to NULL at declaration and after free().

This is especially important if you use a pointer in a loop or do tests for pointer validity.

2. In strdup(), after the call to malloc(), I verify that it returned a valid pointer. If (!outstr) is true when the pointer outstr is a NULL (a 0), which is what malloc will return if it fails.

■ *Verify malloc rule:* Always verify that malloc's returned argument is a valid pointer.

3. In substr(), you see how I have to add the NULL terminator ('\0'), manually. If you are creating your own dynamic strings, ensure that you don't forget that requirement.

4. In main() of string_tst.c, you see the statement:

if (dynamic_name) free(dynamic_name);

With the if statement, I am *protecting the free routine* from getting a null pointer. This is important because giving free a null pointer as an argument will cause the program to crash due to an invalid memory reference (called a segmentation fault on UNIX machines, an access violation on others). This brings us to two more rules for the free() function:

■ *Free() rule 2:* Free() everything you malloc() or calloc().

■ *Free() rule 3:* Always protect your calls to free() with an IF statement. IF (VALID_POINTER) FREE (VALID_POINTER).

8.2. "THINKING DYNAMIC"

Let's think of how a standard payroll application works. Grab an employee's record from disk, do some processing on the record, update the record on disk, and keep going until you have processed all of the employee records. What is wrong with this picture? The problem is that the above application uses a 1960 methodology on 1990 computer systems. A program that assumes that RAM is expensive and limited is a 1960 application, which is when those assumptions were true. The 1990 solution to the problem is "do a block read of ALL the employee records into memory, process all the records with one or multiple processors, and block write all the updated records back to disk." I call the 1990s solution *"thinking dynamic."*

Let's look at some specific examples of thinking dynamic by looking at how we can change the examples of the previous chapters. The first example we will change is the program that sorted and averaged test scores. I am not going to print the whole program over, only the part that needs changing.

```c
/* dynamic_scores.c */
#include <stdio.h>
#include <stdlib.h>
#include <string.h>
#include <ctype.h>

void main()
{
  /* Here is another suggestion, keep all of your same
  data types grouped together. */
  /*** DYNAMIC CHANGE: replace this static declaration
  of a 100 scores with a dynamic pointer.
  double score_array[100]; ***/
  double *score_array=NULL, *temp=NULL;
  double entered_score=0.0, temp=0.0;
  double high=0.0, low=100.0, average=0.0, sum=0.0;

  int i=0,j=0,good_input=0, bad_input=0;

  /*** DYNAMIC CHANGE: add score_max so you know when
  you need to reallocate memory. ***/
  int score_cnt=0, score_max=0;

  char user_input[256];

  /*** DYNAMIC CHANGE: start off by mallocing space for
  the same 100 scores. ***/
  score_array = (double *) malloc(sizeof(double) * 100);
  if (!score_array)
```

Source 8.3.   dynamic_scores.c.

```
{
  fprintf(stderr,"dynamic_scores: FATAL - malloc
  failed!\n");
  exit(0);
}
score_max = 100;

/* explain to the user what the program will do. */
/*** DYNAMIC CHANGE: take away that silly restriction
of a 100 test scores. I would never buy your program
if I had such a limit. ***/
printf("This program will allow you to enter test scores.\n");
printf("Once scores are entered,
I will sort the scores and \n");
printf("calculate the average, high and low score.\n");

/* we will loop until the user types a -1 */
/*** DYNAMIC CHANGE: remove the check for a count of
100 */
while (entered_score != -1.0)
{
  good_input - 0; /* set to false */
  /* it is a good practice to error check all user
  input. This will help prevent GIGO! One way to
  error check user input is to allow him to enter
  characters and then check the characters and
  convert as necessary. */
  while (!good_input)
  {
    bad_input = 0;
    printf("\nEnter a score (-1 to stop): ");
    scanf("%s",user_input);
    /* I will check all the characters in them string
    for the occurence of any alpha or control char */
    for (i = 0; *(user_input+i); i++)
    {
      if ( (isalpha(*(user_input+i))) ||
      (iscntrl(*(user_input+i))) ) bad_input = 1;
      if (bad_input) break;
    }

    if (!bad_input)
```

Source 8.3.   *Continued.*

```
   {
      /* translate the string to a float */
      entered_score = atof(user_input);
      /* error check float */
      if ( ((entered_score>0) &&
            (entered_score<=100)) ||
            (entered_score == -1) )
            good_input = 1;
      else
            good_input = 0;
   }
   else
   {
      /* print an error and try again */
      printf("Incorrect input. Try again (-1 to quit).\n");
      good_input = 0;
   }
} /* while not good input */

if (entered_score != -1)
{
   /* now that we have good input, add it to our
   array. */
   /*** Before we add the record, make sure that we
   have space for it! Realloc in quantities of 100.
   ***/
   if (score_cnt==score_max)
   {
      temp = score_array;
      score_array = (double *) realloc(score_array,
         sizeof(double) * score_max + 100);
      if (!score_array)
      {
         fprintf(stderr,
         "dynamic_scores: FATAL - realloc failed!\n");
         fprintf(stderr,"dynamic_scores: cannot allocate
         any additional memory!\n");
         score_array = temp;
         entered_score = -1;
      }
      else
         score_max += 100;
   }
```

Source 8.3. *Continued.*

```
      if (entered_score != -1)
      {
        score_array[score_cnt] = entered_score;
        score_cnt++;
      }
    }
  } /* while not -1 */
```

Source 8.3.   *Continued.*

Let's discuss the parts that have changed, especially the addition of the realloc() function. The changes to the test_scores program all affect only one area of the program: *flexibility*. Flexibility in the application allows the user more freedom and decision making in how the application will run. In fact, one could argue that the success of modern graphical user interfaces (GUIs) is due to the fact that they allow the user to determine the sequence of his actions (and therefore they are more flexible). The test_scores program previously restricted the user to 100 scores, and the above example shows how we can easily lift that limit by using malloc and realloc. This brings us to the realloc() function. Here is the function definition:

void *realloc(void *ptr, size_t size);

The key points on realloc() are

1. You feed in a previously malloced, calloced, or realloced pointer that you want to change the size of the space it points to. The function will *increase or decrease* the size of the space. If the ptr is NULL, then realloc() works like malloc and allocates size bytes. If the size is zero, then realloc() works like free and returns the previously malloced space to the free list.
2. If realloc() returns a NULL, it was unable to allocate any more free space from the heap; however, the previously allocated memory is left unchanged and can still be accessed. That is why it is important either to realloc() into a new pointer variable or save the pointer to the old block (as I did in the above example with temp) in case realloc() fails.
3. Realloc() returns a pointer because it may have to move the block in order to fulfill a request to increase the block's size. If realloc() does get a new larger block, it copies the contents of the old block into the new one.

Alongside flexibility, the second principle of "thinking dynamic" is *speed*. Simply stated, loading data into memory allows the fastest processing on that data! In the next code example, we will modify the code to incorporate both the benefits of flexibility and speed.

Here is the header file:

```
/* hyper_dict.h */

/*** Remove these horrible limitations
#define SENTENCE_MAX 3
#define ENTRY_MAX 50 ***/

#define MINNUM 50
#define HYPERMIN 10

typedef struct dict_entry dict_entry;
typedef dict_entry *dict_entryp;
struct dict_entry {
 char *keyword;
 char *definition;
 int *hyper_links;
 int hyper_cnt;
 int hyper_max;
} **dictionary;

int entry_count=0;
```

Here is the code (the code has changed so much that we have to include all of it):

```
#include <stdio.h>
#include <stdlib.h>
#include <string.h>
#include <ctype.h>
#include "hyper_dict.h"

/* hyper_dict.c - a dynamic hypertext dictionary */

extern char *get_dynamic_str();
extern char *get_file();
```

Source 8.4.   hyper_dict.c.

```
/*   **************************************************
    FUNCTION NAME: get_definition
    PURPOSE: allocates space on the heap for a dictionary
        entry. Fills the dictionary by calling
        get_dynamic_str and get_file.
    INPUT: none.
    OUTPUT: a dict_entryp which is a pointer to the
        dictionary entry on the heap.
    NOTE: this function MALLOCs memory.
    AUTHOR: MCD
**************************************************** */

/* get_definition - gets one definition and returns a malloced
entry. */
dict_entryp get_definition()
{
  dict_entryp out_entry;
  int i;

  /* malloc space for out_entry */
  out_entry = (dict_entryp) malloc(sizeof(dict_entry));
  if (!out_entry)
  {
    fprintf(stderr,"get_definition: FATAL - malloc
    failed!\n");
    return(NULL);
  }

  printf("\n Enter keyword: ");
  /* use get_dynamic_str() which is similar to gets but
  mallocs the string for us. */
  out_entry->keyword = get_dynamic_str();

  printf("\n Enter the definition: (ctrl-D when finished)\n");
  out_entry->definition = get_file();

  out_entry->hyper_cnt=0;
  out_entry->hyper_max = HYPERMIN;

  /* malloc the space for the hyper links */
  out_entry->hyper_links = (int *) malloc(sizeof(int) * HYPERMIN);
  if (!out_entry->hyper_links)
  {
```

Source 8.4.   *Continued.*

```
      fprintf(stderr,
      "get_definition: FATAL - malloc failed!\n");
      return(NULL);
   }

   return(out_entry);
}

/*   **************************************************
   FUNCTION NAME: display_entry
   PURPOSE: given a pointer to a dictionary entry,
      displays each element of the dictionary entry using
      the arrow operator.
   INPUT: display_rec - a dictionary entry pointer.
   OUTPUT: none.
   AUTHOR: MCD
************************************************** */
/* display_entry */
void display_entry(dict_entryp display_rec)
{
   int i;
   printf("Keyword: %s\n",display_rec->keyword);
   printf("%s\n",display_rec->definition);
   /* display the hyperlinks */
   if (display_rec->hyper_cnt)
   {
      printf(">>—HyperLinks—>\n");
      printf("0) exit to main menu.\n");
      for (i = 0; i < display_rec->hyper_cnt; i++)
      {
         printf("%d) %s\n",i+1,
         dictionary[display_rec->hyper_links[i]]->keyword);
      }
   }
}

/*   **************************************************
   FUNCTION NAME: list_entries
   PURPOSE: lists all the keywords in the dictionary.
   INPUT: none.
   OUTPUT: none.
   AUTHOR: MCD
************************************************** */
```

Source 8.4.   *Continued.*

```
/* list_entries */
void list_entries()
{
  int i;

  printf("Dictionary Entries\n");
  for (i=0; i < entry_count; i++)
    printf("%s\n",dictionary[i]->keyword);
  printf("****** End of Entries ******\n");
}

/*  **************************************************
    FUNCTION NAME: find_entry
    PURPOSE: searches for the input keyword in the
      dictionary.
    INPUT: keyword - a character string to search for.
    OUTPUT: an integer which is the index of the entry on
      success, else -1.
    AUTHOR: MCD
************************************************** */int
find_entry(char *keyword)
{
  int i;

  for (i=0; i < entry_count; i++)
  {
    if (!(strcmp(keyword,dictionary[i]->keyword)))
        return(i);
  }
  return(-1);
}

/*  **************************************************
    FUNCTION NAME: add_hyper_links
    PURPOSE: each dictionary entry will have an array of
      indexes of other entries that have the keyword in
      them. Every time a new entry is added to the
      dictionary, the entire dictionary is checked to see
      if any new hyperlinks need to be added.
    METHOD: a strstr is done on each defininition to see
      if it contains the keyword of the new entry. The
      hyperlink of both the definition and the new_entry
      are updated.
```

Source 8.4.   *Continued.*

```
    INPUT: none.
    OUTPUT: none.
    AUTHOR: MCD
*************************************************** */
void add_hyper_links()
{
   int i=0,target=0;
   int *temp=NULL;

   char *hyper_word=NULL;

   target = entry_count - 1;
   if (target)
   {
     hyper_word = dictionary[target]->keyword;
     for (i=0; i<target; i++)
     {
       if (strstr(dictionary[i]->definition,hyper_word))
       {
         /* update the hyper link of the entry */
         if (dictionary[i]->hyper_cnt == dictionary[i]->
         hyper_max)
         {
           temp = dictionary[i]->hyper_links;
           dictionary[i]->hyper_links = (int *)
             realloc(dictionary[i]->hyper_links,
               sizeof(int) * (dictionary[i]->hyper_max
               + HYPERMIN));
           if (!dictionary[i]->hyper_links)
           {
             fprintf(stderr,
             "add_hyper_links: realloc failed on %d bytes.\n",
             sizeof(int) * (dictionary[i]->hyper_max +
             HYPERMIN));
             dictionary[i]->hyper_links = temp;
           }
           else
             dictionary[i]->hyper_max += HYPERMIN;
         }

         if (dictionary[i]->hyper_cnt < dictionary[i]->
         hyper_max)
         {
```

Source 8.4.   *Continued.*

```
            dictionary[i]->hyper_links[dictionary[i]->
            hyper_cnt] = target;
            dictionary[i]->hyper_cnt++;
          }
        else
          fprintf(stderr,
          "add_hyper_links: cannot allocate any more memory!\n");
        /* update the hyper link of the target */
        if (dictionary[target]->hyper_cnt ==
            dictionary[target]->hyper_max)
        {
          temp = dictionary[target]->hyper_links;
          dictionary[target]->hyper_links = (int *)
            realloc(dictionary[target]->hyper_links,
            sizeof(int) * (dictionary[target]->
            hyper_max + HYPERMIN));
          if (!dictionary[target]->hyper_links)
          {
            fprintf(stderr,"add_hyper_links: realloc
            failed on %d bytes.\n",
            sizeof(int) * (dictionary[target]->
            hyper_max + HYPERMIN));
            dictionary[target]->hyper_links = temp;
          }
          else
            dictionary[target]->hyper_max += HYPERMIN;
        }
        if (dictionary[target]->hyper_cnt <
            dictionary[target]->hyper_max)
        {
          dictionary[target]->
            hyper_links[dictionary[target]->hyper_cnt] = i;
          dictionary[target]->hyper_cnt++;
        }
        else
          fprintf(stderr,
          "add_hyper_links: cannot allocate any more memory!\n");

      } /* if strstr */
    } /* for all entries */
  } /* if target */
}

/* ************************************************
   FUNCTION NAME: main for hyper_dict.c
```

Source 8.4.   *Continued.*

```
   PURPOSE: allocate space for the dictionary, present a
     menu of options, call the appropriate function
     based upon the users choice.
   INPUT: none.
   OUTPUT: none.
   AUTHOR: MCD
*************************************************** */void
main()
{
   int done=0;
   int choice=0,idx=0,entry_max=MINNUM;
   int hyper_choice=0,hyper_count=0;

   char display_kw[80];
   dict_entryp *temp;
   dict_entryp hyper_rec;

   /* malloc space for MINNUM of dictionary entries */
   dictionary = (dict_entryp *)
   malloc(sizeof(dict_entryp) * MINNUM);
   if (!dictionary)
   {
      fprintf(stderr,"hyper_dict: FATAL - malloc failed
      on %d bytes.\n",
      sizeof(dict_entryp) * MINNUM);
      exit(0);
   }

   while (!done)
   {
      printf("<<<< Hyper-Webster >>>>\n");
      printf("1) enter a definition.\n");
      printf("2) list all entries.\n");
      printf("3) display an entry.\n");
      printf("4) exit.\n");
      printf("choice: ");
      scanf("%d",&choice);
      fflush(stdin); /* this is so the \n gets flushed out
                          of the buffer */
      switch (choice) {
        case 1:
          if (entry_count == entry_max)
          {
             /* realloc more space */
```

Source 8.4. *Continued.*

```
        temp = dictionary;
        dictionary = (dict_entryp *)
        realloc(dictionary, sizeof(dict_entryp)
        * (entry_max + MINNUM));
        if (!dictionary)
        {
          fprintf(stderr,
          "hyper_dict: FATAL - realloc failed on %d bytes.\n",
          sizeof(dict_entryp) * (entry_max + MINNUM));
          dictionary = temp;
        }
        else
          entry_max += MINNUM;
      }

      if (entry_count < entry_max)
      {
        dictionary[entry_count] = get_definition();
        if (!dictionary[entry_count])
        {
          fprintf(stderr,
          "hyper_dict: FATAL - get_definition failed!\n");
          exit(0);
        }
        entry_count++;
        /* add hyper links */
        add_hyper_links();
      }
      else
      {
        fprintf(stderr,"hyper_dict: Warning - unable
        to allocate any more memory!\n");
      }
      break;
    case 2:
      list_entries();
      break;
    case 3:
      printf("\n Enter keyword to display: ");
      gets(display_kw);
      if ((idx = find_entry(display_kw)) >= 0)
      {
        display_entry(dictionary[idx]);
        hyper_choice = 1;
```

Source 8.4.   *Continued.*

```
      hyper_count = dictionary[idx]->hyper_cnt;
      while ( (hyper_choice != 0) && (hyper_count) )
      {
        /* jump to hyperlinks */
        printf("choice: ");
        scanf("%d",&hyper_choice);
        fflush(stdin); /* this is so the \n gets
                flushed out of the buffer */
        if (hyper_choice)
        {
          hyper_rec =
          dictionary[dictionary[idx]->hyper_links
          [hyper_choice-1]];
          display_entry(hyper_rec);
          hyper_count = hyper_rec->hyper_cnt;
          idx = dictionary[idx]->hyper_links
          [hyper_choice-1];
        }
      }
    }
    else
      printf("\n %s not found.\n",display_kw);
    break;
  case 4:
    done = 1;
    break;
  default:
    printf("\nInvalid choice - try again.\n");
  } /* switch */
  } /* while not done */
}
```

Source 8.4.   *Continued.*

Here are the two new routines for strings.c:

```
#define STRAVG 40

/*  **************************************************
    FUNCTION NAME: get_dynamic_str
    PURPOSE: a flexible routine to retrieve a string from
      the user of arbitrary size.
    INPUT: none.
    OUTPUT: a character pointer which points to the
      allocated string on the heap.
    NOTE: this function MALLOCs memory.
```

```
   AUTHOR: MCD
*************************************************** */

char *get_dynamic_str()
{
   char *outstr = NULL;
   char inchar;

   int strmax = STRAVG;
   int charcnt = 0;

   /* malloc the outstr */
   /* You should not hard code constants, use a #define */
   outstr = (char *) malloc(sizeof(char) * STRAVG);
   if (!outstr)
   {
     fprintf(stderr,
     "get_dynamic_str: FATAL - malloc failed on %d bytes.\s",
     STRAVG);
     return(NULL);
   }

   while ( (inchar = getchar()) != '\n')
   {
     if (charcnt == strmax)
     {
       outstr = realloc(outstr,sizeof(char) * strmax +
       STRAVG);
       if (!outstr)
       {
         fprintf(stderr,
         "get_dynamic_str: FATAL - realloc failed on %d bytes.\n",
         strmax + STRAVG);
         return(NULL);
       }
       strmax += STRAVG;
     }
     outstr[charcnt] = inchar;
     charcnt++;
   }

   /* null-terminate the string */
   outstr[charcnt] = '\0';

   return(outstr);

}
```

```c
#define LINE 40

/*   ****************************************************
   FUNCTION NAME: get_file
   PURPOSE: get an arbitrary amount of text from stdin
     until the user hits EOF (ctrl-d). The amount of
     text is limited to available memory.
   INPUT: none.
   OUTPUT: a character pointer to the start of the text
     in the heap.
   AUTHOR: MCD
   **************************************************** */
char *get_file()
{
   char *outstr = NULL;
   char inchar;

   int strmax = LINE;
   int charcnt = 0;

   /* malloc the outstr */
   /* You should not hard code constants, use a #define */
   outstr = (char *) malloc(sizeof(char) * LINE);
   if (!outstr)
   {
      fprintf(stderr,
      "get_dynamic_str: FATAL - malloc failed on %d bytes.\s",
      STRAVG);
      return(NULL);
   }

   while ( (inchar = getchar()) != EOF)
   {
      if (charcnt == strmax)
      {
         outstr = realloc(outstr,sizeof(char) * strmax +
         LINE);
         if (!outstr)
         {
            fprintf(stderr,
            "get_dynamic_str: FATAL - realloc failed on %d bytes.\n",
            strmax + LINE);
            return(NULL);
         }
         strmax += LINE;
      }
      outstr[charcnt] = inchar;
```

```
    charcnt++;
}

/* null-terminate the string */
outstr[charcnt] = '\0';

return(outstr);
}
```

Here is a sample run of the program:

<<<< Hyper-Webster >>>>
1) enter a definition.
2) list all entries.
3) display an entry.
4) exit.
choice: 1
   Enter keyword: pointer

   Enter the definition: (ctrl-D when finished)
a memory location that holds an address. Also the subject of a
book entitled *C Pointers and Dynamic Memory Management.*

<<<< Hyper-Webster >>>>
1) enter a definition.
2) list all entries.
3) display an entry.
4) exit.
choice: 2
Dictionary Entries
pointer
****** End of Entries *******

<<<< Hyper-Webster >>>>
1) enter a definition.
2) list all entries.
3) display an entry.
4) exit.
choice: 1

   Enter keyword: address

   Enter the definition: (ctrl-D when finished)
a unique number of a memory location.

<<<< Hyper-Webster >>>>
1) enter a definition.

2) list all entries.
3) display an entry.
4) exit.
choice: 3

    Enter keyword to display: pointer
Keyword: pointer
a pointer is a memory location that holds an address.
it is also the topic of a book entitled C Pointers and Dynamic
Memory Management.

>>—HyperLinks—>
0) exit to main menu.
1) address
choice:

Points to note about hyper_dict.c:

1. In hyper_dict.h, hyper_links is a dynamic array of integers. This is possible because an integer pointer does not just have to point to a single integer but can point to an array of integers; however, unlike character strings there is no termination marker so you have to keep track of how many you have (that is why I use hyper_cnt).

       **dictionary is a pointer pointer that I explain in much greater detail in the next chapter. I had either to use them here to give this program maximum flexibility or restrict the program to a fixed number of entries. For the sake of maximum flexibility I decided to introduce them early. Simply put, a *pointer pointer* is a memory location that *holds the address of a pointer*. A pointer pointer lets you create a dynamic array of pointers. This is what we have in hyper_dict.c: a dynamic array of pointers with each pointer in the array pointing to a dict_entry.

2. In get_definition(), we use our two new dynamic input routines: get_dynamic_str() and get_file(). Both of these routines get characters from stdin and malloc the space in the character string to hold the characters. The only difference between the two routines is that get_dynamic_str() terminates when it hits a '\n', and get_file() terminates at an end of file (EOF).

3. In display_entry(), you see the line

printf("%d) %s\n",i+1,
 dictionary[display_rec->hyper_links[i]]->keyword);

    The second argument in this call to printf looks complicated, but once you dissect it into its component parts it is simple. There are two major components of the expression. Here's how to break it down:

dictionary[display_rec->hyper_links[i]]->keyword
equals,
dictionary[n]->keyword, where n is the number pointed to by
display_rec->hyper_links[i].
dictionary is a pointer pointer.
dictionary[n] is the nth dict_entry pointer.

Each dict_entry has a character string member called keyword. If you use a pointer to a structure, you dereference to the member with the arrow (->) operator.

The number n or "which dictionary entry I want the keyword of" is whatever is stored in the hyper_links array. This means that display_rec->hyper_links[i] will evaluate down to a number. Since we know that the number is one of the entries in the dictionary, we can use the number as a subscript in the dictionary array.

4. The add_hyper_links() routine may look complex, but it is just a matter of knowing what you want to point to in the dictionary. All the routine does is search for the keyword of the entry just entered in all the previous definitions, and if it finds it, then it updates the hyper_link arrays in the structures. Go through the routine slowly, and make sure you understand what pointers are pointing to what dictionary entries. Here is a diagram to help you see what the layout could look like:

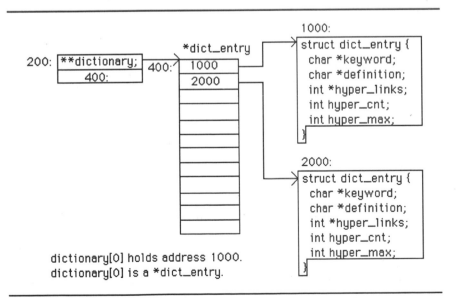

Figure 8.3.   The dictionary pointer pointer.

The above diagram reveals the simple fact that once you malloc space into a pointer pointer, you are creating an array of pointers. Each pointer is then malloced a dictionary entry.

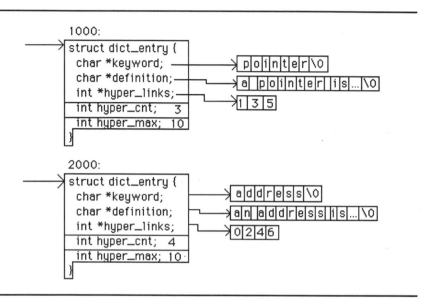

Figure 8.4. The rows of the pointer pointer.

CHAPTER QUESTIONS

1. How can programmers benefit by shifting their programming style?
2. How does the use of the sizeof compile time operator aid portability?
3. Why does the computer need to manage memory as a system resource?
4. What is the memory management philosophy behind using a free list?
5. Why verify the return argument of malloc() since you cannot get any more memory?
6. How is "thinking dynamic" linked to the cost of random access memory?

CHAPTER EXERCISES

1. In substr, simplify the program by adding a pointer that is equivalent to string1 + start.

2. Improve hyper_dict.c to check each new definition for hyperlinks to all previous entries. (Currently, only check if the new keyword is in the old definitions.)

FURTHER READING

Baase, Sara. *Computer Algorithms, Introduction to Design and Analysis*, © 1988, Addison-Wesley.

Tanenbaum, Andrew S. *Modern Operating Systems*, © 1992, Prentice-Hall, Inc.

9

Pointer Pointers and Dynamic Array Initialization

OBJECTIVE: Learn how to use pointer pointers to initialize an array within a function dynamically.

A pointer pointer is a memory location that holds the address of a pointer. Most computer texts mention pointer pointers but do a poor job of describing when you use them. This is a terrible mistake for a feature of the C language that is so valuable! The next chapter will illustrate the power and flexibility of pointer pointers. This chapter will introduce them and detail their use in parameter passing (copying). Here is a diagram of a pointer pointer:

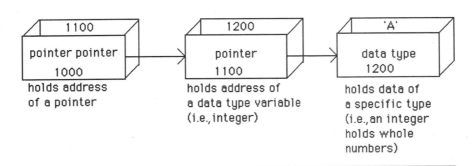

Figure 9.1.　　Pointer pointer as a container.

Here is a small piece of code that demonstrates a pointer pointer:

```
void main()
{
    int number=10;
    int *number_ptr=NULL;
    int **number_ptrptr=NULL;

    printf("the address of number is %p and it holds %d.\n",
        &number,number);
    number_ptr = &number;
    printf("the address of number_ptr is %p and it holds %p.\n",
        &number_ptr,number_ptr);
    printf("number_ptr points to %d.\n",*number_ptr);
    number_ptrptr = &number_ptr;
    printf("the address of number_ptrptr is %p and it holds %p.\n",
        &number_ptrptr, number_ptrptr);
    printf("number_ptrptr points to %p.\n",*number_ptrptr);
    printf("we can double dereference number_ptrptr to get to %d.\n",
        **number_ptrptr);
}
```

ADDRESS	VALUE
003E1F52	10
003E1F4E	003E1F52
003E1F4A	003E1F4E

```
RESULTS:
the address of number is 003E1F52 and it holds 10.
the address of number_ptr is 003E1F4E and it holds 003E1F52.
number_ptr points to 10.
the address of number_ptrptr is 003E1F4A and it holds 003E1F4E.
number_ptrptr points to 003E1F52.
we can double dereference number_ptrptr to get to 10.
```

Figure 9.2.   A paper computer on pointer pointers.

Let's look at why you need pointer pointers. One reason is to enable you to perform dynamic initialization of strings and arrays from within a function. At this point you need to be familiar with how the C language copies the value of function arguments to the stack (if you need a refresher, reread Chapter 2). By copying the functions arguments onto the stack, the compiler creates a stack variable that you then use in your function. Understanding the concept of a "stack variable" and what values you copy to it when you call a function is the key to both parameter passing (copying) and dynamic initialization. Let's look at an example of copying values to the stack with a function call:

```c
/* stack_variable.c */
#include <stdio.h>
#include <stdlib.h>
#include <string.h>
#include <ctype.h>

void func1(int num1, int *numptr, char char1, char *string)
{
  printf("the address of num1 on the stack is: %p\n",
  &num1);
  printf("the address of numptr on the stack is: %p\n",
  &numptr);
  printf("the address of char1 on the stack is: %p\n",
  &char1);
  printf("the address of string on the stack is: %p\n",
  &string);
  printf("num1 holds %d.\n",num1);
  printf("numptr holds %p.\n",numptr);
  printf("char1 holds %c.\n",char1);
  printf("string holds %p.\n",string);
}

void main()
{
  int main_int=50;
  char main_char='m';
  char main_name[] = "mike";

  printf("the address of main_int is %p.\n",&main_int);
  printf("the address of main_char is %p.\n",
  &main_char);
  printf("the address of main_name is %p.\n",
  &main_name);
  printf("main_int holds %d.\n",main_int);
  printf("main_char holds %c.\n",main_char);
  printf("main_name holds %s.\n",main_name);
  func1(main_int,&main_int,main_char,main_name);
}
```

Source 9.1.   stack_variable.c.

A run of the program produces:

the address of main_int is 003E1EAA.
the address of main_char is 003E1EA9.
the address of main_name is 003E1EA4.
main_int holds 50.
main_char holds m.
main_name holds mike.
the address of num1 on the stack is: 003E1E70
the address of numptr on the stack is: 003E1E72
the address of char1 on the stack is: 003E1E76
the address of string on the stack is: 003E1E78
num1 holds 50.
numptr holds 003E1EAA.
char1 holds m.
string holds 003E1EA4.

Here is a diagram of the stack during execution of this program:

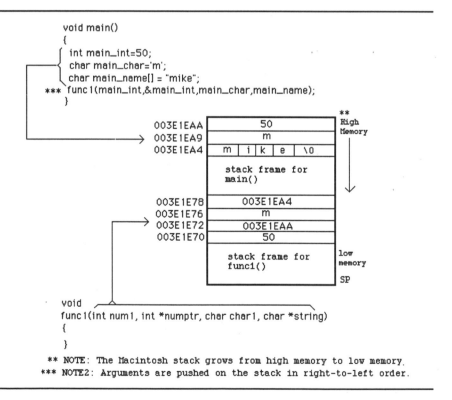

Figure 9.3.   A paper computer on stack_variables.

The essential point of the above program and diagram is that the values of the function arguments get pushed onto the stack. Those values on the stack are local variables to the function, which I like to think of as stack variables! They are variables just like any you would declare in your function. In fact, when you declare variables inside the function, they also reside on the stack, which means that there is no difference between function parameters and variables declared inside your function. So, from now on, you know that parameters are local variables that reside on the stack and get their values from the calling function. To summarize:

1. Function parameters are local variables.
2. The function parameters are initialized to the values of the function arguments in the calling function.

Now that you know what a pointer pointer is and how function parameters work, let's tie the two together with a programming problem that requires a pointer pointer as a function parameter. Here is the problem:

Have a function dynamically initialize an array without using the return value. Although you could use the return value to return the address of the array, it is nice to reserve the return value as an error status. Here is a program that demonstrates this:

```
/* dynamic_initialize.c */
#include <stdio.h>
#include <stdlib.h>
#include <string.h>
#include <ctype.h>

#define TESTNUM 5

extern char *get_dynamic_str();

/*  ***************************************************
   FUNCTION NAME: get_data
   PURPOSE: get data from the user. initialize and
     allocate space on the heap for a date and
     item string
   INPUT: date - a character string pointer pointer to
                  be initialized. The pointer pointer
```

Source 9.2.   dynamic_initialize.c.

```
                     will hold the address of a pointer in
                     the main function.
            item - a character string pointer pointer also
                     to be initialized.
            price - a float
    OUTPUT: an integer. 1 on success, else 0.
    NOTE: It is useful to use the return of the function
      for an error status and at the sametime have the
      function get data for the main program. It is just
      this case where we first encounter "pointer
      pointers".
    AUTHOR: MCD
*************************************************** */

int get_data(char **date, char **item, float *price)
{
  char cdate[80];

  /* let's look at what is on the stack */
  printf("date is %p.\n",date);
  printf("item is %p.\n",item);
  printf("price is %p.\n",price);

  /* Getting the first string in this fashion is
  only used to illustrate filling the dynamic character
  array manually with malloc. We really should use
  get_dynamic_str because it is easier. */
  printf("Enter the date: ");
  scanf("%s",cdate);
  fflush(stdin);

  *date = (char *) malloc(sizeof(char) * (strlen(cdate)
  + 1));
  if (!*date)
  {
    fprintf(stderr,"get_data: FATAL - malloc failed!\n");
    return(0);
  }

  strcpy(*date,cdate);

  /* here is the easier way */
  printf("Enter the item: ");
```

Source 9.2. *Continued.*

```
  *item = get_dynamic_str();
  if (!*item)
  {
    fprintf(stderr,
    "get_data: FATAL - get_dynamic_str failed!\n");
    return(0);
  }

  printf("Enter the price: ");
  scanf("%f",price);

  return(1);
}

/*  ************************************************
  FUNCTION NAME: get_scores
  PURPOSE: get scores from the user and initialize a
    tests array in the main function.
  INPUT: number - an integer which is the number of scores
           to get.
           tests - an integer pointer pointer which holds the
           address of an integer pointer in the main function.
  OUTPUT: an integer, 1 on success, else 0.
  AUTHOR: MCD
*************************************************** */
int get_scores(int number,int **tests)
{
  int i=0;

  *tests = (int *) malloc(sizeof(int) * number);
  if (!*tests)
  {
    fprintf(stderr,"get_scores: FATAL - malloc failed!\n");
    return(0);
  }

  for (i = 0; i < number; i++)
  {
    printf("get score %d: ",i);
    scanf("%d",&((*tests)[i]) );
  }

  return(1);
}
```

Source 9.2. *Continued.*

```
/*   ****************************************************
   FUNCTION NAME: main for dynamic _initialize.c
   PURPOSE: pass off pointers to data retrieval routines
      for "filling." This demonstrates one valuable use
      of pointer pointers.
   INPUT: none.
   OUTPUT: none.
   AUTHOR: MCD
*************************************************** */
void main()
{
   char *main_date=NULL, *main_item=NULL;
   float main_price = 0.0;
   int .i=0,*test_array=NULL;

   /* we already know what the pointers hold. They all
   hold NULL because that is what we initialized
   them to. */

   /* PROBLEM: I want to "fill" the pointers with data
   but since I should program in a modular fashion I
   want a separate function to do the work. How do I get
   a function to malloc space and fill pointers that
   I have declared in this function?
   ANSWER: whenever you want to modify the value of a
   variable inside a function you PASS (COPY) THE
   ADDRESS to the function. Do the same thing for
   pointers. */

   /* let's look at the addresses of our variables. */
   printf("main_date is at address %p.\n",&main_date);
   printf("main_item is at address %p.\n",&main_item);
   printf("main_price is at address %p.\n",&main_price);
   printf("test_array is at address %p.\n",&test_array);

   if (!get_data(&main_date, &main_item, &main_price))
   {
      fprintf(stderr,"main: FATAL - get_data failed!\n");
      exit(0);
   }

   /* let's print out the data get_data provided. */
   printf("date: %s item: %s price: %3.2f\n",
   main_date, main_item, main_price);
```

Source 9.2.   *Continued.*

```
/* let's get 10 scores */
if (!get_scores(TESTNUM, &test_array))
{
  fprintf(stderr,"main: FATAL - get_scores
  failed!\n");
  exit(0);
}

/* print out the scores */
printf("test scores: ");
for (i=0; i<TESTNUM; i++)
{
  if (!i)
    printf("%d",test_array[i]);
  else if (i != (TESTNUM - 1))
    printf(",%d",test_array[i]);
  else
    printf(",%d\n",test_array[i]);
}
}
```

Source 9.2. *Continued.*

Here is a run of the program:

main_date is at address 003E1D08.
main_item is at address 003E1D04.
main_price is at address 003E1D00.
test_array is at address 003E1CFC.
date is 003E1D08.
item is 003E1D04.
price is 003E1D00.
Enter the date: 1/28/93
Enter the item: computer book
Enter the price: 39.95
date: 1/28/93 item: computer book price: 39.95
get score 0: 98
get score 1: 97
get score 2: 96
get score 3: 95
get score 4: 90
test scores: 98,97,96,95,90

Points to note about dynamic array initialization:

1. The goal of the above program is to have a function modify the value of our pointer. To have a function modify *any* variable, you pass (copy) the variables address. If I copy a pointer's address into the stack variable, what does the stack variable become? A pointer pointer!

2. It is very natural to return a zero (0) as an error condition because your if statement can read

    if (NOT function_success)

    then error

    i.e. if (!get_data(...))
    {
            /* error */;
    }

Now that we have our feet wet in pointer pointers, the next chapter reveals some exciting uses.

CHAPTER QUESTIONS

1. Is a pointer pointer different from a pointer?
2. Do we really need pointer pointers?
3. What is a stack variable?
4. Is there any difference between function parameters and local variables?

CHAPTER EXERCISES

1. Define a problem that must be solved by using a pointer pointer.
2. Modify get_scores to get any number of scores the user wants to enter. *HINT*: You will need to use realloc().

10

Pointer Pointers and Pointer Arrays

OBJECTIVE: Explore the flexibility of dynamic two-dimensional arrays and string arrays.

Besides using pointer pointers in function parameters, pointer pointers can be used effectively to create and manipulate dynamic two-dimensional arrays. Here is a diagram of a dynamic two-dimensional array:

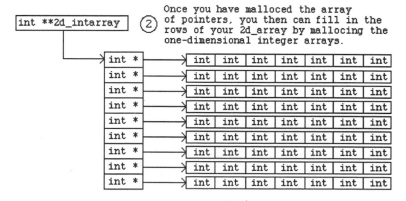

Figure 10.1.   How to set up a pointer array.

Arrays of pointers are often glossed over in C-language books; however, they are extremely useful tools for rapid manipulation of large amounts of data in memory. The diagram above clearly shows the two-step process involved in setting up a dynamic 2d array (what I refer to as a pointer-pointer buf or ppbuf).

"If this is just a two-dimensional array, why do I need a ppbuf? I already know how to declare a two-dimensional array: int 2d_array[10][10]."

What if you don't use all 10 rows of the array. Or more importantly, what if while the program is running you had a need for 15 rows?

"I can see how this can be handy. Continue."

As I was saying, there is a two-step process to create a ppbuf:

1. Allocate an array of pointers.
2. Allocate each array of objects of the chosen data type.

Here is a small program to show you how to construct a ppbuf:

```
/* class_ppbuf.c */
#include <stdlib.h>
#include <stdio.h>
#include <string.h>
#include <ctype.h>

extern char *get_dynamic_str();

/*  **************************************************
    FUNCTION NAME: main for class_ppbuf.c
    PURPOSE: an example on creating a pointer pointer
      buffer (ppbuf).
    INPUT: none.
    OUTPUT: none.
    AUTHOR: MCD
************************************************** */

void main()
{
  int **class_grades=NULL;
  char **student_names=NULL;
  int num_students=0;
  int num_tests=0;
  int i=0,j=0;
```

Source 10.1. class_ppbuf.c.

```
printf("Enter the number of students in your class: ");
scanf("%d",&num_students);
printf("Enter the number of tests you gave this semester: ");
scanf("%d",&num_tests);

if (!num_students || !num_tests)
{
  fprintf(stderr,
  "You entered 0 for one of the fields. Goodbye.\n");
  exit(0);
}

/* malloc the space for ppbufs */
student_names = (char **) malloc(sizeof(char *) *
num_students + 1);
if (!student_names)
{
  fprintf(stderr,
  "class_ppbuf: FATAL - malloc failed!\n");
  exit(0);
}

class_grades = (int **) malloc(sizeof(int *) *
(num_students + 1);
if (!class_grades)
{
  fprintf(stderr,
  "class_ppbuf: FATAL - malloc failed!\n");
  exit(0);
}

for (i=0; i<num_students;i++)
{
  fflush(stdin);
  printf("Enter name of student %d: ",i);
  student_names[i] = get_dynamic_str();

  /* malloc space for the 1d int array */
  class_grades[i] = (int *) malloc(sizeof(int) *
  num_tests);
  if (!class_grades[j])
  {
    fprintf(stderr,"class_ppbuf: FATAL - malloc failed!\n");
```

Source 10.1. *Continued.*

```c
        exit(0);
    }

    for (j=0; j<num_tests; j++)
    {

        printf("Enter the students grade for test %d: ",j);
        scanf("%d",&(class_grades[i][j]));
    }
}

/* print out what we stored. See Exercise 1 to expand
upon this program. We will print out the information
differently than we received it. */
for (i=0; i < num_tests; i++)
{
    printf("On test #%d...\n",i);
    for (j=0; j < num_students; j++)
        printf("\t%s scored %d.\n",
        student_names[j],class_grades[j][i]);
}
}
```

Source 10.1.   class_ppbuf.c.

Here is a run of the program:

Enter the number of students in your class: 3
Enter the number of tests you gave this semester: 3
Enter name of student 0: Mike Daconta
Enter the students grade for test 0: 95
Enter the students grade for test 1: 88
Enter the students grade for test 2: 90
Enter name of student 1: John Doe
Enter the students grade for test 0: 99
Enter the students grade for test 1: 98
Enter the students grade for test 2: 97
Enter name of student 2: Bob Smith
Enter the students grade for test 0: 87
Enter the students grade for test 1: 88
Enter the students grade for test 2: 86
On test #0...
      Mike Daconta scored 95.
      John Doe scored 99.
      Bob Smith scored 87.

On test #1...
 Mike Daconta scored 88.
 John Doe scored 98.
 Bob Smith scored 88.
On test #2...
 Mike Daconta scored 90.
 John Doe scored 97.
 Bob Smith scored 86.

Points to note on class_ppbuf.c:

1. The calls to malloc, that is, malloc(sizeof(char *)...) and malloc(sizeof(int *) ...), give us another example of how important the use of the sizeof macro is for portability. Different machines will have different address sizes and therefore different sizes of the pointer variables that need to hold those addresses.
2. student_names[i] = get_dynamic_str()—Here is our utility program saving us work again and making life easier. Just as there are a ton of generic utility programs for string operations, we programmers need to huddle down with our nose to the grindstone and churn out a slew of generic utilities for dynamic pointer operations and manipulations!
3. class_grades[i] = (int *) malloc(...)—Here's a pop quiz: How would you write this assignment using pointer dereferencing? *(class_grades + i) = (int *) malloc(...);
4. printf("\t% scored %d.\n", student_names[j], class_grades[j][i]); If both student_names and class_grades are two-dimensional arrays, how can I print out the whole row of students_names? I confess that student_names is more than just a two-dimensional array of characters. Each row is NULL-terminated! This makes student_names a dynamic array of strings! With all of the powerful string processing functions at our disposal, you can see why it is easier to manipulate ppbufs of character strings! Here is a diagram of a char ppbuf that will highlight the difference:

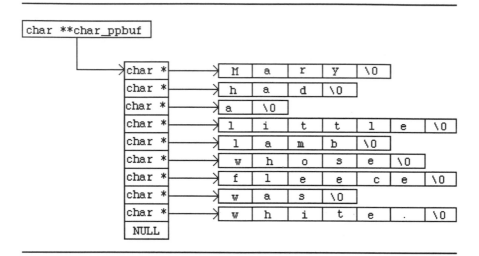

Figure 10.2.   A char ppbuf.

"Hey, what is that NULL pointer doing at the end?"

That is a handy trick we can use to enable us to know the end of our pointer array in the same way that we use the ASCII NUL to know when the string ends.

"You like tagging new items inside examples to see if we catch you, don't ya?"

I take the fifth.

Our definition of a *ppbuf* is *a NULL-terminated array of pointers to NULL-terminated character arrays.* The ppbuf data structure can be a powerful tool for manipulating text files by creating reusable utility programs to manipulate the data structure. I will demonstrate a few of the utilities here and provide more in Chapter 15.

```
/* ppbuf_utils */

#include <stdio.h>
#include <string.h>
#include <stdlib.h>
#include <ctype.h>

extern char *strdup();
```

Source 10.2.   ppbuf_utils.c.

```
/* #define DEBUGPP */

/*  **************************************************
   FUNCTION NAME: file2ppbuf
   PURPOSE: read a text file into a character pointer
     pointer buffer.
   INPUT: filename - a character string of the file to
     open.
   OUTPUT: a character pointer pointer which points to
     the null-terminated ppbuf.
   NOTE: this function MALLOCs memory.
   AUTHOR: MCD
************************************************** */
char **file2ppbuf(char *filename)
{
   FILE *fp;

   char str[512];
   char **buf=NULL;

   int linechunk=100;
   int cnt=0, len=0;

   if (!filename)
   {
     fprintf(stderr,"file2ppbuf:FATAL - filename is
     NULL!\n");
     return(NULL);
   }

   if ((fp = fopen(filename,"r"))==NULL)
   {
     fprintf(stderr,"file2ppbuf: FATAL - cannot open %s!\n",
     filename);
     return(NULL);
   }

   buf = (char **) malloc(sizeof(char *) * linechunk);
   if (!buf)
   {
     fprintf(stderr,"file2ppbuf: FATAL - malloc failed!\n");
     return(NULL);
   }
```

Source 10.2. *Continued.*

```
  cnt = 0;
  while (!feof(fp))
  {
    if (fgets (str,500,fp))
    {
      len = strlen(str);
      buf[cnt] = (char *) malloc(sizeof(char) * len + 1);
      strcpy(buf[cnt],str);
      cnt++;
      if (cnt >= linechunk)
      {
        /* realloc in quantities of 100 */
        buf = (char **) realloc(buf,sizeof(char *) *
        (cnt + 100));
        if (!buf)
        {
          fprintf(stderr,
          "file2ppbuf: FATAL - realloc failed!\n");
          return(NULL);
        }
        linechunk += 100;
      }
    }
  }

  buf[cnt] = NULL;

  fclose(fp);
  return(buf);
}

/*  **************************************************
  FUNCTION NAME: free_ppbuf
  PURPOSE: free each string and the array of pointers
    that make up a ppbuf.
  INPUT: inbuf - a character pointer pointer buffer to
                 be freed.
         count - the number of lines in the ppbuf. If 0
                 it will expect the ppbuf to be
         null-terminated.
  OUTPUT: none.
  AUTHOR: MCD
************************************************** */
void free_ppbuf(char **inbuf, int count)
```

Source 10.2. *Continued.*

```
{
  int i;

  if (inbuf)
  {
    if (count>0)
    {
      for (i = 0; i < count; i++)
        if (inbuf[i]) free(inbuf[i]);
      free(inbuf);
    }
    else
    {
      for (i = 0; inbuf[i]; i++)
        count++;
      for (i = 0; i<count; i++)
        if (inbuf[i]) free(inbuf[i]);
      free(inbuf);
    }
  }
}
```

Source 10.2.   *Continued.*

Here is an example on the use of file2ppbuf():

```
/* dissect.c */
#include <stdio.h>
#include <stdlib.h>
#include <string.h>
#include <ctype.h>

extern char **file2ppbuf();
extern void free_ppbuf();
extern char *get_dynamic_str();

/*  **************************************************
    FUNCTION NAME: main for dissect.c
    PURPOSE: read in any C source file and count the
      number of words, statements, blocks and comments in
      the source file.
    INPUT: none.
```

Source 10.3.   dissect.c.

```
  OUTPUT: none.
  AUTHOR: MCD
************************************************** */
void main()
{
  char *source=NULL;
  char *dot=NULL;
  char **src_ppbuf=NULL;
  char last_char='~';

  int i=0,j=0;
  int words=0, statements=0, blocks=0, comments=0;

  short int alnum=0;

  printf("Source file to dissect? ");
  source = get_dynamic_str();
  if (!source)
  {
    fprintf(stderr,"dissect: FATAL - get_dynamic_str()
    failed!\n");
    exit(0);
  }
  dot = strrchr(source,'.');
  if (!dot || strcmp(dot,".c"))
  {
    fprintf(stderr,
    "dissect: FATAL - source file must end in .c!\n");
    exit(0);
  }
  src_ppbuf = file2ppbuf(source);
  if (!src_ppbuf)
  {
    fprintf(stderr,
    "dissect: FATAL - file2ppbuf failed!\n");
    exit(0);
  }
  printf("Dissecting ... ");
  fflush(stdout);
  /* go through all the lines in the file */
  for (i=0; src_ppbuf[i]; i++)
  {
    for (j=0; src_ppbuf[i][j]; j++)
    {
```

Source 10.3.   *Continued.*

```
      if (isalnum(src_ppbuf[i][j]))
        alnum=1;
      else if (isspace(src_ppbuf[i][j]))
      {
        if (alnum)
        {
          words++;
          alnum=0;
        }
      }
      else if (ispunct(src_ppbuf[i][j]))
      {
        switch (src_ppbuf[i][j]) {
          case ';':
            statements++;
            break;
          case '{':
            blocks++;
            break;
          case '*':
            if (last_char == '/')
              comments++;
            break;
        } /* end of switch */
      } /* end of if */
      last_char = src_ppbuf[i][j];
    } /* end of for all chars on line */
  } /* end of for all lines */

  printf("Done.\n");
  printf("+---------- %s ----------+\n",source);
  printf("Number of words : %d\n",words);
  printf("Number of statements : %d\n",statements);
  printf("Number of blocks : %d\n",blocks);
  printf("Number of comments : %d\n",comments);
  printf("+-----------------------------------+\n");

  free_ppbuf(src_ppbuf,0);
}
```

Source 10.3.   *Continued.*

Here is a sample run of the program on two files. The first data file is called tst_dissect.c, and the second one was the above program, dissect.c. Here is the file tst_dissect.c:

```
/* test_dissect */
#include <stdlib.h>

void main()
{
  int i;

  /* this program will do nothing */
  for (i =0; i<100; i++)
    ;
}
```

Here is the run of the program:

Source file to dissect? tst_dissect.c
Dissecting ... Done.
+——————— tst_dissect.c ———————+
Number of words : 17
Number of statements : 4
Number of blocks : 1
Number of comments : 2
+————————————————————————+

Source file to dissect? dissect.c
Dissecting ... Done.
+——————— dissect.c ———————+
Number of words : 160
Number of statements : 45
Number of blocks : 11
Number of comments : 6
+————————————————————————+

Points to note about dissect.c:

1. The line for (i=0; src_ppbuf[i]; i++) is a good example of how we can take advantage of knowing that the ppbuf is NULL-terminated. src_ppbuf[i] is the ith character pointer in the character pointer array. As i is incremented, src_ppbuf[i] will eventually hit the NULL terminator and terminate the for loop.
2. The line for (j=0; src_ppbuf[i][j]; j++) takes advantage of the fact that the character string in the ith row is NULL-terminated. The two subscripts, [i] and [j], illustrate how the ppbuf is just a dynamic two-dimensional, NULL-terminated array.

Using the other ppbuf utilities is left to you as exercises. There are many useful applications for ppbufs in parsing, message passing, and data manipulation. I encourage you to add more ppbuf utilities, improve the ones I have given you, and create even better pointer pointer data structures!

Before we leave ppbufs, there is a special case pointer pointer where you may not have realized you were dealing with a pointer pointer: the argv portion of the command line arguments. Here is a program to demonstrate:

```
/* cmd_line.c */
#include <stdio.h>
#include <stdlib.h>
#include <string.h>
#include <ctype.h>

/* the next include is only necessary to allow
   command line arguments in THINK C */
#include <console.h>

/*  ************************************************
    FUNCTION NAME: main for cmd_line.c
    PURPOSE: demonstrate how argv is a pointer pointer.
    INPUT: none.
    OUTPUT: none.
    AUTHOR: MCD
************************************************** */
void main(int argc, char *argv[])
{
  int i,j;

  char **my_arg=NULL;

  /* the next statement is just THINK C's way of allowing
  command line arguments in the mac's window environment. */
  argc = ccommand(&argv);

  my_arg = argv;

  /* print out as strings */
  for (i=0; i<argc; i++)
    printf("argv[%d] = %s.\n",i,my_arg[i]);
```

Source 10.4.   cmd_line.c.

```
  /* print out as characters */
  for (i=0; i<argc; i++)
  {
    /* wouldn't it have been easier if they made the
    argv pointer pointer NULL terminated? */
    for (j=0; *((*(my_arg+i)) + j); j++)
      printf("character[%d] of the row[%d] is
      %c.\n",j,i,my_arg[i][j]);
  }
}
```

Source 10.4. *Continued.*

Here is a run of the program with the command line "cmd_line –s src –d dst":

argv[0] = cmd_line.
argv[1] = -s.
argv[2] = src.
argv[3] = -d.
argv[4] = dst.
character[0] of the row[0] is c.
character[1] of the row[0] is m.
character[2] of the row[0] is d.
character[3] of the row[0] is _.
character[4] of the row[0] is l.
character[5] of the row[0] is i.
character[6] of the row[0] is n.
character[7] of the row[0] is e.
character[0] of the row[1] is -.
character[1] of the row[1] is s.
character[0] of the row[2] is s.
character[1] of the row[2] is r.
character[2] of the row[2] is c.
character[0] of the row[3] is -.
character[1] of the row[3] is d.
character[0] of the row[4] is d.
character[1] of the row[4] is s.
character[2] of the row[4] is t.

Points to note about cmd_line.c:

1. Although the function ccommand() is specific to THINK C, notice what is passed into the function (&argv). What is that? Yep! A pointer pointer pointer! Why was the address of argv passed (copied

to the stack)? The answer is that the function command needs to malloc into argv!

2. The first for loop simply prints out the arguments passed in. It should be very clear that argv is a char pointer pointer and argv[i] is a char pointer. To prove this is the case, I substituted my own pointer pointer (my_arg) for argv.

3. The doubly nested loops are used to print out the characters of the argv array. In the inner for loop I use the pointer method of array access as my termination test:

*((*my_arg + i)) + j)

Let's look at how that expression breaks down in our paper computer:

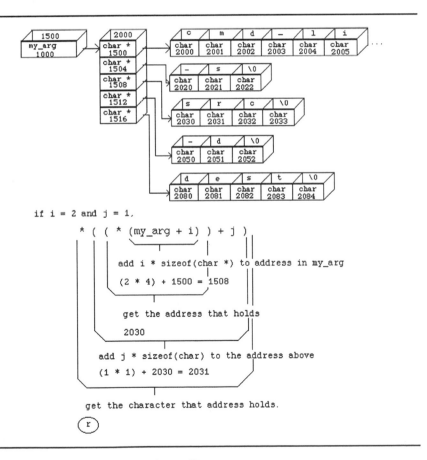

Figure 10.3.   Paper computer on **argv.

4. Last, I make the suggestion that argv would be simpler to handle if it was NULL-terminated just like our ppbufs. If we passed (copied) it to our dupppbuf() function (listed in Chapter 15), the ppbuf returned would be NULL-terminated. You should try this as an exercise.

CHAPTER QUESTIONS

1. When allocating space for a dynamic two-dimensional array, why do you malloc the row of pointers first?
2. What benefit do we gain by attaching an extra NULL pointer to the end of our ppbuf?
3. Is there any limit on the size of the file we can process using file2ppbuf?
4. What benefit is there in passing argv to dupppbuf()?

CHAPTER EXERCISES

1. Enhance the program class_ppbuf.c to average all the students' test scores for one test or average all the scores for a single student.
2. Improve the function file2ppbuf() to make it more flexible by eliminating the static character array str.
3. Create a program that uses ppbuf_utils to strip comments and empty lines from a C source file.
4. Create a program that uses ppbuf_utils to translate a file of keywords into a skeleton C program. For example, the keyword "for" would be expanded into

```
for ( = 0, < ; i++)
{
}
```

5. Create a dynamic overlay from a ppbuf by using the following structure:

```
typedef struct Soverlay Soverlay;
typedef Soverlay *Soverlayp;
struct Soverlay {
    char *name;
    char ***overlay;
};
```

An overlay is an array of pointers for each line of a ppbuf. The pointers should hold the start addresses for items of the "overlay type." Useful overlays to create are word overlays (breaking down a text block into its syntactical structure—noun overlay, verb overlay), number overlays, address overlay, phone overlay. The purpose of overlays will be autorecognition of multiple ownership sets for portions of a text document that can trigger automatic actions. For example, a modification of an address in a letter that has an address overlay associated with it would trigger an automatic update of an address database.

6. Create a generic function that takes the command line ppbuf and will return a specific option by passing the function the option character. For example, if the command line is myprog –s source –d dest, the function would be char *get_opt(char optchar). If you passed in the letter s, you would get back an allocated string that pointed to "source."

11

Pointers and Abstract Data Types

OBJECTIVE: Examine pointer manipulations in abstract data types and learn how to create generic models of ADTs.

This book is not designed to instruct you on the purpose, design, and benefits of various abstract data types (ADTs); instead, this chapter will reveal how pointers are at the core of most common data structures. Also, we will only look at the three most common ADTs: stacks, lists, and trees.

11.1. STACKS

In Chapter 2, we discussed the run time stack used to copy arguments from a calling function to the called function. Here is an implementation of a stack using a ppblock structure:

Here is the header file:

```
/* string_stack.h */
#define STACK_GROW 50

typedef struct ppstack ppstack;
typedef ppstack *ppstackp;
struct ppstack {
 char **queue;
```

```
    int top;
    int stack_qty;
    int stack_max;
  };
```

Here is the implementation of the stack:

```
/* string_stack.c */
#include <stdio.h>
#include <stdlib.h>
#include <string.h>
#include <stdarg.h>
#include "string_stack.h"

extern char *strdup();

/*  *************************************************
  FUNCTION NAME: init_ppstack
  PURPOSE: allocates memory for and initializes a
    pointer pointer stack structure.
  INPUT: none.
  OUTPUT: a pointer to ppstack structure in the heap.
  NOTE: this function MALLOCs memory.
  AUTHOR: MCD
***************************************************
*/ppstackp init_ppstack()
{
  ppstackp outstack;

  /* malloc space for the stack structure */
  outstack = (ppstackp) malloc(sizeof(ppstack));
  if (!outstack)
  {
    fprintf(stderr,"init_stack: FATAL - malloc failed!\n");
    return(NULL);
  }

  /* fill in the initial values of this stack */
  outstack->queue = (char **) malloc(sizeof(char *) *
  (STACK_GROW + 1));
  if (!outstack->queue)
  {
```

Source 11.1.   string_stack.c.

```
      fprintf(stderr,"init_stack: FATAL - malloc
      failed!\n");
      if (outstack) free(outstack);
      return(NULL);
   }

   outstack->top = -1;
   outstack->stack_qty = 0;
   outstack->stack_max = STACK_GROW;

   return(outstack);
}

/*  **************************************************
   FUNCTION NAME: pushstr
   PURPOSE: add a string to the stack.
   METHOD: the queue represents a stack that will grow
      at one end. The bottom of our stack will be the 0th
      entry and the top of the stack will be the last
      entry added. We will realloc as necessary.
   INPUT: thestack - a ppstack pointer which is the
                      stack to push the string onto.
         data - a character string to push on the stack.
   OUTPUT: an integer as an error status. 1 on success,
      else 0.
   AUTHOR: MCD
************************************************** */
int pushstr(ppstackp thestack, char *data)
{
   char **temp;

   if (!data)
   {
     fprintf(stderr,
     "pushtr: FATAL - data argument is NULL!\n");
     return(0);
   }

   if (!thestack)
   {
     fprintf(stderr,
     "pushtr: FATAL - stack pointer is NULL!\n");
     return(0);
   }
```

Source 11.1.   *Continued.*

```
/* make a copy of the data string and push it onto
the stack */
/* first check if there is enough room on the stack */
if ( (thestack->stack_qty + 1) >= thestack->stack_max)
{
   /* grow the stack before adding, realloc in chunks
   of STACK_GROW */
   temp = (char **) realloc(thestack->queue,
           sizeof(char *) * (thestack->stack_max +
           STACK_GROW));
   if (!temp)
   {
   fprintf(stderr,
   "pushstr: FATAL - unable to GROW STACK!\n");
   return(0);
   }

   thestack->queue = temp;
   thestack->stack_max += STACK_GROW;
}

/* increment top pointer now that we know the stack
has enough room */
thestack->top++;

/* malloc the space for this new element */
thestack->queue[thestack->top] = (char *)
malloc(sizeof(char) * (strlen(data) + 1));
if (!thestack->queue[thestack->top])
{
   fprintf(stderr,"pushstr: FATAL - unable to store data,
   malloc failed!\n");
   return(0);
}

/* copy the data */
strcpy(thestack->queue[thestack->top],data);

/* increment stack quantity */
thestack->stack_qty++;

return(1);
}
```

Source 11.1. *Continued.*

```
/*   ******************************************************
  FUNCTION NAME: popstr
  PURPOSE: pop the top string off the stack.
  METHOD: strdup the top of the stack, free the top and
    decrement the top.
  INPUT: thestack - a pointer to the ppstack to pop from.
  OUTPUT: a copy of the string off the top of the
    stack.
  AUTHOR: MCD
******************************************************
*/char *popstr(ppstackp thestack)
{
  char *data;

  /* check if the stack pointer is valid */
  if (!thestack)
  {
    fprintf(stderr,
    "popstr: FATAL - stack pointer is NULL!\n");
    return(NULL);
  }

  /* check if there is anything on the stack */
  if ( (thestack->top<0) || (thestack->stack_qty<1) )
  {
    fprintf(stderr,
    "popstr: FATAL - you cannot pop an empty stack!\n");
    return(NULL);
  }

  /* give the user a copy of the data then free it */
  data = strdup(thestack->queue[thestack->top]);

  /* free the top of the stack */
  if (thestack->queue[thestack->top]) free(thestack->
  queue[thestack->top]);

  /* decrement the top and the stack quantity */
  thestack->top--;
  thestack->stack_qty--;

  return(data);
}
```

Source 11.1. *Continued.*

```
/*   **************************************************
   FUNCTION NAME: mpush
   PURPOSE: push multiple strings onto the stack.
   METHOD: follows the same methodology as pushstr
      except that it wraps the method in a while loop
      that retrieves each argument off of the variable
      argument list.
   INPUT: thestack - a pointer to the ppstack to push
      arguments on. The call to this routine must end
      with a NULL. For example,
      mpush(mystack,"joe","john",NULL);
   OUTPUT: an integer as an error status. 1 on success,
      else 0.
   AUTHOR: MCD
************************************************** */
/* multiple push. Null terminate end of the list. */
int mpush(ppstackp thestack,...)
{
  char **temp;
  char *next,*data;

  va_list args;

  if (!thestack)
  {
    fprintf(stderr,
    "mpush: FATAL - stack pointer is NULL!\n");
    return(0);
  }

  va_start(args, thestack);

  while (next = va_arg(args,char *))
  {
    data = strdup(next);
    /* make a copy of the data string and push it onto
    the stack */
    /* first check if there is enough room on
    the stack */
    if ( (thestack->stack_qty + 1) >= thestack->stack_max)
    {
    /* grow the stack before adding, realloc in chunks
    of STACK_GROW */
```

Source 11.1. *Continued.*

```
    temp = (char **) realloc(thestack->queue,
            sizeof(char *) * (thestack->stack_max +
            STACK_GROW));
    if (!temp)
    {
      fprintf(stderr,
      "mpush: FATAL - unable to GROW STACK!\n");
      return(0);
    }

    thestack->queue = temp;
    thestack->stack_max += STACK_GROW;
    }

    /* increment top pointer now that we know the stack
    has enough room */
    thestack->top++;

    /* malloc the space for this new element */
    thestack->queue[thestack->top] = (char *)
    malloc(sizeof(char) * (strlen(data) + 1));
    if (!thestack->queue[thestack->top])
    {
    fprintf(stderr,
    "mpush: FATAL - unable to store data, malloc failed!\n");
    return(0);
    }

    /* copy the data */
    strcpy(thestack->queue[thestack->top],data);

    /* increment stack quantity */
    thestack->stack_qty++;
    if (data) free(data);
  }

  return(1);
}

/*  ***********************************************
  FUNCTION NAME: mpop
  PURPOSE: pop a multiple number of strings off of the
    stack.
```

Source 11.1. *Continued.*

```
  METHOD: follows the same method as popstr except that
    it repeats the process number_topop times.
  INPUT: thestack - a pointer to the ppstack to pop from.
          number_topop - integer with the number of
              strings to pop from the stack.
  OUTPUT: a pointer pointer buffer with the strings
    from the stack.
  AUTHOR: MCD
************************************************** */
char **mpop(ppstackp thestack,int number_topop)
{
  char **data;
  int i=0;

  /* check if the stack pointer is valid */
  if (!thestack || !number_topop)
  {
    fprintf(stderr,
    "mpop: FATAL - invalid input arguments!\n");
    return(NULL);
  }

  /* check if there is anything on the stack */
  if ( (thestack->top<0) || (thestack->stack_qty<1) )
  {
    fprintf(stderr,
    "mpop: FATAL - you cannot pop an empty stack!\n");
    return(NULL);
  }
  /* check if there are enough items to pop */
  if ( thestack->stack_qty < number_topop )
  {
    fprintf(stderr,
      "mpop: FATAL - you requested %d items,
      when there are only %d!\n", number_topop,
      thestack->stack_qty);
    return(NULL);
  }

  /* initialize the output buffer */
  data = (char **) malloc(sizeof(char *) *
  (number_topop + 1));
  if (!data)
  {
```

Source 11.1. *Continued.*

```
      fprintf(stderr,"mpop: FATAL - malloc failed!\n");
      return(NULL);
    }

  for (i = 0; i < number_topop; i++)
  {
    /* give the user a copy of the data then free it */
    data[i] = strdup(thestack->queue[thestack->top]);

    /* free the top of the stack */
    if (thestack->queue[thestack->top]) free(thestack->
    queue[thestack->top]);

    /* decrement the top and the stack quantity */
    thestack->top--;
    thestack->stack_qty--;
  }

  data[number_topop] = NULL;
  return(data);
}

/*  **************************************************
  FUNCTION NAME: print_ppstack
  PURPOSE: prints each entry in the stack.
  INPUT: thestack - a pointer to the stack to be
    printed.
  OUTPUT: none.
  AUTHOR: MCD
**************************************************** */
void print_ppstack(ppstackp thestack)
{
  int i;

  /* check if the stack pointer is valid */
  if (!thestack)
  {
    fprintf(stderr,
    "print_ppstack: FATAL - stack pointer is NULL!\n");
    return;
  }

  /* check if there is anything on the stack */
  if ( (thestack->top<0) || (thestack->stack_qty<1) )
```

Source 11.1.   *Continued.*

```
  {
    fprintf(stderr,"print_ppstack: FATAL - you cannot
    print an empty stack!\n");
    return;
  }

  printf("_____< TOP OF STACK >_____\n");
  for (i = thestack->top; i>=0; i-)
    printf("\t%s\n",thestack->queue[i]);
  printf("_____\n");
}

/*  **************************************************
  FUNCTION NAME: free_ppstack
  PURPOSE: deallocates all the memory used by a ppstack.
  INPUT: thestack - a pointer to the ppstack to be freed.
  OUTPUT: none.
  AUTHOR: MCD
************************************************** */
void free_ppstack(ppstackp thestack)
{
  int i;

  /* check if the stack pointer is valid */
  if (!thestack)
  {
    fprintf(stderr,
    "free_ppstack: FATAL - stack pointer is NULL!\n");
    return;
  }

  /* check if there is anything on the stack */
  if ( (thestack->top<0) || (thestack->stack_qty<1) )
  {
    fprintf(stderr,"the_ppstack: FATAL - you cannot
    free an empty stack!\n");
    return;
  }

  for (i = thestack->top; i>=0; i-)
    if (thestack->queue[i]) free(thestack->queue[i]);
  if (thestack->queue) free(thestack->queue);
  if (thestack) free(thestack);
}
```

Source 11.1. *Continued.*

Here is a test program:

```
/* test_stack.c */
#include <stdio.h>
#include <stdlib.h>
#include <string.h>
#include "string_stack.h"

extern ppstackp init_ppstack();
extern int pushstr();
extern char *popstr();
extern void print_ppstack();
extern void free_ppstack();
extern int mpush(ppstackp thestack,...);
extern char **mpop();

/*  **************************************************
   FUNCTION NAME: main for test_stack.c
   PURPOSE: test all the stack functions.
   INPUT: none.
   OUTPUT: none.
   AUTHOR: MCD
************************************************** */
main()
{
  ppstackp test_stack;
  char *data;
  char **mdata;

  char buf[80];

  test_stack = init_ppstack();
  if (!test_stack)
  {
  fprintf(stderr,"init_ppstack failed!\n");
    exit(0);
  }

    printf("test_stack initialized!\n");

    if (!pushstr(test_stack,"mike"))
  {
```

Source 11.2.   test_stack.c.

```c
        fprintf(stderr,"pushstr failed!\n");
        exit(0);
    }

    if (!pushstr(test_stack,"frank"))
    {
      fprintf(stderr,"pushstr failed!\n");
      exit(0);
    }

    if (!pushstr(test_stack,"Kris"))
    {
      fprintf(stderr,"pushstr failed!\n");
      exit(0);
    }
      if (!pushstr(test_stack,"Joe"))
    {
      fprintf(stderr,"pushstr failed!\n");
      exit(0);
    }

    if (!pushstr(test_stack,"John"))
    {
      fprintf(stderr,"pushstr failed!\n");
      exit(0);
    }

    if (!pushstr(test_stack,"chris"))
    {
      fprintf(stderr,"pushstr failed!\n");
      exit(0);
    }

    if (!pushstr(test_stack,"cj"))
    {
      fprintf(stderr,"pushstr failed!\n");
      exit(0);
    }

    print_ppstack(test_stack);

    printf("press return\n");
    scanf("%s",buf);
```

Source 11.2. *Continued.*

```
data = popstr(test_stack);
if (data)
  printf("popped data is %s\n",data);
else
  printf("popstr failed!\n");

data = popstr(test_stack);
if (data)
  printf("popped data is %s\n",data);
else
  printf("popstr failed!\n");

data = popstr(test_stack);
if (data)
  printf("popped data is %s\n",data);
else
  printf("popstr failed!\n");

data = popstr(test_stack);
if (data)
  printf("popped data is %s\n",data);
else
  printf("popstr failed!\n");

  print_ppstack(test_stack);

data = popstr(test_stack);
if (data)
  printf("popped data is %s\n",data);
else
  printf("popstr failed!\n");

data = popstr(test_stack);
if (data)
  printf("popped data is %s\n",data);
else
  printf("popstr failed!\n");

  print_ppstack(test_stack);

data = popstr(test_stack);
if (data)
  printf("popped data is %s\n",data);
```

Source 11.2.   *Continued.*

```
      else
        printf("popstr failed!\n");

        print_ppstack(test_stack);

    data = popstr(test_stack);
    if (data)
        printf("popped data is %s\n",data);
    else
        printf("popstr failed!\n");

        print_ppstack(test_stack);

        printf("press return\n");
        scanf("%s",buf);

        printf("multiple push ... \n");
        mpush(test_stack,"mike","frank","joe","john",
        "cj",NULL);
        print_ppstack(test_stack);

        printf("multiple pop ... \n");
        mdata = mpop(test_stack,2);
        print_ppstack(test_stack);

        printf("multiple pop ... \n");
        mdata = mpop(test_stack,2);
        print_ppstack(test_stack);

        printf("multiple push ... \n");
        mpush(test_stack,"lori","kristine",NULL);
        print_ppstack(test_stack);

        printf("press return\n");
        scanf("%s",buf);

        printf("multiple pop ... \n");
        mdata = mpop(test_stack,2);
        print_ppstack(test_stack);

        printf("multiple pop ... \n");
        mdata = mpop(test_stack,2);
        print_ppstack(test_stack);
}
```

Source 11.2.   *Continued.*

Here is a run of the test program:

```
test_stack initialized!
_____< TOP OF STACK >_____
    cj
    chris
    John
    Joe
    Kris
    frank
    mike

_____
popped data is cj
popped data is chris
popped data is John
popped data is Joe
_____< TOP OF STACK >_____
    Kris
    frank
    mike

_____
popped data is Kris
popped data is frank
_____< TOP OF STACK >_____
    mike

_____
popped data is mike
print_ppstack: FATAL - you cannot print an empty stack!
popstr: FATAL - you cannot pop an empty stack!
popstr failed!
print_ppstack: FATAL - you cannot print an empty stack!
multiple push ...
_____< TOP OF STACK >_____
    cj
    john
    joe
    frank
    mike

_____
multiple pop ...
_____< TOP OF STACK >_____
    joe
    frank
    mike

_____
multiple pop ...
_____< TOP OF STACK >_____
```

mike

---

multiple push ...
____< TOP OF STACK >____
   kristine
   lori
   mike

---

multiple pop ...
____< TOP OF STACK >____
   mike

---

multiple pop ...
mpop: FATAL - you requested 2 items, when there are only 1!
____< TOP OF STACK >____
   mike

Notes on string_stack.c:

1. In string_stack.h, observe how the ppstack structure is very similar to the ppblock structure in Chapter 15. The queue pointer pointer holds the stack data while the integer top holds the index of the string on top of the stack.

   The main idea to implementing a stack is to create a data storage structure that only grows and shrinks at one end. Here is a picture of how a ppbuf can function as a stack:

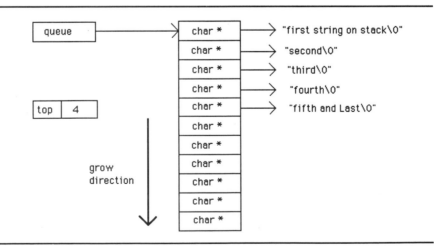

Figure 11.1.   The string stack.

2. The function init_ppstack() initializes a ppstack structure. Question: Why is outstack->top initialized to –1? (*HINT:* Go back to Chapter 5, section 5.1).
3. In pushstr(), I should have used strdup() to replace the calls to malloc() and strcpy().
4. The function popstr() is straightforward.
5. The function mpush() allows the caller to push multiple arguments onto the stack. To accomplish this, the function allows a variable number of arguments. The variable arguments are popped off the variable arguments list and pushed on the string stack until a NULL argument is popped off the variable argument list.

   WARNING: If the last argument to the mpush() function call is not a NULL, the behavior of this function is undefined (I always hated when I read that—what is undefined?). Translation of undefined: CRASH AND BURN!
6. The function mpop() allows the user to pop multiple arguments from the stack and returns a NULL-terminated ppbuf.
7. The functions print_ppstack(), free_ppstack(), and main() are straightforward.
8. A nontrivial use of the string stack can be found in the sortppbuf() routine in Chapter 15.

11.2. LINKED LISTS

A linked list is nothing more than a flexible structure for storing and manipulating an indeterminate and changing quantity of data items. You create a structure of the data you want to store with one item of the structure (usually the last) a pointer to another structure of the same type. The chain of structures is continued for all the stored items, and the last one stores a NULL pointer. Here is a diagram of a linked list of addresses:

```
struct address_struct {
  char *name;
  char *street;
  char *city;
  char *state;
  int zip;
  struct  address_struct *next;
};
```

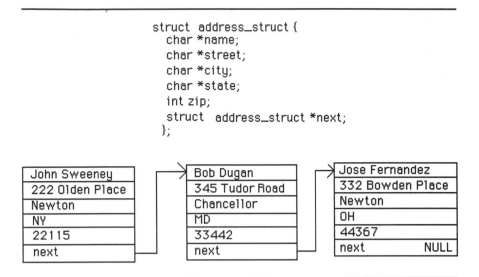

Figure 11.2.   A sample linked list.

Linked lists are very easy to construct and manipulate and many C textbooks provide instruction on how to build a linked list. The problem with this approach is that you have to duplicate the same creation, addition, and manipulation functions for every linked list you create. Because each linked list you build is built using a specific data structure, you need to create an add_element, delete_element, and delete_list for every different type of list you want to create. Luckily, using pointers and variable arguments, we can build a generic linked list structure that is flexible enough to work on any data structure. Here is the code for these generic linked lists.

Here is the header file:

```
/* gll.h */

#ifndef GLL_LIST
#define GLL_LIST

struct genericlist {
 int ns,ni,nf;
 char **Strings;
 int *Integers;
 float *Floats;
 struct genericlist *next;
};
```

```
typedef struct genericlist *glptr;
/* Here is the utility routines to create and manipulate
generic linked lists.*/
glptr initgll(int numstr,int numint, int numflt,...);
int addgll_node(glptr start, ...);
void printgll();
glptr srchgll(glptr start, int numkeys, ...);
glptr delgll_node(glptr start, glptr searchptr);
int extractgll_node(glptr start, glptr searchptr, ...);
void delgll();
glptr sortgll(glptr start, int numkeys, ...);
#endif
```

Here is the library code for gll.c:

```
#include <stdlib.h>
#include <stdio.h>
#include <stdarg.h>
#include <ctype.h>
#include <string.h>

#include "gll.h"

/*  ************************************************
   FUNCTION NAME: initgll
   PURPOSE: allocate space for and initialize a generic
     linked list structure.
   INPUT: numstr - integer which is the number of
                   strings in the generic structure, also
                   represents the number of strings that
                   will follow in the variable argument list.
          numint - integer which is the number of
                   integers in the generic structure, also
                   represents the number of integers that
                   will follow in the variable argument
                   list.
          numflt - integer which is the number of floats
                   in the generic structure, also represents
                   the number of floats that will follow in
                   the variable argument list.
```

Source 11.3.   gll.c.

```
    OUTPUT: a pointer to the start of the generic linked
       list.
    AUTHOR: MCD
*************************************************** */
glptr initgll(int numstr,int numint,int numflt,...)
{
  glptr head;
  int i,j,k;
  va_list args;
  char *shold;
  int ihold;
  float fhold;

  if ( (numstr<0) || (numint<0) || (numflt<0) )
  {
    fprintf(stderr,
    "initgll: parameter count less than 0.\n");
    return(NULL);
  }
  else
    head = (glptr) malloc(sizeof(struct genericlist));
  if (!head)
  {
      fprintf(stderr,
      "initgll: error mallocing structure memory.\n");
    return(NULL);
  }

  va_start(args,numflt);

  /* store the counts in the structure. */
  head->ns = numstr; head->ni = numint; head->nf =
  numflt;

  /* malloc the memory for the structure, based upon
     the counts. After the memory for the structure is
     malloced. Loop through the field count, malloc the
     memory for the fields and assign the fields. */
  if (numstr>0)
  {
    head->Strings = (char **) malloc(sizeof(char *) *
    numstr);
    if (!head->Strings)
    {
```

Source 11.3.   *Continued.*

```
      fprintf(stderr,
       "initgll: error mallocing structure memory.\n");
      return(NULL);
   }

   for (i = 0; i < numstr; i++)
   {
     shold = va_arg (args,char *);
     head->Strings[i] = (char *)malloc(sizeof(char) *
     (strlen(shold) + 1));
     strcpy(head->Strings[i], shold);
   }
 }

 if (numint>0)
 {
   head->Integers = (int *) malloc(sizeof(int) *
   numint);
   if (!head->Integers)
   {
     fprintf(stderr,
      "initgll: error mallocing structure memory.\n");
     return(NULL);
   }

   for (j = 0; j < numint; j++)
   {
    ihold = (int) va_arg(args,double);
    head->Integers[j] = ihold;
   }
 }

 if (numflt>0)
 {
    head->Floats = (float *) malloc(sizeof(float) *
    numflt);
    if (!head->Floats)
   {
      fprintf(stderr,
      "initgll: error mallocing structure memory.\n");
     return(NULL);
   }

   for (k = 0; k < numflt; k++)
```

Source 11.3.   *Continued.*

```
  {
    fhold = (float) va_arg(args,double);
    head->Floats[k] = fhold;
  }
}

va_end(args);

/* now assign the next pointer to null */

head->next = NULL;

/* now return the head pointer */

return(head);
}

/*  **************************************************
  FUNCTION NAME: addgll_node
  PURPOSE: add a record to the generic linked list.
  INPUT: start - a generic linked list pointer to the
         start of the generic list.
         ... - variable arguments which must match the
         same type and number of arguments specified
         in the initgll called.
  OUTPUT: an integer as an error status. 1 on success,
    else 0.
  AUTHOR: MCD
************************************************** */
int addgll_node(glptr start, ...)
{
  glptr node;
  glptr traverse;
  int i,j,k;
  va_list args;
  char *shold;
  int ihold;
  float fhold;
  int nums,numi,numf;

  if (!start)
  {
    fprintf(stderr,
      "\a\aaddgll_node: list pointer is NULL.\n");
```

Source 11.3. *Continued.*

```
        return(0);
}

/* retrieve the field counts from the head node */
nums = start->ns;
numi = start->ni;
numf = start->nf;

/* traverse to the end of the list */
for (traverse = start; traverse->next;
traverse = traverse->next)
;

/* malloc space for the new node */
node = (glptr) malloc(sizeof(struct genericlist));
if (!node)
{
    fprintf(stderr,"addgll_node: error mallocing
    structure memory.\n");
    return(0);
}
va_start(args,start);

/* store the counts in the structure. */
node->ns = nums; node->ni = numi; node->nf = numf;

/* malloc the memory for the structure, based upon
   the counts. After the memory for the structure is
   malloced. Loop through the field count, malloc the
   memory for the fields and assign the fields. */
if (nums>0)
{
   node->Strings = (char **) malloc(sizeof(char *) *
   nums);
   if (!node->Strings)
  {
    fprintf(stderr,"addgll_node: error mallocing
    structure memory.\n");
    return(0);
  }

  for (i = 0; i < nums; i++)
 {
    shold = va_arg(args,char *);
```

Source 11.3. *Continued.*

```
        node->Strings[i] = (char *) malloc(sizeof(char) *
        (strlen(shold) + 1));
        strcpy(node->Strings[i], shold);
   }
 }

if (numi>0)
{
    node->Integers = (int *) malloc(sizeof(int) *
    numi);
   if (!node->Integers)
  {
     fprintf(stderr,"addgll_node: error mallocing
      structure memory.\n");
     return(0);
  }
   for (j = 0; j < numi; j++)
   {
     ihold = (int) va_arg(args,double);
     node->Integers[j] = ihold;
   }
 }

if (numf>0)
{
    node->Floats = (float *) malloc(sizeof(float) *
    numf);
   if (!node->Floats)
  {
     fprintf(stderr,"addgll_node: error mallocing
     structure memory.\n");
     return(0);
  }

   for (k = 0; k < numf; k++)
   {
     fhold = (float) va_arg(args,double);
     node->Floats[k] = fhold;
   }
 }
 va_end(args);

 /* now assign the next pointer to null */
```

Source 11.3. *Continued.*

```
    node->next = NULL;

    /* now connect this new node to the list */

    traverse->next = node;

    /* return success */
    return(1);
}
/*    **************************************************
   FUNCTION NAME: printgll
   PURPOSE: prints each node of the input generic linked
      list.
   INPUT: start - a generic linked list pointer to the
          start of the list to be printed.
          fptr - where the output should go, either
          stdout or a file pointer.
   OUTPUT: none.
   AUTHOR: MCD
************************************************** */
void printgll(glptr start,FILE *fptr)
{
   glptr traverse;
   int ns, ni, nf;
   int i,j,k,cnt;

   /* retrieve the number of fields from the start node */
   ns = start->ns;
   ni = start->ni;
   nf = start->nf;

   for (traverse = start,cnt=1; traverse;
traverse = traverse->next,cnt++)
   {
           fprintf(fptr,
           "——— node %d ———\n",cnt);
     for (i = 0; i < ns; i++)
        fprintf(fptr,"%s\n",traverse->Strings[i]);
     for (j = 0; j < ni; j++)
       fprintf(fptr,"%d,",traverse->Integers[j]);
      fprintf(fptr,"\n");
     for (k = 0; k < nf; k++)
        fprintf(fptr,"%f,",traverse->Floats[k]);
```

Source 11.3.   *Continued.*

```
      fprintf(fptr,"\n");
   }
      fprintf(fptr,"—————————————————————\n");
}


/*  **************************************************
  FUNCTION NAME: srchgll
  PURPOSE: searches for a specific node within the
    generic linked list.
  METHOD: the function allows any number of keys to be
    entered as criteria for the search. a key has three
    fields - a key type (string, integer or float), a
    position in the generic structure, and the value of
    the key to compare to the generic structure. The
    keys are read in from the variable argument list
    and then the generic linked list is searched until
    all keys are matched or the list is exhausted.
  INPUT: start - a generic linked list pointer of the
                   list to be searched.
         numkeys - an integer which represents the
                   number of key groups to follow.
                   a key group has three fields as
                   described above.
         ... - the keys.
  OUTPUT: a generic linked list pointer to the node
           that matches all of the keys. Returns
           NULL if no node matches the keys.
  AUTHOR: MCD
************************************************** */
glptr srchgll(glptr start, int numkeys, ...)
{
  struct key{
    char keytype;
    int keypos;
     void *keyval; /* a typeless key value */
  };
  struct key **keys;
  va_list args;
  char *shold;
  int i,ihold;
  float fhold;
  glptr traverse;
  int keysmatch=0;
```

Source 11.3.   *Continued.*

```
 if (!start)
{
  fprintf(stderr,
    "\a\asrchgll: linked list pointer is NULL.\n");
  return(NULL);
}

 if ((!numkeys) || (numkeys < 0))
{
  fprintf(stderr,
    "\a\asrchgll: number of keys cannot be 0 or
    negative.\n");
  return(NULL);
}

/* malloc the space for numkeys */

keys = (struct key **) malloc(sizeof(struct key *) *
numkeys);
if (!keys)
{
  fprintf(stderr,
    "\a\asrchgll: mallocing error.\n");
  return(NULL);
}

va_start(args, numkeys);

/* loop through and retrieve key values */
for (i = 0; i < numkeys; i++)
{
  keys[i] = (struct key *) malloc(sizeof(struct key));
  keys[i]->keytype = (char) va_arg(args, int);
  keys[i]->keypos = (int) va_arg(args,double);
  switch (keys[i]->keytype) {
 case 's':
    shold = (char *) va_arg(args,char *);
    keys[i]->keyval = (char *) malloc(sizeof(char) *
    (strlen(shold) + 1));
    strcpy(keys[i]->keyval, shold);
  break;
 case 'i':
    keys[i]->keyval = (int *) malloc(sizeof(int));
```

Source 11.3.   *Continued.*

```
        ihold = (int) va_arg(args,double);
        memcpy(keys[i]->keyval,&ihold,sizeof(int));
      break;
    case 'f':
        keys[i]->keyval = (float *) malloc(sizeof(float));
        fhold = (float) va_arg(args,double);
        memcpy(keys[i]->keyval,&fhold,sizeof(float));
      break;
    default:
        fprintf(stderr,
        "\a\asrchgll: key case is incorrect.\n");
        return(NULL);
  }
}


/* now we can traverse the list and check if any of the
   nodes match all of the keys. The node must match ALL
   of the specified key values exactly! */

  for (traverse = start; traverse; traverse=traverse->
  next)
{
  keysmatch = 0;
  for (i = 0; i < numkeys; i++)
  {
      switch (keys[i]->keytype) {
    case 's':
    if (!(strcmp(traverse->Strings[(keys[i]->
    keypos)-1],
    keys[i]->keyval)))
    keysmatch++;
    break;
    case 'i':
    memcpy(&ihold,keys[i]->keyval,sizeof(int));
    if ( (traverse->Integers[(keys[i]->keypos)-1])
    == ihold)
    keysmatch++;
    break;
    case 'f':
        memcpy(&fhold,keys[i]->keyval,sizeof(float));
        if ( (traverse->Floats[(keys[i]->keypos)-1])
        == fhold)
        keysmatch++;
```

Source 11.3. *Continued.*

```
        break;
      }
      if(keysmatch < (i + 1)) break;
      }
        if (keysmatch == numkeys)
      }
   for (i = 0; i < numkeys; i++)
   if (keys[i]) free(keys[i]);
   if (keys) free (keys);
   return(traverse);
   }
   for (i = 0; i < numkeys; i++)
   if (keys[i]) free(keys[i]);
   if (keys) free (keys);
   return(NULL);
}


/*  **************************************************
   FUNCTION NAME: delgll_node
   PURPOSE: delete a specific node from the generic
     linked list.
   INPUT:    start - the start of the linked list from
             which the node will be deleted.
             searchptr - a generic linked list pointer to
             the node to be deleted.
   OUTPUT: a generic linked list pointer to the start of
     the list in case the node to be deleted is the
     first one.
   AUTHOR: MCD
**************************************************** */
glptr delgll_node(glptr start, glptr searchptr)
{
   glptr traverse;
   glptr temp;
   int i,j,k;

   if ( (!start) || (!searchptr) )
  {
       fprintf(stderr,
         "\a\adelgll_node: argument pointer set to NULL\n");
       return(NULL);
  }
    if (start == searchptr)
```

Source 11.3.   *Continued.*

```
{
  temp = start->next;
  /* free the heap space used */
    if (start->ns > 0)
    {
      for (i = 0; i< start->ns; i++)
          if (start->Strings[i]) free(start->
          Strings[i]);
      if (searchptr->Strings) free (searchptr->
      Strings);
    }
   if (start->ni > 0)
   {
     if (searchptr->Integers) free (searchptr->
     Integers);
  }
  if (start->nf > 0)
  {
    if (searchptr->Floats) free (searchptr->Floats);
  }
  free(start);
  start = temp;
  return(start);
}

  for (traverse=start; traverse; traverse=traverse->
  next)
{
    if (traverse->next == searchptr)
    {
    traverse->next = searchptr->next;
    /* free the heap space used */
    if (start->ns > 0)
    {
      for (i = 0; i< start->ns; i++)
        if (searchptr->Strings[i]) free(searchptr->
        Strings[i]);
      if (searchptr->Strings) free(searchptr->Strings);
    }
    if (start->ni > 0)
    {
      if (searchptr->Integers) free(searchptr->
      Integers);
```

Source 11.3. *Continued.*

```
    }
    if (start->nf > 0)
    {
      if (searchptr->Floats) free(searchptr->Floats);
    }
    free(searchptr);
    return(start);
    }
  }
  return(NULL);
}

/*  **************************************************
  FUNCTION NAME: extractgll_node
  PURPOSE: extract the data fields from a node of the
    generic linked list. Used in conjunction with
    srchgll_node.
  INPUT: start - a generic linked list pointer to the
                  start of the generic linked list.
         searchptr - a pointer to the node to extract
                     the data from.
         ... - the variable argument list must consist
               of pointers to the variables to be
               assigned the data.
  OUTPUT: an integer as an error status. 1 on success,
    else 0.
  AUTHOR: MCD
**************************************************** */
int extractgll_node(glptr start, glptr searchptr, ...)
{
  glptr traverse;
  va_list args;
  int numstr,numint,numflt;
  char *sptr;
  int *iptr;
  float *fptr;
  int i,j,k;
  if ( (!start) || (!searchptr) )
{
    fprintf(stderr,
      "\a\aextractgll_node: argument pointer set to NULL\n");
    return(0);
}
```

Source 11.3. *Continued.*

```c
  for (traverse=start; traverse; traverse=traverse->
  next)
{
  if (traverse == searchptr)
  {
  va_start(args,searchptr);

  /* store the counts */
  numstr = start->ns; numint=start->ni; numflt=start->nf;

  if (numstr>0)
  {
    for (i = 0; i < numstr; i++)
   {
      sptr = va_arg (args, char *);
      strcpy(sptr,traverse->Strings[i]);
   }
  }

  if (numint>0)
  {
    for (j = 0; j < numint; j++)
   {
      iptr = va_arg(args,int *);
      memcpy(iptr,&(traverse->Integers[j]),
      sizeof(int));
   }
  }

  if (numflt>0)
  {
#ifdef DEBUG_EXTRACTGLL_NODE
    printf("extractgll_node: Extracting the floats.\n");
#endif

    for (k = 0; k < numflt; k++)
   {
      fptr = va_arg(args,float *);
      memcpy(fptr,&(traverse->Floats[k]),
      sizeof(float));
   }
  }

  va_end(args);
```

Source 11.3. *Continued.*

```
      return(1);
     } /* if */
   } /* for */
   return(0);
}


/*  **************************************************
   FUNCTION NAME: delgll
   PURPOSE: delete an entire generic linked list.
   INPUT: start - a pointer to the start of the generic
                  linked list to delete.
   OUTPUT: none.
   AUTHOR: MCD
************************************************** */
void delgll(glptr start)
{
   int i,j,k;
   glptr traverse = 0L;
   glptr temp = 0L;

    if(!start)
   {
      fprintf(stderr,
        "delgll: Cannot free a NULL linked list.\n");
      return;
   }

   for(traverse = start;traverse->next;traverse =
   temp)
   {
      temp = traverse->next;

      /* free the heap space used */

      for (i = 0; i < traverse->ns; i++)
      free(traverse->Strings[i]);

      if(traverse->ns > 0) free(traverse->Strings);
      if(traverse->ni > 0) free(traverse->Integers);
      if(traverse->nf > 0) free(traverse->Floats);

      free(traverse);
   }
}
```

Source 11.3.   *Continued.*

Here is a test program for the gll library:

```
/* tstgll.c */
#include <stdio.h>
#include <stdlib.h>
#include <string.h>
#include <ctype.h>

#include "gll.h"

/*  *************************************************
    FUNCTION NAME: main for tstgll.c
    PURPOSE: test all the generic linked list functions.
    INPUT: none.
    OUTPUT: none.
    AUTHOR: MCD
************************************************** */
void main()
{
  glptr studentgll=NULL,searchptr=NULL;

  char name[80], street[80], city[32], state[3];

  int zip, age;

  float grade;

  /* a list of student records */
  studentgll = initgll(4,2,1,"Jack Bright",
          "222 Golden lane", "Tinseltown","LA",
          (double) 32341, (double) 21, (double) 3.9);
  if (!studentgll)
  {
    fprintf(stderr,"tstgll: FATAL - initgll failed!\n");
    exit(0);
  }
  if (!addgll_node(studentgll,"Cindy Society",
          "323 Spruce st.","Holyoake","MA",
          (double) 22113, (double) 22, (double) 3.2))
  {
    fprintf(stderr,
    "tstgll: FATAL - addgll_node failed!\n");
```

Source 11.4.   tstgll.c.

```
    exit(0);
}

if (!addgll_node(studentgll,
"John Green","323 Oak st.","Beantown","VT",
        (double) 10743, (double) 19, (double) 3.0))
{
  fprintf(stderr,
  "tstgll: FATAL - addgll_node failed!\n");
  exit(0);
}
if (!addgll_node(studentgll,"Guy Studly",
"221 Boulder st.","Dolittle","DE",
        (double) 22543, (double) 20, (double)
          2.5))
{
  fprintf(stderr,
  "tstgll: FATAL - addgll_node failed!\n");
  exit(0);
}

printgll(studentgll,stdout);

if ((searchptr = srchgll(studentgll,1,'s',(double) 1,
"John Green")) == NULL)
{
  printf("srchgll could not find John Green.\n");
}
else
  printf("srchgll found John Green\n");

studentgll = delgll_node(studentgll,searchptr);

if (!studentgll)
{
  fprintf(stderr,"tstgll: FATAL - delgll_node failed!\n");
  exit(0);
}

printgll(studentgll,stdout);

if ((searchptr = srchgll(studentgll,1,'s',(double) 1,
"Cindy Society")) == NULL)
```

Source 11.4.   *Continued.*

```
  {
    printf("srchgll could not find Cindy Society.\n");
  }
  else
    printf("srchgll found Cindy Society\n");
  if (!extractgll_node(studentgll,searchptr,name,
  street,city,state,&zip,&age,&grade))
  {
    fprintf(stderr,
    "tstgll: FATAL - extractgll_node failed!\n");
    exit(0);
  }

  printf("name is %s.\n",name);
  printf("street is %s.\n",street);
  printf("city is %s.\n",city);
  printf("state is %s.\n",state);
  printf("zip is %d.\n",zip);
  printf("age is %d.\n",age);
  printf("grade is %f.\n",grade);

  delgll(studentgll);
}
```

Source 11.4.   *Continued.*

Here is the run of the test program:

```
————————— node 1 —————————
Jack Bright
222 Golden lane
Tinseltown
LA
32341,21,
3.900000,
————————— node 2 —————————
Cindy Society
323 Spruce st.
Holyoake
MA
22113,22,
3.200000,
```

——————————— node 3 ———————————
John Green
`323 Oak st.`
Beantown
VT
10743,19,
3.000000,
——————————— node 4 ———————————
Guy Studly
221 Boulder st.
Dolittle
DE
22543,20,
2.500000,

—————————————————————————

srchgll found John Green
——————————— node 1 ———————————
Jack Bright
222 Golden lane
Tinseltown
LA
32341,21,
3.900000,
——————————— node 2 ———————————
Cindy Society
323 Spruce st.
Holyoake
MA
22113,22,
3.200000,
——————————— node 3 ———————————
Guy Studly
221 Boulder st.
Dolittle
DE
22543,20,
2.500000,

—————————————————————————

srchgll found Cindy Society
name is Cindy Society.
street is 323 Spruce st..
city is Holyoake.
state is MA.
zip is 22113.
age is 22.
grade is 3.200000.

Notes on gll.c:

Before I discuss specific points about the gll library, it is important to understand why these and all generic tools are useful. Generic code forces you to understand a concept fully by having to implement a full suite of functions to support it. Generic code also makes you write better code because the goal of the code is to have as many developers use the code as possible. Anytime you have the opportunity to write reusable code, take advantage of it. The experience and potential time savings far outweigh any learning curve. The motivation for this library came from the desire to create a single set of functions to handle multiple-linked lists within the same application. I encourage you to improve this library for your own use.

1. The generic list structure is designed to store any type of data record. For completeness, you should add long and double pointers to handle large numbers. Integers and floats suited my applications.
2. The initgll() function is used to lay out the structure of the generic list as well as create the first node of our list. The data is popped off the variable argument list and stored in the linked list structure.
3. The addgll_node() function mallocs and attaches a new node to the end of the list. Here is a diagram of the add operation:

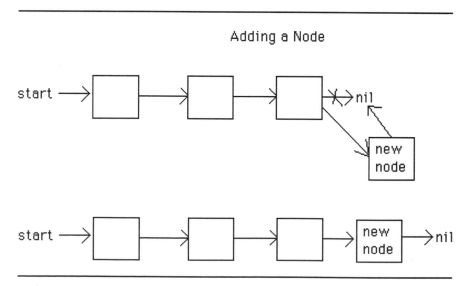

Adding a Node

Figure 11.3.   Adding a node to a linked list.

The addgll_node() function is not efficient because it traverses through all the nodes of the list (to find the end of the list) every time it wants to add a new node. A better implementation would always save a pointer to the last node and pass it into addgll_node(). This is left for you as an exercise.

4. Printgll() traverses the list and prints each node.

5. The srchgll() function finds a node in the linked list by matching one or more key values. A key has a type (string, int, or float), a position in the generic structure (which member in the array of strings, ints, or floats that I compare the key value to), and a key value. Notice that since the key value can be either a string, integer, or float, we use a generic pointer (also called a void pointer) to store the value. The best way to think about the generic pointer is that it simply points to a series of bytes; therefore, to use the data in those bytes, you must either cast the pointer to a specific type or memcpy the bytes into a variable. Both methods are used in srchgll().

6. The function delgll_node() disconnects a node from the list, then frees the node's memory. Here is a diagram of this operation:

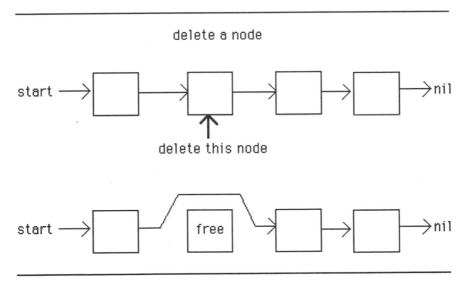

Figure 11.4.   Deleting a node from a linked list.

The delgll_node() function makes a distinction between freeing the first node of the list and freeing any other node only because if the first node is freed, the head of the list (start in the diagram) changes and a new head-of-list pointer must be returned.

7. The function extractgll_node() simply takes a pointer to a generic node (previously found by srchgll()) and copies the contents of the node into the parameters passed (copied) to the function.

8. The delgll() function traverses the entire list and frees all the allocated memory. The method used is to free from the start of the list forward to the end. In the for loop, notice that we have to store the pointer to the next node in the list before we free the current node.

9. The tstgll() program is straightforward.

11.3.   BINARY TREES

A binary tree is a hierarchical structure that allows for rapid searching by imposing rules on the nodes of the tree. The hierarchical structure is based on the family tree model with parents and children. In a binary tree, each parent has a left and right child. A rule is imposed on the children that forces the child less than the parent on the left and the child greater than the parent on the right. This rule and the tree's triangular structure allow an average search time of $\log_2 n$ (where n is the number of nodes). Here is a diagram of a tree with 15 nodes:

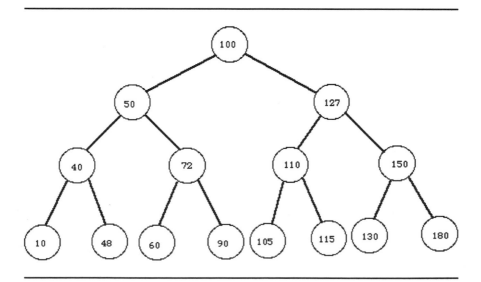

Figure 11.5.   A sample binary tree.

It is easy to see how, for 15 nodes, it will take no more than an inspection of 4 nodes to find any member of the tree. For the above reason, binary search trees are widely used. However, in order to get the fast search time, the tree must be balanced with the height of the left subtrees equaling the height of the right subtrees. The height of any tree is the number of nodes to traverse to get to the bottom of the tree (four in the above example).

Balanced trees can be more efficient than linked lists, but the balancing algorithms are much more complex. We will not cover these algorithm complexities here because they add nothing to our discussion of pointers, and there are many fine books that discuss the details of creating fast, balanced trees; however, to show the basic pointer manipulations with trees, here is a simple example.

Here is the header file:

```
/* generic_tree.h */

typedef struct generic_tree generic_tree;
typedef generic_tree *generic_treep;
struct generic_tree {
  short balance;
  short lheight;
  short rheight;
  short ns, nl, nd;
  char keytype;
  short keypos;
  char **Strings;
  long *Longs;
  double *Doubles;
  generic_treep left,right,parent;
};
```

Here is the code:

```
#include <stdio.h>
#include <stdlib.h>
#include <string.h>
#include <stdarg.h>
#include <ctype.h>

#include "generic_tree.h"
```

Source 11.5.   generic_tree.c.

```
/*  *************************************************
    FUNCTION NAME: gcmp
    PURPOSE: allow any of the three keytypes to be
      compared by specifying the keytype and its position
      within the generic tree structure.
    INPUT: keytype - character which represents the
        keytype, 's' for strings, 'l' for long. 'd' for
        double.
      keypos - integer representing the position of the
        key within the generic tree structure.
      Strings1 - array of strings of the first tree node.
      Longs1 - array of longs of the first tree node.
      Doubles1 - array of doubles of the first tree node.
      Strings2 - array of strings of the second tree node.
      Longs2 - array of longs of the second tree node.
      Doubles2 - array of doubles of the second tree node.
    OUTPUT: an integer representing the result of the
      comparison. A 1 if key 1 is greater than key 2, a 0
      if equal, and a -1 if key 1 is less than key 2.
    AUTHOR: MCD
    ************************************************* */
int gcmp(char keytype, int keypos, char **Strings1,
        long *Longs1, double *Doubles1,char **Strings2,
        long *Longs2, double *Doubles2)
{
   switch (keytype) {
     case 's':
       return (strcmp(Strings1[keypos],Strings2[keypos]));
       break;
     case 'l':
       if (Longs1[keypos] == Longs2[keypos])
         return(0);
       else
         return( Longs1[keypos] > Longs2[keypos] ? 1 : -
         1);
       break;
     case 'd':
       if ( Doubles1[keypos] == Doubles2[keypos] )
         return(0);
       else
         return( Doubles1[keypos] > Doubles2[keypos] ? 1
         : -1);
       break;
```

Source 11.5. *Continued.*

```
    } /* end of switch */
}

/*  **************************************************
    FUNCTION NAME: init_gtree
    PURPOSE: allocate memory for and initialize the root
      node of the generic tree.
    INPUT: keytype - a character represented what part of
        the generic structure (strings, longs or doubles)
        will be the key used for tree ordering and
        traversal.
      keypos - an integer which is the position of the
      key in the generic structure.
      nums - integer which is the number of strings in
      the generic structure. Must have this number of
        strings in the variable argument list.
      numl - integer which is the number of longs in the
        generic structure. Must have this number of longs
        in the variable argument list.
      numd - integer which is the number of doubles in
        the generic structure. Must have this number of
        doubles in the variable argument list.
      ... - the variable arguments are the fields
        representing the data for the root node.
    OUTPUT: a generic tree pointer that points to the
      root of the tree. NULL on error.
    AUTHOR: MCD
    ************************************************** */
generic_treep init_gtree(char keytype, short keypos,
            short nums, short numl, short numd, ...)
{
  generic_treep head;
  int i,j,k;
  va_list args;
  char *shold;
  long lhold;
  double dhold;

    if ( (nums<0) || (numl<0) || (numd<0) )
  {
      fprintf(stderr,"initgll: input paramaters invalid.\n");
     return(NULL);
  }
```

Source 11.5.   *Continued.*

```
else
  head = (generic_treep) malloc(sizeof(struct
  generic_tree));

 if (!head)
 {
    fprintf(stderr,
    "init_gtree: error mallocing structure memory.\n");
    return(NULL);
 }
  head->balance=0;
  head->lheight=0;
  head->rheight=0;
  head->keytype = keytype;
  head->keypos = keypos;

  va_start(args,numd);

  /* store the counts in the structure. */
  head->ns = nums; head->nl = numl; head->nd = numd;

  if (nums>0)
  {
    head->Strings = (char **) malloc(sizeof(char *) *
    nums);
    if (!head->Strings)
    {
      fprintf(stderr,"init_gtree: error mallocing
      structure memory.\n");
      return(NULL);
    }

    for (i = 0; i < nums; i++)
    {
      shold = va_arg (args,char *);
      head->Strings[i] = (char *)malloc(sizeof(char)
      * (strlen(shold) + 1));
      strcpy(head->Strings[i], shold);
    }
  }

   if (numl>0)
   {
```

Source 11.5. *Continued.*

```
      head->Longs = (long *) malloc(sizeof(long) * numl);
   if (!head->Longs)
   {
      fprintf(stderr,"init_gtree: error mallocing
      structure memory.\n");
      return(NULL);
   }
    for (j = 0; j < numl; j++)
   {
      lhold = (long) va_arg(args,double);
      head->Longs[j] = lhold;
   }
   }
   if (numd>0)
   {
      head->Doubles = (double *)
      malloc(sizeof(double) * numd);
      if (!head->Doubles)
   {
        fprintf(stderr,"init_gtree: error mallocing
        structure memory.\n");
        return(NULL);
   }

    for (k = 0; k < numd; k++)
   {
     dhold = (double) va_arg(args,double);
     head->Doubles[k] = dhold;
   }
  }
}

va_end(args);

/* now assign the children pointers to null */

head->left = NULL;
head->right = NULL;
head->parent = NULL;

/* now return the head pointer */

return(head);
}
```

Source 11.5.   *Continued.*

```
/*   **************************************************
   FUNCTION NAME: add_node
   PURPOSE: add a node to the generic tree.
   METHOD: first the space for the node is allocated and
       the node retrieved from the variable argument list.
       Secondly, the tree is traversed to place the node
       in its correct place according to the rules of a
       binary tree (right is greater than root and left is
       less than). Lastly, we traverse back up the tree to
       insure the balancing information is correct. There
       are three pieces of information to the balancing:
       the height of the left subtree, the height of the
       right subtree and the balance is the difference
       between the two.
   INPUT: root - a generic tree pointer to the root of
       the tree to add the node.
       ... - the variable argument list will have the
       node data to be adding and must correspond
       exactly to the way the generic tree structure was
       laid out in the init_gtree function.
   OUTPUT: an integer as an error status. 1 on success,
     else 0.
   AUTHOR: MCD
************************************************** */
int add_node(generic_treep root, ...)
{
   generic_treep new=NULL,traverse=NULL,predecessor=NULL;
   int nums, numl, numd,i,j,k,stat;
   char keytype;
   short keypos;
   char *shold;
   long lhold;
   double dhold;
   va_list args;
   short tot_height=0;

   if (!root)
   {
     fprintf(stderr,
     "add_node: FATAL - root may not be NULL!\n");
     return(0);
   }
   /* malloc space for the new node */
   new = (generic_treep) malloc(sizeof(generic_tree));
```

Source 11.5. *Continued.*

```
  if (!new)
  {
    fprintf(stderr,"add_node: FATAL - malloc failed!");
    return(0);
  }

  /* read the counts from the root */
  keytype = new->keytype = root->keytype;
  keypos = new->keypos = root->keypos;
  nums = new->ns = root->ns;
  numl = new->nl = root->nl;
  numd = new->nd = root->nd;

  /* read in all of the variable arguments */
  va_start(args,root);

if (nums>0)
{
    new->Strings = (char **) malloc(sizeof(char *) *
    nums);
    if (!new->Strings)
  {
    fprintf(stderr,"init_gtree: error mallocing
    structure memory.\n");
    return(0);
  }

  for (i = 0; i < nums; i++)
  {
    shold = va_arg (args,char *);
    new->Strings[i] = (char *)malloc(sizeof(char) *
    (strlen(shold) + 1));
    strcpy(new->Strings[i], shold);
  }
}

if (numl>0)
{
  new->Longs = (long *) malloc(sizeof(long) * numl);
  if (!new->Longs)
  {
    fprintf(stderr,"init_gtree: error mallocing
    structure memory.\n");
```

Source 11.5.   *Continued.*

```
      return(0);
 }

  for (j = 0; j < numl; j++)
 {
    lhold = (long) va_arg(args,double);
    new->Longs[j] = lhold;
 }
}

if (numd>0)
{
    new->Doubles = (double *) malloc(sizeof(double) *
    numd);
    if (!new->Doubles)
   {
      fprintf(stderr,
      "init_gtree: error mallocing structure memory.\n");
      return(0);
   }

    for (k = 0; k < numd; k++)
   {
      dhold = (double) va_arg(args,double);
      new->Doubles[k] = dhold;
   }
}

va_end(args);

/* now assign the children pointers to null */
  new->left = NULL;
  new->right = NULL;

  /* now traverse the tree */
  traverse = root;
  while (traverse)
  {
    if ( (stat = gcmp(keytype,keypos,new->Strings,
              new->Longs,
                new->Doubles,
                traverse->Strings,
                traverse->Longs,
                traverse->Doubles)) > 0)
```

Source 11.5. *Continued.*

```
    {
      if (traverse->right)
      {
        tot_height++;
        traverse = traverse->right;
      }
      else
      {
        /* add node here */
        tot_height++;
        traverse->rheight++;
        traverse->balance =
              traverse->rheight - traverse->lheight;
        traverse->right = new;
        new->parent = traverse;
        new->balance = 0;
        new->lheight=0;
        new->rheight=0;
        traverse=NULL; /* terminate loop */
      }
    }
    else
    {
      if (traverse->left)
      {
        tot_height++;
        traverse = traverse->left;
      }
      else
      {
        /* add node here */
        tot_height++;
        traverse->lheight++;
        traverse->balance =
              traverse->rheight - traverse->lheight;
        traverse->left = new;
        new->parent = traverse;
        new->balance = 0;
        new->rheight=0;
        new->lheight=0;
        traverse=NULL; /* terminate loop */
      }
    }
  } /* end of while */
```

Source 11.5.   *Continued.*

```
/* traverse back up the tree and insure the balance
counts are correct. */
predecessor=new;
for (i=1; i <= tot_height; i++)
{
  traverse = predecessor;
  predecessor = predecessor->parent;
  if ( (stat = gcmp(keytype,keypos,traverse->Strings,
      traverse->Longs,traverse->Doubles,
      predecessor->Strings,predecessor->Longs,
      predecessor->Doubles)) > 0)
  {
    /* a right node */
    if (predecessor->rheight < i)
    {
      predecessor->rheight = i;
      predecessor->balance =
        predecessor->rheight - predecessor->lheight;
    }
  }
  else
  {
    /* a left node */
    if (predecessor->lheight < i)
    {
      predecessor->lheight = i;
      predecessor->balance =
        predecessor->rheight - predecessor->lheight;
    }
  }
} /* end of for */

return(1);
}


/*  **************************************************
  FUNCTION NAME: print_key
  PURPOSE: prints the key and balance information of
    the input generic tree node.
  INPUT: keytype - a character representing the key
      type (string, long, double). keypos - the position
      of the key in the generic tree structure.
    balance - the difference between the height of the
      left and right subtree.
```

Source 11.5.   *Continued.*

```
      lheight - the height of the left subtree.
      rheight - the height of the right subtree.
      Strings - the strings of the generic tree node.
      Longs - the longs of the generic tree node.
      Doubles - the doubles of the generic tree node.
    OUTPUT: none.
    AUTHOR: MCD
*************************************************** */
void print_key(char keytype, int keypos,short
balance,short lheight, short rheight,
char **Strings, long *Longs, double *Doubles)
{
  switch (keytype) {
    case 's':
      printf("K:%s B:%d L:%d R:%d\n",
             Strings[keypos],balance,lheight,rheight);
      break;
    case 'l':
      printf("K:%ld B:%d L:%d R:%d\n",
             Longs[keypos],balance,lheight,rheight);
      break;
    case 'd':
      printf("K:%f B:%d L:%d R:%d\n",
             Doubles[keypos],balance,lheight,rheight);
      break;
  }
}
/*  *************************************************
    FUNCTION NAME: print_tree_keys
    PURPOSE: a recursive function to print a sideways
      tree that lets you visually see the tree structure.
    INPUT: r - a generic tree pointer which will point to
                the current node to print.
           l - an integer which is the level of the tree
                and used to determine how much spacing to
                print.
    OUTPUT: none.
    AUTHOR: MCD
*************************************************** */
void print_tree_keys(generic_treep r, int l)
{
  int i;

  if (!r) return;
```

Source 11.5. *Continued.*

```
    print_tree_keys(r->left, l+1);
    for (i = 0; i < l;++i) printf(" ");
    print_key(r->keytype,r->keypos,r->balance,r->lheight,
            r->rheight,r->Strings,r->Longs,r->Doubles);
    print_tree_keys(r->right,l+1);
}

/*  **********************************************
    FUNCTION NAME: main for generic_tree.c
    PURPOSE: test the generic tree function by allowing a
      simplified tree to be entered consisting of just
      doubles.
    INPUT: none.
    OUTPUT: none.
    AUTHOR: MCD
/*  **********************************************
void main()
{
    char s[80];
    long int num=0;

    generic_treep root = NULL;

    do {
      printf("enter a number: ");
      gets(s);
      num = atol(s);

      if (s[0])
      {
        if (!root) root =
        init_gtree('l',0,0,1,0,(double)num);
        else add_node(root,(double)num);
      }
    } while (s[0]);
    print_tree_keys(root,0);
}
```

Source 11.5. *Continued.*

Here is a short run of the program:

enter a number: 500
enter a number: 200
enter a number: 700

```
enter a number: 100
enter a number: 900
enter a number:
        K:100 B:0 L:0 R:0
    K:200 B:-1 L:1 R:0
K:500 B:0 L:2 R:2
    K:700 B:1 L:0 R:1
        K:900 B:0 L:0 R:0
```

Notes on generic_tree.c:

1. Note the similarities and differences between the generic_tree structure and the generic linked list structure. The generic tree has similar storage variables for the generic structure—Strings, Longs, and Doubles and the corresponding counts ns, nl, and nd. The pointers in the structure are two children (left and right) and a parent pointer for easy traversal up the tree. This is a "plain vanilla" binary tree; however, understand that there are many different variations on tree structure, each with different costs and benefits. Last, notice the key specifiers and the balancing information. The key specifiers (keytype and keypos) tell us which piece of information in our generic structure is the key (used for comparison and traversal). The balancing information (balance, lheight, and rheight) illustrate the idea of balanced versus unbalanced trees by keeping track of just how "balanced" your tree is. The add_node() function updates the balance information as you build the tree. The print_tree_keys() function will print out your tree and the balance information on each node. After visualizing balanced and unbalanced trees, the interested reader can turn to the algorithm texts under Further Reading to implement the fairly complex "balancing algorithms."

2. The function gcmp() will take two "generic structures" and the key specifier and compare the two keys returning 1 for the first greater than the second, 0 for equal, and –1 for the first less than the second.

3. The init_gtree() function is almost identical to the init_gll() function.

4. The add_node() function can be divided into three parts:
   a. Creating the new node via malloc and retrieving the variable arguments
   b. Putting the new node in the proper place in the tree by traversing the tree and comparing the key with the existing node's key
   c. After inserting the node, traversing back up to the root of the tree to update the balance information.

CHAPTER QUESTIONS

1. In init_ppstack(), how could you keep track of the stack size without the stack_size variable?
2. Why does a stack only grow in one direction?
3. What are the benefits of a generic linked list implementation?
4. What are the advantages of generic code?
5. What is the average search time of a balanced binary tree?
6. What does it mean for a tree to be balanced?

CHAPTER EXERCISES

1. Write wrap routines to pushstr() and popstr() that will convert, push, and pop integers, floats, and doubles to and from the string stack.
2. Modify popstr() and mpop() to not strdup() the return arguments. The strdup() is unnecessary and a waste of code.
3. Write an implementation of addgll_node() that will create a linked list if none is there to add to. This will eliminate the need for initgll().
4. Change addgll_node() to not traverse the entire list to find the end of the list. *HINT:* Pass (copy) in a pointer to the end of the list.
5. Create an enhanced implementation of srchgll() to allow other relational operators like OR, AND, and NOT. The current implementation assumes the AND relationship for all the keys.
6. Create two new routines to add to the generic linked list library: next() and prev() that retrieve the successor and predecessor node of a generic linked list.
7. Rewrite delgll_node() using recursion. Your implementation should snake through the linked list recursively, and when it hits the end of the list, it returns, freeing each node passed into it. The recursive approach is neat because it resembles a snake eating its own tail.

FURTHER READING

Aho, Alfred V., John E. Hopcroft, and Jeffrey D. Ullman. *Data Structures and Algorithms*, © 1983, Addison-Wesley.

Augenstein, Moshe J. and Aaron M. Tenenbaum. *Data Structures Using Pascal*, © 1981, Prentice-Hall.

Knuth, Donald E. *The Art of Computer Programming, Volume 1, Fundamental Algorithms*, © 1973, Addison-Wesley.

Weisfeld, Matt. *C: Building Portable Libraries*, © 1993, QED Publishing Group.

12

Function Pointers

OBJECTIVE: Learn the concepts, syntax, and applications of function pointers.

Function pointers are probably the least understood (and therefore least used) component of the C language. Why the confusion? Most high-level languages do not have function pointers so there is nothing to relate this mechanism to. Also, it is a subject not covered well in the current computer literature. Here we have another fine example where C delves beneath high-level programming into assembly-level power!

We will examine function pointers in three ways: the general concept, the syntax (which often turns programmers off), and then applications. In the end you should see function pointers as a veritable gold mine of programming opportunity! Let's jump right in!

12.1. CONCEPT OF FUNCTION POINTERS

We have studied the function stack and therefore understand that function arguments are placed onto the stack and not really passed to a separate, isolated block of code. In that same vein, a function is not a separate, isolated block of code but simply the address of the start point (often called the entry point) to a series of computer instructions that you bunched together and wrapped up with a high-level construct called a function. At the assembly level a function is just a sequence of instructions with a known starting point. This "known starting point" is nothing more than the address of the first instruction. That brings us to function pointers.

A function pointer is a pointer that stores the entry-point address of a function. Second, if you dereference a function pointer, it is the same as calling the function. Now we are ready for the syntax.

12.2.   SYNTAX OF FUNCTION POINTERS

The easiest way to understand the syntax of function pointers is to contrast them to the syntax of a function declaration. Let's declare a function:

char *strdup (char *instr);

We can break this declaration into three parts: the return type (char *), the function name (strdup), and the function arguments (char *instr). In assembler thinking, the return type is the type of the returned argument, the function name is the ADDRESS OF THE ENTRY POINT, and the arguments will be copied to the stack. Knowing this, it is easy to construct a function pointer declaration by simply replacing a pointer declaration with the function name.

char **funcp (char *instr); /* this is wrong !!! */

The above example is wrong for a purpose. It shows you the need to separate the pointer declaration from the type of the return value. To separate the two we wrap the pointer declaration in a set of parentheses. This gives us the correct declaration:

char *(*funcp) (char *instr);

Following this method it is easy to construct any type of function pointer you want. Let's declare an array of function pointers:

char *(*funcp[10]) (char *instr);

or a function pointer pointer,

char *(funcp) (char *instr);**

Here is a simple program to illustrate the function pointer concept and syntax:

```
/* funcptr.c */
#include <stdio.h>
#include <stdlib.h>
#include <string.h>
#include <ctype.h>

long add_em(int a, int b)
{
  return((a+b));
}

long sub_em(int a, int b)
{
  return((a-b));
}

long mult_em(int a, int b)
{
  return((a*b));
}

void upcase(char **instr)
{
  int i,len;

  if (instr);
  {
    len = strlen(*instr);
    for (i=0; i < len; i++)
    {
      if (islower((*instr)[i]))
        (*instr)[i] = toupper((*instr)[i]);
    }
  }
}

char *reverse_em(char *instr)
{
  int i,j,len;

  char *outstr;

  if (instr)
```

Source 12.1.   funcptr.c.

```
  {
    len = strlen(instr);
    outstr = (char *) malloc(sizeof(char) * (len + 1));
    if (outstr)
    {
      for (i = 0, j = len - 1; i < len; i++, j-)
        outstr[i] = instr[j];
    }
    outstr[len] = '\0';
  }
  return(outstr);
}

void main()
{
  long (*math) (int a, int b);

  long (*math_array[3]) (int a, int b);

  enum ops {add,sub,mult};

  void (*fp) (char **str);

  char *(*fp2) (char *str);

  char *str1;

  int var1, var2, i, j;
  long answer;
  fp = upcase;
  fp2 = reverse_em;

  printf("address of upcase function is %p.\n",fp);
  printf("address of reverse_em function is
  %p.\n",fp2);

  str1 = (*fp2) ("junk");
  printf("after dereferencing fp2, str1 is %s.\n",str1);
  (*fp) (&str1);
  printf("after dereferencing fp, str1 is %s.\n",str1);

  math_array[add] = add_em;
  math_array[sub] = sub_em;
  math_array[mult] = mult_em;
```

Source 12.1. *Continued.*

```
   var1 = 1; var2 = 2;
   printf("var1 is %d, var2 is %d.\n",var1,var2);

   for (i = 0; i < 10; i++)
   {
      for (j = 0; j < 3; j++)
      {
         answer = (*math_array[j]) (var1, var2);
         var1 = answer;
      }
      printf("answer is %ld.\n",answer);
   }
}
```

Source 12.1. *Continued.*

Here is the program result:

address of upcase function is 00207C86.
address of reverse_em function is 00207C8E.
after dereferencing fp2, str1 is knuj.
after dereferencing fp, str1 is KNUJ.
var1 is 1, var2 is 2.
answer is 2.
answer is 4.
answer is 8.
answer is 16.
answer is 32.
answer is 64.
answer is 128.
answer is 256.
answer is 512.
answer is 1024.

Notes on funcptr.c:
The functions add_em, sub_em, mult_em, upcase, and reverse_em
are trivial functions to illustrate function pointers. Let's move right to
the main function.

1. After the declarations, observe how you can assign directly to the
   function pointer (i.e., fp = upcase). Does this remind you of assigning an array name to a pointer? It should because array names are
   address tags just as function names are address tags! From now on
   if you see an array name or a function, think ADDRESS!

2. Dereferencing a function pointer "calls" the function it points to. (*fp) (&str1) is the same as upcase(&str1).

3. The nested for loops are an example of how function pointers allow you to call functions "flexibly." By flexibly I mean as many times as you want and in any order. This fact used creatively can lead to many dynamic and innovative programs! That brings us to applications of function pointers.

12.3. APPLICATIONS OF FUNCTION POINTERS

This chapter will be part example, part free thinking. I hope to spur your interest in function pointers and get your creative juices flowing! The more you dig into function pointers, the more golden opportunities you will discover! Here are some of the ideas I came up with, and I'm sure you can do better than I did:

1. More generic code—using function pointers you can write utility functions that work on different data types. This will increase code reusability. Here is a common function pointer example that provides a sorting routine to sort both strings and numbers:

```c
/* generic_compare.c */
#include <stdio.h>
#include <stdlib.h>
#include <string.h>
#include <ctype.h>

/*  **************************************************
   FUNCTION NAME: numcmp
   PURPOSE: treat two strings as numbers, translate them
     and compare them.
   INPUT: a - character string containing first number.
          b - character string containing second number.
   OUTPUT: an integer representing the result of the
     compare: a 1 if a > b, 0 if a = b,
     else -1.
   AUTHOR: MCD
   ************************************************** */
int numcmp(char *a, char *b)
{
   double v1,v2;
```

Source 12.2.   generic_compare.c.

```
  v1 = atof(a);
  v2 = atof(b);

  if (v1==v2)
    return (0);
  else
    return( (v1<v2) ? -1:1);
}

/*  ************************************************
  FUNCTION NAME: swap
  PURPOSE: a function to swap two character strings.
  INPUT:  a - a pointer pointer which is the address of
              the string from the calling function.
          b - a pointer pointer which is the address of
              the string from the calling function.
  OUTPUT: none.
  AUTHOR: MCD
************************************************ */
void swap(char **a, char **b)
{
  char *temp;

  temp = *a; *a = *b; *b = temp;
}

/*  ************************************************
  FUNCTION NAME: isort
  PURPOSE: an insertion sort that will work on both
    character strings and numbers.
  INPUT:  cmp - a function pointer to a compare function.
          data - a character pointer pointer which
                 points to the string array.
          length - the number of strings in the string
                   array.
  OUTPUT: none.
  AUTHOR: MCD
************************************************ */
/* here is a generic insertion sort. */
void isort(int (*cmp)(char *, char *),
char **data, int length)
{
  int i,j;
```

Source 12.2.   *Continued.*

```
  for (i = 2; i < length; i++)
  {
    j = i;
    while ( (j > 0) && ( ((*cmp)(data[j],
    data[j-1])) == -1 ))
    {
      swap(&(data[j]), &(data[j-1]));
      j--;
    }
  }
}

/*  **************************************************
  FUNCTION NAME: main for generic_compare.c
  PURPOSE: test the generic insertion sort on test data.
  INPUT: none.
  OUTPUT: none.
  AUTHOR: MCD
  *************************************************** */
void main()
{
  char *ages[10] = { "23", "56", "45", "55", "87",
  "12", "44", "99", "10", "17"};
  char *names[10] = { "john","joe","mike",
  "bill","bob","mack","mary","alice",
  "margaret","lynne"};
  int i;

  isort((int (*) (char *, char *)) strcmp, names, 10);
  for (i = 0; i < 10; i++) printf("%s ",names[i]);
  printf("\n");

  isort((int (*) (char *, char *)) numcmp, ages, 10);
  for (i = 0; i < 10; i++) printf("%s ",ages[i]);
  printf("\n");
}
```

Source 12.2.   *Continued.*

Here is a run of the program:

alice bill bob john joe lynne mack margaret mary mike
10 12 17 23 44 45 55 56 87 99

The idea behind the above generic code is to pass a function
pointer into a routine that allows you to use a data-type specific

function to go along with the specific data you want the function to work on.

2. Quicker coding—function pointers can eliminate long switch statements in your code by creating a "function dispatcher":

```c
/* dispatcher.c */

#include <stdlib.h>
#include <stdio.h>
#include <string.h>
#include <ctype.h>

void func1(char *arg1)
{
  printf("performing action 1 on %s.\n",arg1);
}

void func2(char *arg1)
{
  printf("performing action 2 on %s.\n",arg1);
}

void func3(char *arg1)
{
  printf("performing action 3 on %s.\n",arg1);
}

void func4(char *arg1)
{
  printf("performing action 4 on %s.\n",arg1);
}

void (*action[4]) (char *arg1) = {func1, func2, func3,
func4};

void do_action(int type, char *instr)
{
  if ( (type >= 0) && (type <= 3) )
    (*action[type]) (instr);
}

void main()
{
```

Source 12.3.   dispatcher.c.

```
   int i=0;

   for (i = 0; i < 4; i++)
     do_action(i, "object");
}
```

Source 12.3.   *Continued.*

Here is a run of the program:

performing action 1 on object.
performing action 2 on object.
performing action 3 on object.
performing action 4 on object.

   The function do_action is our function dispatcher that would save us a lot of typing if we used it for 20 or 30 functions. These dispatcher-type functions are very common in parsers.

3. An "adaptive" program flow—by using function pointers you could change the order in which you call functions based on an external signal or internal evaluation function. The program below demonstrates changing the order of function call based on a change of priorities:

```
/* changeprio.c */

#include <stdlib.h>
#include <stdio.h>
#include <string.h>
#include <ctype.h>

void func1(char *arg1)
{
   printf("performing action 1 on %s.\n",arg1);
}

void func2(char *arg1)
{
   printf("performing action 2 on %s.\n",arg1);
}

void func3(char *arg1)
{
```

Source 12.4.   changeprio.c.

```
    printf("performing action 3 on %s.\n",arg1);
}

void func4(char *arg1)
{
    printf("performing action 4 on %s.\n",arg1);
}

void (*initial[4]) (char *arg1) = {func1, func2, func3,
func4};
void (**action) (char *arg1);

void do_action(int type, char *instr)
{
    if ( (type >= 0) && (type <= 3) )
        (*action[type]) (instr);
}

void main()
{
    int i=0,j=0;

    action = (void (*) ()) malloc(sizeof(void (*) ()) * 4);
    for (i = 0; i < 4; i++)
        action[i] = initial[i];

    printf("Before priority adjustment.\n");
    for (i = 0; i < 4; i++)
        do_action(i, "object");

    /* reverse priorities */
    for (i = 0, j = 3; i < 4; i++,j-)
        action[i] = initial[j];

    printf("After priority adjustment.\n");
    for (i = 0; i < 4; i++)
        do_action(i, "object");
}
```

Source 12.4. *Continued.*

Here is a run of the program:

Before priority adjustment.
performing action 1 on object.
performing action 2 on object.

performing action 3 on object.
performing action 4 on object.
After priority adjustment.
performing action 4 on object.
performing action 3 on object.
performing action 2 on object.
performing action 1 on object.

You may have noticed that the above function is very similar to the dispatcher routine; however there are three crucial differences:

a. The function pointers are stored twice. The function pointer array "initial" holds the starting order, and the array "action" will store the modified order.

b. To illustrate dynamic allocation of function pointers, action is a function pointer pointer that we malloc into. The succeeding ideas will take advantage of this powerful capability!

c. Since action is an array of functions, we can change the order of functions by simply assigning function pointers to new array indexes. Think of the many different areas in which this could be useful:

—a program that customizes itself to different user preferences

—a program that adjusts its difficulty based on user progress

—a program that adjusts to its computer disk, memory, and cpu environment

4. Some IMAGINATIVE ideas for function pointers—let's let our imaginations go free for a moment! What if we use function pointers in our abstract data types? A linked list of function pointers could be used as the event queue for a simulation. What could we do with "function trees" or "function stacks"? Could we organize function pointers into broad "function groups" and have our programs handle unknown input by experimenting on them? If you have every function typed in a data structure, could you build a program that constructed its order on the fly? I'd better stop here before I get lost in the ether!

CHAPTER QUESTIONS

1. Why are function pointers not well understood?
2. What is a function pointer?
3. Why do we wrap the function pointer declaration in an extra set of parentheses?
4. How are function names and array names similar?
5. List some of the ways function pointers can improve your applications?

CHAPTER EXERCISES

1. In funcptr.c, create a function pointer pointer and assign it the address of fp2, then double dereference it to call the function fp2 points to.
2. Write a simple parser that uses a function dispatcher once it identifies a token. (*HINT:* initialize a structure that has both the tokens to identify and the corresponding function to call.)

13

Memory Management Internals

OBJECTIVE: To understand how the functions malloc() and free() work by writing debug versions that include error checking.

You may think, "Do I really need to know how they work? Why can't I just know the rules (do's and don'ts) for using them?" Just following the rules is fine if you are not going to use and depend extensively on memory management in your applications; however, if you intend to write robust applications, you WANT to use memory. Therefore, when coding large pieces of software that depend on memory, it is extremely frustrating not to understand those tiny functions that so easily crash your code! The BOTTOM LINE: Using malloc() and free() as black boxes that you entrust your applications to is not acceptable because you have given up control! So, let's open up those black boxes and build some safety mechanisms into malloc() and free().

Before we jump into analyzing the code, there are four points common to most memory management schemes.

1. Sawing off a block of memory, just like cutting up a block of cheese— as explained in Chapter 8, memory is a computer system resource that the system controls. The C memory management routines are layered on top of any operating system memory management routines with the philosophy that we want to ask the system for memory as little as possible (and the assumption that your program will prob-

ably have many requests for a small amount of memory). Memory management routines work by getting a large chunk of memory from the system and divying it up for your program. That is what the memory management routines are managing—a large chunk of system memory.

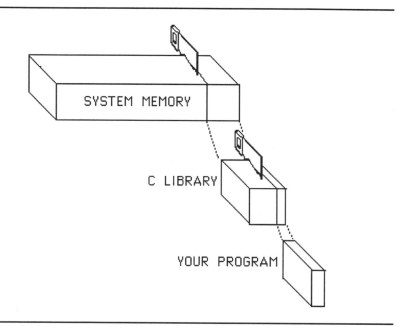

Figure 13.1.   Memory management methodology.

What is this process of "sawing off a chunk of memory"? Nothing more than reserving address space for only one user (by user we mean one process, program, or malloc request). Reserving address space is just sectioning off addresses; for example, if my computer had 1000 bytes of memory with addresses from 0 to 999, it would give my program 100 bytes by reserving the address space from 900 through 999. The C library would then have this space to work with and would reserve space for each malloc request. There is no physical handoff of memory; it is just convention! Once you understand this, the "mystery" behind memory management vanishes, and what is left are routines that act like a hotel desk clerk assigning spare rooms.

2. Alignment concerns—designers of microprocessors build their CPUs to perform arithmetic and logic operations on data fetched from

memory and stored in registers. In order to increase performance, some CPU designers put restrictions on where the data can be stored in memory. For example, the computer may store all doubles at even-addresses that are multiples of 8, or it may just require all data to start on a word (two-byte) boundary (which means on an even address). It is unnecessary to worry about how and why a CPU designer forces these restrictions on us programmers. The important thing to understand is that alignment restrictions exist so we must know two things: how to return aligned memory and how to find out what the restrictions are for the machines we are interested in programming on. Most books don't deal with the subject of alignment except to state that requirements exist and malloc must be able to return a chunk of memory that can store any data type without crashing the computer! In *The C Programming Language*, Kernighan and Ritchie tell you to deal with alignment problems by discovering the "most restrictive type" and then making sure that the space your memory allocator returns follows those guidelines. That is good advice, except it doesn't tell you how to determine what the "most restrictive type is," nor does it give me a good understanding of what makes something "aligned." P. J. Plauger in *The C Standard Library* talks about alignment as a requirement for certain data types to begin on some multiple of bytes. This gives us an idea of how to align data but still doesn't help us on finding out what the most restrictive type is. Let's cement this discussion by explaining in detail the two key points on alignment: multiples and worst-case alignment.

a. Multiple of—malloc() needs to make sure that any address it returns can handle the worst-case alignment. The worst-case alignment restriction is guaranteed to be some power of two that we will need to round up a memory request to. Therefore the "problem of alignment" really boils down to returning a "multiple of" the storage requirement. You will see this multiple of calculated in one of two ways:

new_size = (size / alignment + 1) * alignment;

or

MULTIPLE_OF(x) ((x % alignment) ? (alignment - (x % alignment)) + x : x)

The MULTIPLE_OF macro is less efficient, but I think it illustrates the point better by asking, "Is x already a multiple of the worst-case alignment?" If so, then do nothing else round up.

So, once you find out what the worst-case alignment is, the problem is simple. The user asks for 9 bytes, and the alignment is on 2-byte boundary, you give him at least 10 bytes.

b. Worst-case alignment—I found the solution to the problem of worst-case alignment by studying the GCC compiler code from the Free Software Foundation (see Further Reading for more information on the Free Software Foundation). Here is a small piece of code that demonstrates the solution:

```
/* fooalign.c */
#include <stdio.h>
#include <stdlib.h>

/* the following two macros are from obstack.c © 1988
Free Software Foundation, Inc. */
struct fooalign {char x; double d;};
#define DEFAULT_ALIGNMENT ( (char *) & ((struct
fooalign *) 0)->d - (char *) 0)

union fooround {long x; double d;};
#define DEFAULT_ROUNDING (sizeof (union fooround))

void main()
{
  printf("For this machine, DEFAULT_ALIGNMENT IS %ld.\n",
DEFAULT_ALIGNMENT);
  printf(" , DEFAULT_ROUNDING IS %ld.\n",
DEFAULT_ROUNDING);
}
```

Source 13.1.   fooalign.c.

Here is the result of compiling and running this code on four computers:

Table 13.1.   Default alignment and rounding on common computer systems.

Machine	Default Alignment	Default Rounding
SUN IIC	8	8
INTEL 386	1	8
MACINTOSH 68030	2	12
VAX 3800	1	8

Two questions come to mind:

a. "Why do we look at both DEFAULT ROUNDING and DEFAULT ALIGNMENT?" DEFAULT ALIGNMENT is what malloc() should align memory on, while DEFAULT ROUNDING is what a "less smart" malloc() would align to.

b. "How do DEFAULT ALIGNMENT and DEFAULT ROUNDING work?" DEFAULT ALIGNMENT uses the compiler's requirement to align the members of a structure properly to determine what the machine alignment requirement is. The ingenious part of the macro is to create a structure that it never intends to use and examine how the compiler aligns the structure members. Here is a diagram of how it works:

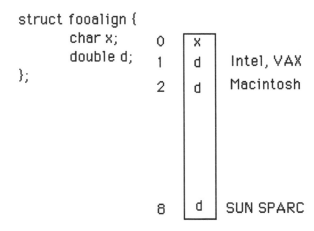

Figure 13.2.   The fooalign structure.

The fooalign structure has a char as its first element and then a double. The char is necessary just because we don't want the double to be the first element because the trick is to say that the structure starts at address 0. By making the structure start at address 0 and a char be the first element, the compiler will align the double (the largest and therefore most restrictive type) a minimum of 1 byte away from the start of the structure at the next suitable address. The difference between the address where the compiler aligns a double and 0 (the start of our fictional structure) is the number of bytes for the DEFAULT ALIGNMENT.

3. The free list and fragmentation—once a small chunk of memory is reserved for your program, the memory management routines no longer keep track of it. Why? Simply because there are too many to keep track of efficiently. Your program may malloc() 1,000, 2,000, or 10,000 tiny memory blocks that would waste precious CPU cycles keeping them properly linked together and gain very little for all that extra work. Since it is too wasteful to keep track of memory once it has been allocated, the memory management routines really manage the AVAILABLE MEMORY OR FREE MEMORY. The most common method for managing the free blocks is on a circular linked list. You should remember the diagram in Chapter 8:

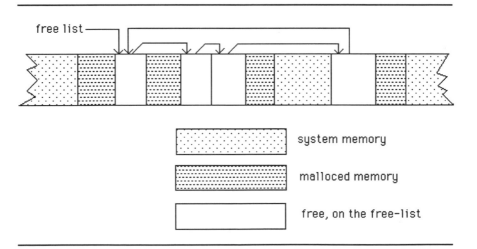

Figure 13.3.   A noncoalesced free list.

The above diagram has an error in it. The error is that two free blocks are adjacent to each other. This is not efficient because you may receive a malloc request for which you don't have a big enough block and would have to go out to the system to get more system memory. When memory is littered with many tiny memory blocks that are too small to satisfy your malloc request *and there is no more system memory*, the heap is said to be *fragmented*. The ideal management of free memory would be to have only one large free block at all times. That is an impossible goal, but it is easy to understand that one large free block will be able to satisfy the majority of malloc() requests. Here are two common strategies to avoid fragmentation:

a. Coalesce adjacent blocks. The above free list diagram corrected looks like this:

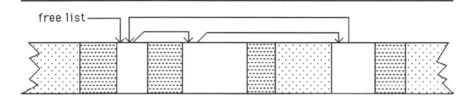

Figure 13.4.   A coalesced free list.

This is accomplished by checking for adjacent free blocks every time the program frees a previously allocated block. If there are adjacent free blocks (either after, before, or both), the new free block is merged with the adjacent ones.

b. Start your search of the free list from where you left off. If your memory management routine always looked for a free block at the start of the free list, the blocks at the beginning of the list would quickly become fragmented; however, by starting from the point of the last freed block, you get a more homogeneous spread of free blocks.

4. Search techniques and speed—for each malloc request the free list is searched for a free block that is big enough to satisfy the request. Most malloc() routines are categorized based on how they perform this search. The most common searches on a free list are first fit and best fit. Both algorithms are simple: first fit chooses the first block that is equal to or greater than the requested size, while best fit searches the entire list to find a free block closest to the requested size. It is generally faster and causes less fragmentation to use first fit.

Now let's examine our debug-version of malloc() and free(); however, unlike the other explanations of source code where we first presented the entire program, we will discuss each block of code separately and in greater detail. The routines implement five safety techniques:

a. The dbg_malloc() checks for a reasonably-sized memory request.

b. The dbg_malloc() checks the integrity of the heap as it searches for a large enough block. It is able to insure the integrity of each block of memory because it "wraps" the blocks with magic numbers. Either a FREE or MALLOC magic number is the first part of the header and the last part of the block. A "magic number" is nothing more than a unique number used for identification. The technique is widely used in the UNIX operating system to differentiate different file types.

c. The dbg_free() does not crash for freeing a NULL.

d. The dbg_free() does not crash or allow a double free.

e. The dbg_free() does not allow freeing of a nonmalloced pointer. This ability takes advantage of the fact that a block to be freed must start and end with a MALLOC-MAGIC number.

Now we are ready for a line-by-line dissection of each header and function in our memory manager. Here is the header:

```
/* debug_memory.h */

#ifndef _DEBUG_MEMORY
#define _DEBUG_MEMORY
/* Alignment defines */
struct fooalign {char x; double d;};
#define DEFAULT_ALIGNMENT ((char *) &((struct fooalign *)
0)->d - (char *) 0)
/* DEFAULT_ALIGNMENT macro is from GNU-C source by the
Free Software Foundation */
#define MULTIPLE_OF(x) ( ((x)%DEFAULT_ALIGNMENT) ? \
    ((DEFAULT_ALIGNMENT - ((x)%DEFAULT_ALIGNMENT)) +
    (x)) : (x))

/* header block */
typedef struct header header;
typedef header *headerp;
struct header {
```

Source 13.2. debug_memory.h.

```
  unsigned header_magic;
  headerp next;
  unsigned size;
};

/* Start & End Bytes */
#define START_BYTES (MULTIPLE_OF(sizeof(header)))
#define END_BYTES (MULTIPLE_OF(sizeof(unsigned)))
/* s is the number of bytes the user requested */
#define TOT_BYTES(s) (MULTIPLE_OF(s) + START_BYTES +
END_BYTES)
#define END_OFFSET(s) (MULTIPLE_OF(s) + START_BYTES)
/* x is a total number of bytes available, like from
get_mem */
#define USABLE_BYTES(x) (x - (START_BYTES + END_BYTES))

/* magic numbers */
#define MAGIC_MALLOC 0x1212
#define MAGIC_FREE 0x2323
#define MALLOCFLAG 1
#define FREEFLAG 0

/* macros */
#define ret_addr(ptr) ( (void *) ((char *)ptr +
START_BYTES) )
#define header_magic(ptr) (((headerp)((char *)ptr -
START_BYTES))->header_magic)
#define header_size(ptr) (((headerp)((char *)ptr -
START_BYTES))->size)
#define end_magic(ptr) (* (unsigned *) ((char *)ptr +
MULTIPLE_OF(header_size(ptr))))

/* default sizes */
#define DEFAULT_BLOCK_SIZE 1024
#define DEBUG_BOUND 65535

/* free list */
static header freelist; /* freelist */
static headerp lfree = NULL; /* last freed block */

/* malloc statistics */
struct heap_info {
  unsigned long current_heap_size;
  unsigned free_blocks;
```

Source 13.2.   debug_memory.h.

```
  unsigned used_blocks;
  unsigned largest_free_block;
  unsigned long total_free_mem;
} stats = {0,0,0,0,0};

/* debug routines */
void set_mem(char *ptr, unsigned size,short flag);
headerp get_mem(unsigned size);
int check_magic(headerp ptr, short flag);
int check_free_list(unsigned *largest);
void print_free_list(void);
void memory_map(void);
int check_heap(void);
void *dbg_malloc(unsigned num_bytes);
void dbg_free(void *ptr);
void *dbg_realloc(void *ptr, unsigned num_bytes);
char *dbg_strdup(char *instr);
#endif
```

Source 13.2.   *Continued.*

Notes on debug_memory.h:

1. DEFAULT_ALIGNMENT and MULTIPLE_OF have already been covered.
2. The header block is key to understanding memory management because it is a "hidden" structure that is strictly for management purposes. The header is "hidden" from the user (your program) who is returned an address that immediately follows the header: All memory management routines think of a block of memory as being composed of two parts: a header (used exclusively by the memory manager) and the body (returned to the calling program). Our header structure has three elements:
   a. The header-magic number for debugging purposes
   b. A pointer to the next block in the free list
   c. The size of the body (returned memory)

Our header file contains many #defines and macros to simplify the code and make it more readable. Here is a description and explanation of each #define:

START_BYTES—While most memory managers divide each chunk of memory into two parts (header and body), we will divide it into three parts (header, body, and tail). In that context, START_BYTES is the number of bytes (properly aligned) required for the header.

END_BYTES—Number of properly aligned bytes for the tail. The tail only holds a magic number for debugging purposes. The beginning and end magic can be thought of as a "corruption guard" against overrunning array bounds. Here is a diagram of a typical malloced memory block:

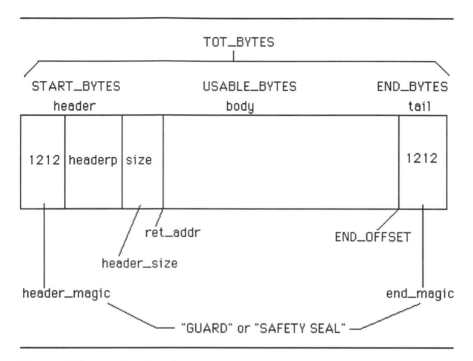

Figure 13.5. A malloced memory block.

TOT_BYTES(s)—Given the size(s) of the user request, TOT_BYTES is the total number of bytes required to fulfill the user's request.

END_OFFSET(s)—Given the size(s), END_OFFSET is the address where the tail magic number is stored.

USABLE_BYTES(x)—This macro is the number of bytes available to the user in a memory block of size x.

MAGIC_MALLOC—The magic number (hexadecimal 1212) used to denote a malloced block.

MAGIC_FREE—A magic number (hexadecimal 2323) used to denote a block that has been freed.

MALLOCFLAG—A flag used to set the magic numbers to MAGIC_MALLOC.

FREEFLAG—A flag used to set the magic numbers to MAGIC_FREE.

ret_addr(ptr)—Given the pointer to the starting address of a memory block, this macro will give you the address of the user's block (the body).

header_magic(ptr)—Given the pointer to the starting address of a memory block, this macro will give you the value of the magic number in the header.

header_size(ptr)—Given the pointer to the starting address of a memory block, this macro will give you the value of the body size as stored in the header.

end_magic(ptr)—Given the pointer to the start of the block, this macro gives you the value of the magic number in the tail (can also be referred to as the footer).

DEFAULT_BLOCK_SIZE—This is the minimum number of bytes (1024) the memory manager will ask the system for when it needs more memory.

DEBUG_BOUND—This is the largest number of bytes for a reasonable memory request (less than 64k). Obviously this is application dependent and should be increased for memory-hungry applications. You would also have to increase the size field in the header to an unsigned long.

The next items in the header file concern the free list:

1. free list is an empty structure that is necessary because malloc assumes a free list exists even before it requested any memory from the system. The degenerate (empty) free list structure enables us not to have to distinguish between a nonexistent (empty) free list and one that is fragmented.
2. lfree is a header pointer that will point to the block before the last freed block (i.e., if traverse->next is the a block just freed, lfree equals traverse).

Last, malloc statistics are kept to check for heap fragmentation. In general, if you have a large number of free blocks (unfortunately, "large" is relative to the maximum size of your heap) and the largest unallocated block is tiny, the heap is approaching fragmentation.

Here is the code:

```
/* debug_memory.c */

#include <stdlib.h>
#include <stdio.h>
#include <string.h>
```

Source 13.3.   set_mem function.

```
#include <ctype.h>

#include "debug_memory.h"

/* set the memory with header and debug info */
void set_mem(char *ptr, unsigned size,short flag)
{
  headerp hptr;
  unsigned *eptr;
  /* given the pointer to the start of mem, assign the
  magic numbers and the size. */
  hptr = (headerp) ptr;
  hptr->header_magic = flag ? MAGIC_MALLOC : MAGIC_FREE;
  hptr->size = size;
  eptr = (unsigned *) ((char *)ptr + END_OFFSET(size));
  *eptr = flag ? MAGIC_MALLOC : MAGIC_FREE;
}
```

Source 13.3.   *Continued.*

The above routine, set_mem(), sets the magic numbers in the header and tail (footer) of our memory block. The pointer passed in is a character pointer that we cast to what we need. After we set the header magic and header size, we calculate the pointer to our end magic. To calculate the address we use a character pointer that is only one byte long and add the number of bytes to get to the end_offset, which gives us the starting address of our magic number. We assign the magic number into the dereferenced address (assign it to what the address points to which is an unsigned number). It is very important to feel comfortable with the statement

eptr = (unsigned *) ((char *)ptr + END_OFFSET(size));

because calculating addresses in this manner is the cornerstone of memory management. As we said at the beginning of the chapter, all our memory manager really does is manage the assignment of address space. There is no real physical chopping off or passing; they are just analogies for the pointer arithmetic in the above statement.

```
/* get "raw" system memory */
headerp get_mem(unsigned size)
{
```

Source 13.4.   get_mem function.

```
unsigned tsize=0,bsize=0;

char *ptr=NULL;

tsize = TOT_BYTES(size);

for (bsize = DEFAULT_BLOCK_SIZE; ; bsize >>= 1)
{
  if (bsize < tsize)
    bsize = tsize;

  /* NewPtr is a Macintosh system function to grab a
  block of memory. A UNIX, VMS and DOS implementation
  would use sbrk(). A DOS implementation may want to
  use LocalAlloc() or GlobalAlloc() depending on the
  use for the memory debugger. */
  if ( (ptr = (char *)NewPtr(bsize)) != NULL)
    break;
  else if (bsize == tsize)
    return(NULL);
}

/* update the stats */
stats.current_heap_size += bsize;
stats.used_blocks++;

/* set the memory, i.e. give the block structure */
set_mem(ptr,USABLE_BYTES(bsize),MALLOCFLAG);
dbg_free(ret_addr(ptr)); /* free the new block to
attach it to the free list */
return(lfree);
/* return the block prior to the one just freed */
}
```

Source 13.4.   *Continued.*

The above routine, get_mem(), requests memory from the system. The size of the request from the system depends on several factors:

1. We ask for the DEFAULT_BLOCK_SIZE unless the size the user requested is larger than our DEFAULT_BLOCK_SIZE. Actually it is not the user requested size, TOT_BYTES(user_requested_size), which is the user's size aligned plus an aligned header and footer.
2. If the user's request is small, but the system cannot give us DEFAULT_BLOCK_SIZE, we halve the request by using the for loop and a shift (a shift right by 1 divides by 2).

3. We will continue halving the size of our request but not below tsize. If the system cannot give us tsize bytes, then we return a NULL, which means the system is out of memory.

After acquiring the memory from the system, get_mem() performs four more functions:

1. Update statistics on heap size and used blocks.
2. Call set_mem() to update the header and footer of the block. You can think of this as "stamping" or "shaping" our unformed memory (similar to unformed clay).
3. Free the block to add it to the free list. This is what free is designed to do so it really makes no difference whether this memory is freshly allocated from the system or has been allocated 30 minutes ago (free() just deals with addresses—it doesn't care where it gets that address space!). This point cannot be stressed enough—it's all just managing addresses! A memory block is nothing more than the memory space between a start address and an end address!
4. Return the address in lfree. Remember that free() assigns this to the address just before the freed block. When we get to dbg_malloc(), you will see why this is just what we need.

```
int check_magic(headerp ptr, short flag)
{
    int head=0,foot=0;

    head = flag? (ptr->header_magic == MAGIC_MALLOC) :
                 (ptr->header_magic == MAGIC_FREE);

    foot = flag? (end_magic(ret_addr(ptr)) == MAGIC_MALLOC) :
                 (end_magic(ret_addr(ptr)) == MAGIC_FREE);

    return ((head&&foot));
}
```

Source 13.5.   check_magic function.

The above routine, check_magic(), checks whether the current memory blocks' magic numbers are correct. The flag passed in determines whether the routine checks for a MALLOC or FREE block (1 being malloc, 0 being free). The header magic is easy to check as part of the header structure; however, the end magic is a little more difficult. The end_magic macro expects the pointer to the start of the body, so we need to translate the pointer passed in into the correct pointer using the ret_addr() macro. This macro within a macro looks straightforward, but just be thankful you do not have to look at how it expands because it is not a pretty sight. If you have the ability to preprocess source code, I recommend expanding the program to see how a simple-looking expression expands into severely ugly code. Notice the terminology I used—head and foot. You may like this better than head and tail, or you may want to use header and footer. The concept remains the same, but the question is which terminology makes the most sense to you. Finally, we return the ANDed result of the head and foot. We want the ANDed result because if one of them is 0, we return a failure, and only when both are a success do we return a success.

```
/* check free list traverses the free-list, checks for
corruption and returns the number of blocks in the
free-list and the largest unallocated block. */
int check_free_list(unsigned *largest)
{
  headerp traverse;
  unsigned biggest=0;
  int cnt=0;

  for (traverse = freelist.next; !(traverse ==
  &freelist); traverse = traverse->next)
  {
    if (!check_magic(traverse,FREEFLAG))
    {
      printf("check_free_list: BAD MAGIC NUMBER!
      CORRUPTED HEAP! ABORT!\n");
      exit(0);
    }

    cnt++;
    if (traverse->size > biggest)
      biggest = traverse->size;
  }

  *largest = biggest;
  return(cnt);
}
```

Source 13.6. check_free_list function.

The above routine, check_free_list(), checks the freelist for corruption and returns the number of free blocks and the largest unallocated block. It is important to understand the for loop used to traverse the free list.

for (traverse = freelist.next; !(traverse == &freelist); traverse = traverse->next)

Why do we initialize traverse to freelist.next instead of &freelist? Remember what freelist is, and you should understand the consequences of that action. Freelist is only the start of the list and an empty structure. The function check_magic would think the heap was corrupted if you sent it &freelist because there is no memory block corresponding to that address. The freelist structure only points to the start of the free list and is NOT a free block itself. Knowing this, it is easy to skip over this first entry. The for loop will exit if the traverse pointer equals the address of freelist. The operations in the loop are to check the integrity of the free list by calling check_magic(), to count the number of free blocks, and save the largest block found.

```
void print_free_list(void)
{
  headerp traverse;
  int cnt=0;

  printf("FREELIST\n");
  for (traverse = freelist.next; !(traverse ==
  &freelist); traverse = traverse->next)
  {
    if (!check_magic(traverse,FREEFLAG))
    {
      printf("check_free_list: BAD MAGIC NUMBER!
      CORRUPTED HEAP! ABORT!\n");
      exit(0);
    }
    cnt++;
    printf("block[%d]->size(%d) ",cnt,traverse->size);

    if (!(cnt % 3)) printf("\n");
  }
  printf("\n");
}
```

Source 13.7.   print_free_list function.

The above routine, print_free_list(), prints each free block and its size. The function traverses the free list in the same manner as check_free_list().

```
void memory_map(void)
{
  headerp traverse,inbetween;
  int cnt=0, block_cnt=stats.used_blocks;

  printf("\n");
  for (traverse = freelist.next; !(traverse ==
  &freelist); traverse = traverse->next)
  {
    cnt++;
    printf("[%d]%p: FREE (%d)
    ",cnt,ret_addr(traverse),traverse->size);
    if (!(cnt % 3))
      printf("\n");
    else
      fflush(stdout);

    inbetween = (headerp) ( (char *) traverse +
    TOT_BYTES(traverse->size));
    if (inbetween != traverse->next)
    {
     if (traverse->next != &freelist)
     {
      while (inbetween < traverse->next)
      {
        /* if we hit a non-malloced block, which could
        occur if there is only one free block, and when
        the heap is not contiguous. get out and go to
        the next free block. (if any) */
        if (inbetween->header_magic != MAGIC_MALLOC)
          break;
        else
        {
          if (end_magic(ret_addr(inbetween)) !=
          MAGIC_MALLOC)
          {
            printf("memory_map: CORRUPTED HEAP! ABORT!\n");
            exit(0);
          }
        }
```

Source 13.8. memory_map function.

```
      cnt++;
      printf("[%d]%p:MALLOC(%d)",cnt,
      ret_addr(inbetween),
              inbetween->size);
      if (!(cnt % 3))
        printf("\n");
      else
        fflush(stdout);

      inbetween = (headerp) ( (char *) inbetween +
      TOT_BYTES(inbetween->size));
    } /* end of while */
}/* if traverse->next ! = &freelist */
else /* traverse->next does equal &freelist */
{
   /* find out how many malloced blocks are left
   to be printed out. */
   while (block_cnt)
   {
   /* if we hit a non-malloced block, which could
   occur if there is only one free block, and when
   the heap is not contiguous, get out and go to the
   next free block. (if any) */
   if (end_magic(ret_addr(inbetween))!= MAGIC_MALLOC)
    break;
   else
   {
    if (end_magic(ret_addr(inbetween))!=
     MAGIC_MALLOC)
     {
     printf("memory_map: CORRUPTED HEAP! ABORT!\n");
     exit(0);
    {
   {

   cnt++;
   printf("[%d]%p:MALLOC(%d)",cnt,ret_addr(inbetween),
   inbetween->size);
   if (!(cnt % 3))
      printf("\n");
   else
      fflush(stdout);

   /* decrement # of malloced blocks printed out. */
```

Source 13.8.   *Continued.*

```
        block_cnt--;
        inbetween = (headerp) ((char*) inbetween +
        TOT_BYTES(inbetween->size));
        } /* while block_cnt */
    } /* if traverse->next == &freelist */
} /* inbetween ! = traverse->next */

} /* end of for */
printf("\n");
}
```

Source 13.8. *Continued.*

The above routine, memory_map(), uses the debugging magic_numbers to print every block (both malloced and free) in the heap. The methodology used to do this is to print each block in the free list and all malloced blocks in between. If the "in between" block does not have the MALLOC magic number, we have either hit the end of the heap (in other words, there are no more free blocks), or the heap is noncontiguous, so we hit a chunk of system memory. Traversing the free list is done in the same manner as the check_free_list() and print_free_list() routines. The pointer variable in between is calculated to check for malloced blocks in between free blocks. It is important to understand how we calculate the start location of the malloced block.

> **inbetween = (headerp) ((char *) traverse + TOT_BYTES (traverse->size));**

The pointer inbetween is the address of the next block, which we calculate by adding the total number of bytes used for this block to the starting address of this block. That simple pointer arithmetic gives us the address of the next block, which we cast to a header pointer. We have to cast it back to a header pointer because we cast it to a character pointer to add the number TOT_BYTES. What would happen if we left traverse as a header pointer and then added the number returned by TOT_BYTES? That would give us the address for (address of traverse + (sizeof(header) * TOT_BYTES(traverse->size))) instead of what we want, which is (address of traverse + (1 byte * TOT_BYTES(traverse->size))). This is the concept of the compiler automatically "scaling" the pointer arithmetic based on the type of pointer it is performing the arithmetic on. If the pointer to do arithmetic on is a character, the number is multiplied by sizeof(char). If the pointer is a structure pointer, we multiply by the sizeof(struct). The type of the pointer that determines this "scaling factor" is often called the "scalar."

```
int check_heap(void)
{
  headerp traverse,inbetween;
  int block_cnt = stats.used_blocks;

  for (traverse = freelist.next; !(traverse ==
  &freelist); traverse = traverse->next)
  {

    if (!check_magic(traverse,FREEFLAG))
      return(0);

    inbetween = (headerp) ( (char *) traverse +
    TOT_BYTES(traverse->size));
    if (inbetween != traverse->next)
    {
     if (traverse->next! = &freelist)
     {
      while (inbetween < traverse->next)
      {
        if (inbetween->header_magic != MAGIC_MALLOC)
          break;
        else
        {
          if (end_magic(ret_addr(inbetween)) != MAGIC_MALLOC)
            return(0);
        }

        /* decrement # of malloced blocks printed out. */
        block_cnt-;
        inbetween = (headerp) ( (char *) inbetween +
        TOT_BYTES(inbetween->size));
      } /* end of while */
    } /* if traverse->next! = &freelist */
    else /* traverse->next does equal &freelist */
    {
     /* find out how many malloced blocks are left
     to be printed out. */
```

Source 13.9. check_heap function.

```
        while (block_cnt)
        {
        /* if we hit a non-malloced block, which could
           occur if there is only one free block, and when
           the heap is not contiguous, get out and go to
           the next free block. (if any) */
        if (inbetween->header_magic != MAGIC_MALLOC)
           break;
        else
        {
         if (end_magic(ret_addr(inbetween)) !=
         MAGIC_MALLOC)
           {
            return(0);
           }
        }

        /* decrement # of malloced blocks printed out. */
        block_cnt—;
        inbetween = (headerp) (char*) inbetween —
        TOT_BYTES(inbetween->size));
       } /* while block_cnt */
      } /* if traverse->next == &freelist */
     }
   } /* end of for */

   return(1);
}
```

Source 13.9. *Continued.*

The above routine, check_heap(), has all of the same logic as memory_map(), except check_heap() does not print out the heap. The purpose of check_heap is to check the integrity of every block (malloced and free) in the heap.

```
void *dbg_malloc(unsigned num_bytes)
{
   headerp traverse, previous_ptr;
```

Source 13.10. dbg_malloc function.

```
    if (num_bytes == 0)
    {
      printf("dbg_malloc: FATAL - num_bytes is 0!\n");
      exit(0);
    }

    /* check if num_bytes is outlandish */
    if (num_bytes > DEBUG_BOUND)
    {
      printf("dbg_malloc: FATAL - requested %ld bytes :
      %ld over upper bound of %ld.\n",
          num_bytes, DEBUG_BOUND - num_bytes,
          DEBUG_BOUND);
      exit(0);
    }

    if ( (previous_ptr = lfree) == NULL)
    {
      freelist.next = previous_ptr = lfree = &freelist;
      freelist.size = 0;
    }

    /* search for a memory block big enough. */
    for (traverse = previous_ptr->next; ; previous_ptr =
    traverse,
      traverse = traverse->next)
    {
      if (traverse != &freelist)
      {
        if (!check_magic(traverse,FREEFLAG))
        {
          printf("dbg_malloc: BAD MAGIC NUMBER! CORRUPTED
          HEAP! ABORT!\n");
          exit(0);
        }
      }
      /* traverse->size is a count of the USABLE BYTES */
      if ( (traverse->size == MULTIPLE_OF(num_bytes)) ||
        (traverse->size >= TOT_BYTES(num_bytes)) )
        /* looking for first memory equal to or bigger.*/
      {
        if (traverse->size == MULTIPLE_OF(num_bytes))
        /* exact match */
```

Source 13.10.   *Continued.*

```
      {
        previous_ptr->next = traverse->next; /* delink
        from free list */
        set_mem((char *)traverse,traverse->
        size,MALLOCFLAG);
      }
      else
      {
        /* reduce size of current block so we can strip
        off the end. */
        traverse->size -= TOT_BYTES(num_bytes);
        /* set the memory of the reduced free block */
        set_mem((char *)traverse,traverse->
        size,FREEFLAG);
        traverse = (headerp) ( (char *) traverse +
        TOT_BYTES(traverse->size));
        /* set the memory of the tail portion. */
        set_mem((char *)traverse,
        MULTIPLE_OF(num_bytes),MALLOCFLAG);
      }

      /* set previous ptr to the place before the
      just-malloced memory so that if that memory
      gets freed right away, we will be ready at that
      spot. */
      lfree = previous_ptr;

      /* update the stats */
      stats.used_blocks++;

      return(ret_addr(traverse));

    } /* end of if */

    if (traverse == lfree)
      if ( (traverse = get_mem(num_bytes)) == NULL)
        return(NULL);

  } /* end of for */
}
```

Source 13.10.   *Continued.*

The above routine, dbg_malloc(), searches for a large enough block of memory on the free list and, if found, returns a pointer to the user's portion (body) of that memory. The function declares two variables:

1. traverse—used to traverse the free list.
2. previous_ptr—always points to the block before traverse, this is necessary to be able to delink a block.

To perform the above service, the routine performs the following steps:

1. Check if the request is reasonable. It is unreasonable if greater than DEBUG_BOUND.
2. Now that we have a valid request for memory, we check if lfree is NULL. If lfree is NULL, we know that this is the first malloc request and there is no free list to search. We initialize the pointers to &freelist, which is the address of our degenerate free list.
3. We traverse the free list using a for loop that has no end condition. There is no end condition because we will end as soon as we find a large enough free block or when we have checked the entire list.
4. While traversing the free list, we call check_magic() to insure the integrity of our free list.
5. We check the size of all the free blocks for a size that either exactly matches the aligned requested size or where the body is big enough to carve out a new block.
6. If the size exactly matches the request, we just delink the free block from the linked list and return the pointer to the user's portion (the body). "Delinking" from the free list is nothing more than taking the pointer that points to "the block to delink" and making it point to the block "the delinked block" points to. In other words, if A points to B and B points to C, to delink B we just make A point to C.
7. If the size of the free block is greater than the total number of bytes for the requested block, we can carve off a hunk of this free block. This "carving off a hunk" is nothing more than changing the size of the free block, resetting the magic numbers on the old block, setting traverse to the new block's address with some pointer arithmetic, and then setting the magic numbers (with set_mem()) on the new block. Here is a diagram of this process:

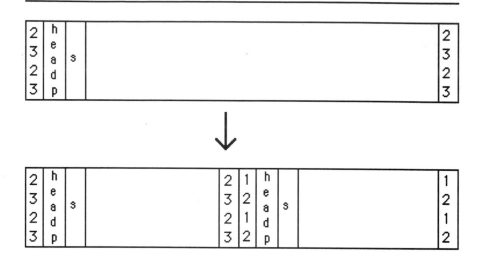

Figure 13.6. Carving off a memory hunk.

8. After the exact match or "carving off a hunk," we set lfree to the free block before the block to return (so we can start where we left off for our next search, which will evenly distribute the malloced and free blocks). Then we update the count of used blocks for our statistics and return the ret_addr() of the new block to the calling function.

9. If we have looped through the entire free list and not found a block of the right size, we call get_mem() to request more memory from the system.

```
void dbg_free(void *ptr)
{
  headerp block_header=NULL,traverse;

  if (!ptr)
  {
    printf("dbg_free: Attempt to free a NULL pointer!\n");
    return;
  }
  else
```

Source 13.11. dbg_free function.

```
block_header = (headerp) ((char *)ptr -
START_BYTES);

/****** *check to make sure the pointer passed in has
a MALLOC_MAGIC ***** */

if (block_header->header_magic != MAGIC_MALLOC)
{
  if (block_header->header_magic == MAGIC_FREE)
  {
    printf("dbg_free: Trying to free a freed pointer!\n");
    return;
  }
  else
  {
    printf("dbg_free: Trying to free a NON-MALLOCED
    pointer!\n");
    return;
  }
}

/* update the stats */
stats.used_blocks—;

/* find where this block fits in the list. Should be
inbetween two elements in the list. */
for (traverse = lfree;
!(block_header > traverse && block_header < traverse->
next);
traverse = traverse->next)
{
  /* if traverse is greater then its next pointer, we
  are at the end of the list. AND block header must be
  either greater then the end or before the beginning. */
  if (traverse >= traverse->next && (block_header >
                traverse || block_header <
                traverse->next)) break;
}

/* if the end_of_this_block equals the start of the
next, connect to upper */
if (((char *) block_header + TOT_BYTES(block_header->
      size)) ==        (char *) traverse->next)
```

Source 13.11. *Continued.*

```
{
  block_header->size += TOT_BYTES(traverse->next->
  size);
  block_header->next = traverse->next->next;
  set_mem((char *)block_header,block_header->
  size,FREEFLAG);
}
else
{
  set_mem((char *)block_header,block_header->
  size,FREEFLAG);
  block_header->next = traverse->next;
}

/* If the end of the previous block equals this
blocks address, connect to lower */
if (((char *) traverse + TOT_BYTES(traverse->size))
                       == (char *) block_header)
{
  traverse->size += TOT_BYTES(block_header->size);
  traverse->next = block_header->next;
  set_mem((char *)traverse,traverse->size,FREEFLAG);
}
else
  traverse->next = block_header;

lfree = traverse;
}
```

Source 13.11.   *Continued.*

The above routine, dbg_free(), returns a previously malloced block to the free list by inserting it in its proper place and coalescing free blocks if possible. The function declares two variables:

1. block_header—this is a header pointer to the start of the block to be freed. Remember that the pointer your application uses is the pointer to the start of the body.
2. traverse—a header pointer used to traverse the free list.

To return the block to the free list, the function performs the following operations:

1. Checks if the pointer passed in is NULL. If the pointer is NULL, then the function returns (some free() functions will crash if given a NULL pointer), or the block_header pointer is calculated.
2. Since the pointer is not NULL, we know that we have an address so we now insure that this pointer is indeed a block to be freed. The function insures the block is a previously malloced block and not already freed or a non-malloced pointer. Double freeing a pointer or freeing a non-malloced pointer are two very common situations that most implementations of free do not check for because of the extra overhead. Here we can catch these errors by using our magic numbers!
3. Update the statistics by decrementing the used block count.
4. The end condition in the for loop is the key code in the free-list traversal.

!(block_header> traverse && block_header<traverse->next)

In English, this means STOP when the block to be freed is greater than the current pointer and less than the next pointer. In other words, stop when we are *in between* two free blocks. Inside the loop we simply check if the block to be freed is at the beginning or end of the list (not in between two blocks) in which we break out of the loop. It is very IMPORTANT to feel comfortable with comparing addresses, adding to, and subtracting from addresses as these are the "core requirements" of memory management. Luckily, adding, subtracting, and comparing addresses is exactly the same as adding, subtracting, and comparing integers, which is EASY! SO SMILE—we got this beat!

5. Once we know that our block is at the correct position in the free list, we now check if there are free blocks directly adjacent to our block. If the end of this block equals the start of the next, we "combine" this block with the upper block. Remember that "combine" or "coalesce" is nothing more than adjusting the size, rearranging the list pointers, and setting the magic numbers. If there are malloced blocks in between, then we just set the magic numbers and point to the next free block. We then check if we bump against the previous block; if so, we coalesce the two blocks, or just connect.
6. Finally, set lfree to the block before our freed block. We do this so that if we are putting a block in the free list from get_mem, malloc will catch it on its next pass. Study malloc's loop to see how this would work.

```c
void *dbg_realloc(void *ptr, long size)
{
  headerp block_header,freeblock;
  void *newp=NULL;

  if (!ptr)
    return(dbg_malloc(size));

  block_header = (headerp) ((char *)ptr - START_BYTES);
  if (block_header->size < MULTIPLE_OF(size))
  {
    /* get a larger block */
    newp = dbg_malloc(size);

    if (!newp)
      return(NULL);
    memcpy(newp,ptr,block_header->size);

    dbg_free(ptr);
    return(newp);
  }
  else if (block_header->size < TOT_BYTES(size))
    return(ptr);
  else
  {
    /* chop off the end of the block */
    freeblock = (headerp) ((char *) block_header +
    TOT_BYTES(size));
    set_mem((char *)freeblock, block_header->size -
    TOT_BYTES(size),MALLOCFLAG);
    dbg_free(ret_addr(freeblock));
    set_mem((char *)block_header,MULTIPLE_OF(size),
    MALLOCFLAG);
    return(ptr);
  }
}
```

Source 13.12.   dbg_realloc function.

The function dbg_realloc() is just a combination of malloc() and free() and there is not much new to it.

```
/* strdup will malloc a copy of the input string. */
char *dbg_strdup(char *instr)
{
  char *outstr=NULL;

  if (!instr)
  {
    fprintf(stderr,
    "strdup: FATAL - NULL argument!\n");
    return(NULL);
  }

  outstr = (char *) dbg_malloc(sizeof(char) *
  (strlen(instr) + 1) );
  if (!outstr)
  {
    fprintf(stderr,
    "strdup: FATAL - malloc failed!\n");
    return(NULL);
  }

  strcpy(outstr, instr);

  return(outstr);
}
```

Source 13.13.   dbg_strdup function.

The above routine, dbg_strdup(), mallocs memory for an input string and returns the malloced string.

```
void print_stats(void)
{
  stats.free_blocks =
  check_free_list(&(stats.largest_free_block));
  stats.total_free_mem = (unsigned long) FreeMem();

  printf("HEAP STATISTICS\n");
  printf(" - current heap size : %ld\n",
  stats.current_heap_size);
  printf(" - free blocks : %d\n",stats.free_blocks);
```

Source 13.14.   print_stats function.

```
    printf(" - used blocks : %d\n",stats.used_blocks);
    printf(" - largest free block : %d\n",
    stats.largest_free_block);
    printf(" - system memory left : %ld\n",
    stats.total_free_mem);
}
```

Source 13.14. *Continued.*

The above routine, print_stats(), is straight forward.
Here is a header for the test program:

```
/* memory.h */

/* debug routines */
int check_free_list(unsigned *largest);
void print_free_list(void);
void memory_map(void);
int check_heap(void);
void *dbg_malloc(unsigned num_bytes);
void dbg_free(void *ptr);
char *dbg_strdup(char *instr);

#define malloc(x) dbg_malloc(x)
#define free(x) dbg_free(x)
#define strdup(x) dbg_strdup(x)
```

Here is the code for the test program:

```
/* memory_test.c */
#include <stdlib.h>
#include <stdio.h>
#include <string.h>
#include <ctype.h>

#include "memory.h"

void main()
{
  char *str1, *str2, *str3, *str4, *str5;
  char *never_malloced;
```

Source 13.15. memory_test.c.

```
unsigned blocks, largest;
int i,len;
char bad_string[] = "this is a string too long to be      |
stuffed into st1.";

printf("case 1: malloc memory of varying sizes.\n");
str1 = strdup("This is sentence one.");
str2 = (char *) malloc(400);
str3 = strdup("This is sentence Three and rather
lengthy and long and very long.");                         |
str4 = (char *) malloc(600);
str5 = strdup("This is sentence Five.");

if (!str1 || !str2 || !str3 || !str4 || !str5)
{
  printf("malloc failed!\n");
  exit(0);
}

memory_map();
print_free_list();
print_stats();

printf("case 2: free some memory.\n");
free(str2);
free(str4);

memory_map();
print_free_list();
print_stats();

printf("case 3: test free on errors.\n");
free(NULL);
free(str4);
never_malloced = str1 + 5;
free(never_malloced);

printf("case 4: free memory and coalesce small blocks     |
into big blocks.\n");
free(str3);

memory_map();
print_free_list();
print_stats();
```

Source 13.15. *Continued.*

```
  printf("case 5: check the heap for corruption. Should
  be good.\n");
  if (!check_heap())
    printf("HEAP IS CORRUPTED!\n");
  else
    printf("HEAP IS OK!\n");

  printf("case 6: corrupt the heap!\n");

  /* we will corrupt the heap by overwriting str3. */
  str2 = strdup("this is string2.");
  str3 = strdup("this is string3.");
  str4 = strdup("this is string4.");
  strcpy(str2,bad_string);

  if (!check_heap())
    printf("HEAP IS CORRUPTED!\n");
  else
    printf("HEAP IS OK!\n");

  memory_map();
  print_free_list();
  print_stats();
}
```

Source 13.15.   *Continued.*

Here is the result of the test program:

```
case 1: malloc memory of varying sizes.

[1]001D60E4: FREE (496) [2]001D62DE:MALLOC(66)
[3]001D632A:MALLOC(400)
[4]001D64C4:MALLOC(22) [5]001D64EC: FREE (370)
[6]001D6668:MALLOC(24)
[7]001D668A:MALLOC(600)
FREELIST
block[1]->size(496) block[2]->size(370)
HEAP STATISTICS
- current heap size : 2048
- free blocks : 2
- used blocks : 5
- largest free block : 496
- system memory left : 314704
case 2: free some memory.
```

```
[1]001D60EC: FREE (496) [2]001D62E6:MALLOC(66)
[3]001D6332: FREE (400)
[4]001D64CC:MALLOC(22) [5]001D64F4: FREE (370)
[6]001D6670:MALLOC(24)
[7]001D6692: FREE (600)
FREELIST
block[1]->size(496) block[2]->size(400) block[3]->
size(370)
block[4]->size(600)
HEAP STATISTICS
- current heap size : 2048
- free blocks : 4
- used blocks : 3
- largest free block : 600
- system memory left : 313864
case 3: test free on errors.
dbg_free: Attempt to free a NULL pointer!
dbg_free: Trying to free a freed pointer!
dbg_free: Trying to free a NON-MALLOCED pointer!
case 4: free memory and coalesce small blocks into big
blocks.

[1]001D60E4: FREE (982) [2]001D64C4:MALLOC(22)
[3]001D64EC: FREE (370)
[4]001D6668:MALLOC(24) [5]001D668A: FREE (600)
FREELIST
block[1]->size(982) block[2]->size(370) block[3]->
size(600)

HEAP STATISTICS
- current heap size : 2048
- free blocks : 3
- used blocks : 2
- largest free block : 982
- system memory left : 314044
case 5: check the heap for corruption. Should be good.
HEAP IS OK!
case 6: corrupt the heap!
HEAP IS CORRUPTED!

[1]001D60E4: FREE (982) [2]001D64C4:MALLOC(22)
[3]001D64EC: FREE (286)
[4]001D6614:MALLOC(18) [5]001D6630:MALLOC(18)
memory_map: CORRUPTED HEAP! ABORT!
```

I encourage you to examine the memory map closely because it gives you a good idea of what a heap looks like. Even better than that is to experiment on your own using debug_memory.c as your "insurance policy" in your own applications. Using the techniques described above should provide adequate protection on your projects by catching the majority of memory management defects.

CHAPTER QUESTIONS

1. What are the benefits of studying the memory management internals?
2. What are the four points common to most memory management schemes?
3. Why are there alignment restrictions on data storage?
4. What are the two key characteristics of alignment?
5. What is ingenious about the DEFAULT_ALIGNMENT macro?
6. How come the memory manager does not keep track of all the allocated blocks?
7. What is the cornerstone of the debug_memory protection scheme?
8. Why is calculating addresses important to understand?
9. In the memory_map() routine, when will the "in between" method fail?
10. Why do we cast the headerp to a (char *) before calculating an address?
11. Since we do not use any part of the freelist structure except the next pointer, why not just make freelist a headerp instead of a header?
12. In dbg_malloc(), why not just check if traverse->size is greater than MULTIPLE_OF(num_bytes) instead of checking if it is greater than TOT_BYTES(num_bytes)?

CHAPTER EXERCISES

1. Change dbg_malloc() to use the best-fit algorithm.
2. Increase DEBUG_BOUND to 1 megabyte and modify the header and memory management routines to handle this larger size. *HINT:* Change the size field in the header to an unsigned long.

FURTHER READING

The DEFAULT_ALIGNMENT and DEFAULT_ROUNDING macros are from obstack.c © 1988 by the Free Software Foundation. The GCC compiler and source code can be acquired for a small distribution fee by writing to the Free Software Foundation, 675 Massachusetts Avenue, Cambridge, MA 02139.

Heller, Martin. *Advanced Windows Programming*, © 1992, John Wiley and Sons, Inc.

Tanenbaum, Andrew S. *Operating Systems, Design and Implementation*, © 1987, Prentice Hall.

14

Pointer Traps and Pitfalls

OBJECTIVE: A discussion of pointer traps to avoid.

This chapter is designed to save the beginning and intermediate programmers the MANY HOURS of frustration that I and numerous other programmers suffered through while stumbling into the pointer traps we will discuss. Some of the traps are just stupid mistakes, while others are subtle logic bombs. We will cover the traps in four ways: give an example of the trap, dissect all the parts of the trap (drag them into the sunlight), give an example of the correct solution to the problem, and last, suggest a checking program or method to assist you in avoiding the problem.

14.1. TRAP ONE: FORGETTING THE NULL TERMINATOR

As the title suggests, this is simply a stupid mistake—an "aw, shucks"—but it should be the first thing you check for on your debug run. Here is an example:

```
/* forget_null.c */
#include <stdlib.h>
#include <stdio.h>
```

Source 14.1.   forget_null.c.

```c
#include <string.h>
#include <ctype.h>

char *strip_trailing_blanks(char *instr)
{
  int len=0,i=0,j=0;
  char *outstr;
  if (instr)
  {
    len = strlen(instr);

    for (i = len - 1; ((instr[i] == ' ') && (i >= 0));
    i--);

    i++;
    outstr = malloc(sizeof(char) * (i+1));
    if (!outstr)
    {
      fprintf(stderr,
      "strip_trailing_blanks: FATAL - malloc failed!\n");
      return(NULL);
    }

    printf("last blank is %d.\n",i);

    for (j = 0; j < i; j++)
      outstr[j] = instr[j];

    /* *** here is where we are forgetting
    something *** */

  }
  return(outstr);
}

void main()
{
  char myname[] = "Jack Waste Space ";
  char *stripped = NULL;
  int mlen = 0, slen = 0;

  mlen = strlen(myname);
  printf("length of myname is %d.\n",mlen);
```

Source 14.1. *Continued.*

```
stripped = strip_trailing_blanks(myname);
slen = strlen(stripped);
printf("stripped is <%s> with length
%d.\n",stripped,slen);
}
```

Source 14.1.   *Continued.*

If you run this program on your machine, its behavior is UNDE-FINED! However, to make this program safe, simply add outstr[j] = '\0'; right below the comment "here is where we are forgetting something." You may think, "That's a really simple error! I would never do that!"

First of all, *NEVER say never.* Although this is just a problem of forgetting to do something that you may not think is a trap, the problem is so widespread that it deserves a brief mention.

14.2.   TRAP ONE DISSECTION

The problem lies in filling in the outstr array without terminating the array with an ASCII NUL.

```
for (j = 0; j < i; j++)
     outstr[j] = instr[j];
/* *** here is where we are forgetting something *** */
```

14.3.   TRAP ONE SOLUTION

There are two good solutions to the problem:

1.   The simplest is to add this line after the for loop:

outstr[j] = '\0';

2.   Use a function that appends the NULL for you, like strcpy or strdup. You could replace the for loop with

strcpy(outstr,instr);

14.4.   TRAP TWO: ASKING MALLOC FOR THE WRONG NUMBER OF BYTES

This trap is more subtle because the program does not crash when the offensive act of getting the wrong amount of memory is done, but later when you attempt to free or use space that was never malloced! Here is an example:

```
/* bad_request.c */
#include <stdlib.h>
#include <stdio.h>
#include <string.h>

extern char *strdup();

void free_ppbuf(char **inbuf, int count)
{
  int i;

  if (inbuf)
  {
    if (count>0)
    {
      for (i = 0; i < count; i++)
        if (inbuf[i]) free(inbuf[i]);
      free(inbuf);
    }
    else
    {
      /* ********* HERE IS WHERE THE PROGRAM WILL
CRASH! ****** */
      for (i = 0; inbuf[i]; i++)
        if (inbuf[i]) free(inbuf[i]);
      free(inbuf);
    }
  }
}

char **reverse_ppbuf(char **inbuf)
{
  int count=0,i=0,j=0;
  char **outbuf;

  if (inbuf)
  {
    for (count = 0; inbuf[count]; count++);
    /* ******** HERE IS THE BAD REQUEST ********** */
```

Source 14.2.   bad_request.c.

```
      outbuf = (char **) malloc(sizeof(char *) * count + 1);
      if (!outbuf)
      {
        fprintf(stderr,"reverse_ppbuf: FATAL - malloc
        failed!\n");
        return(NULL);
      }
      for (i=0,j=count-1; i < count; i++,j--)
        outbuf[i] = strdup(inbuf[j]);

      /* null terminate the ppbuf */
      outbuf[count] = NULL;

      return(outbuf);
  }
}

void main()
{
  char **mybuf=NULL;
  char **reversed=NULL;

  int i=0;

  mybuf = malloc(sizeof(char *) * 4);
  if (!mybuf)
  {
    fprintf(stderr,
    "bad_request: FATAL - malloc failed!\n");
    exit(0);
  }

  mybuf[0] = strdup("one");
  mybuf[1] = strdup("two");
  mybuf[2] = strdup("three");
  mybuf[3] = NULL;

  reversed = reverse_ppbuf(mybuf);

  for (i = 0; reversed[i]; i++)
    printf("%s\n",reversed[i]);

  free_ppbuf(reversed,0);
}
```

Source 14.2.   *Continued.*

14.5. TRAP TWO DISSECTION

As the title of the trap suggests, the trap is the consequence of allocating the wrong number of bytes from malloc, so let's examine the malloc request in reverse_ppbuf:

outbuf = (char **) malloc(sizeof(char *) * count + 1);

Now it is obvious that when I first wrote this piece of code I did not intentionally wish to crash my program. My initial intention for the malloc request was to malloc enough memory to store every line of the ppbuf (count is the number of lines in the ppbuf) plus one extra character pointer to store a NULL (to NULL terminate my ppbuf). Have you caught my error yet? If you are thinking that the error is in my order of operations for my arithmetic operators, you are correct. Let's calculate the number of bytes that I asked for and then see how many I really needed.

If sizeof(char *) is 4 bytes, and count is 3,
then sizeof(char *) * count + 1 =
4 * 3 + 1 =
12 + 1 = 13

Question: Can you store 4 character pointers in 13 bytes?
Answer: Heck, NO!
What do I need to store four character pointers?

sizeof(char *) * (count + 1) =
4 * (3 + 1) =
4 * 4 = 16.

So you see that I needed 16 bytes but only asked for 13 because the compiler correctly performed the multiplication before the addition. How would this mistake affect the program?

It only affected the program because if you pass free_ppbuf a 0 for the count, the function assumes the ppbuf is NULL terminated. By NULL terminated we mean the last pointer is a zero. Let's examine how free_ppbuf makes this assumption that leads to a bus error (on the Macintosh, this means we tried to put an invalid address on the address bus).

for (i = 0; inbuf[i]; i++)
**   if (inbuf[i]) free(inbuf[i]);**

The danger lies in the termination condition of the for loop, inbuf[i], which evaluates to a character pointer and will only terminate when the ith character pointer is a NULL! We know two bytes of the last character pointer are 0, but what about the other two bytes? On the mac, they were an FFFF, which was an illegal address!

14.6.   TRAP TWO SOLUTION

The solution is simple: If you want x objects plus one object, don't ask for x objects plus one byte! In C code,

   malloc(sizeof(any_object) * (count + 1))

14.7.   TRAP TWO CATCHER

When you allocate less memory than you use, you are overwriting someone else's memory (called "stomping on memory"). The quickest way to stop this is to catch yourself from overwriting memory you did not allocate! This was one of the design goals in debug_memory.c, and therefore we can use this to catch our error! Here is how you write the code using debug_memory to catch the trap:

```c
/* bad_request2.c */
#include <stdlib.h>
#include <stdio.h>
#include <string.h>
#include "memory.h"

extern char *strdup();
extern void memory_map();
extern int check_heap();

void free_ppbuf(char **inbuf, int count)
{
  int i;

  if (inbuf)
  {
    if (count>0)
    {
      for (i = 0; i < count; i++)
        if (inbuf[i]) free(inbuf[i]);
      free(inbuf);
    }
```

Source 14.3.   bad_request2.c.

```
      else
      {
        /* ********* HERE IS WHERE THE PROGRAM WILL
        CRASH! ****** */
        for (i = 0; inbuf[i]; i++)
          if (inbuf[i]) free(inbuf[i]);
        free(inbuf);
      }
    }
}

char **reverse_ppbuf(char **inbuf)
{
  int count=0,i=0,j=0;
  char **outbuf;
  if (inbuf)
  {
    for (count = 0; inbuf[count]; count++);
    /* ******** HERE IS THE BAD REQUEST ********** */
    outbuf = (char **) malloc(sizeof(char *) * count + 1);
    if (!outbuf)
    {
      fprintf(stderr,
      "reverse_ppbuf: FATAL - malloc failed!\n");
      return(NULL);
    }

    for (i=0,j=count-1; i < count; i++,j--)
      outbuf[i] = strdup(inbuf[j]);

    printf("reverse_ppbuf: the memory_map before we
    corrupt the heap!\n");
    memory_map();

    /* null terminate the ppbuf - **** Here we corrupt
    the heap! */
    outbuf[count] = NULL;

    return(outbuf);
  }
}

void main()
```

Source 14.3. *Continued.*

```
{
  char **mybuf=NULL;
  char **reversed=NULL;

  int i=0;

  mybuf = malloc(sizeof(char *) * 4);
  if (!mybuf)
  {
    fprintf(stderr,
    "bad_request: FATAL - malloc failed!\n");
    exit(0);
  }

  mybuf[0] = strdup("one");
  mybuf[1] = strdup("two");
  mybuf[2] = strdup("three");
  mybuf[3] = NULL;

  memory_map();

  reversed = reverse_ppbuf(mybuf);

  if (!check_heap())
  {
    printf("reverse_ppbuf CORRUPTED the HEAP - ABORTING!\n");
    printf("Here is the corrupt heap!\n");
    memory_map();
    exit(0);
  }

  for (i = 0; reversed[i]; i++)
    printf("%s\n",reversed[i]);

  free_ppbuf(reversed,0);
}
```

Source 14.3.   *Continued.*

Here is the run with trap catcher:

```
[1]001DBED8: FREE (944) [2]001DC292:MALLOC(6)
[3]001DC2A2:MALLOC(4)
[4]001DC2B0:MALLOC(4) [5]001DC2BE:MALLOC(16)
```

```
reverse_ppbuf: Here is the memory_map before we corrupt
the heap!
[1]001DBED8: FREE (876) [2]001DC24E:MALLOC(4)
[3]001DC25C:MALLOC(4)
[4]001DC26A:MALLOC(6)  [5]001DC27A:MALLOC(14)
[6]001DC292:MALLOC(6)
[7]001DC2A2:MALLOC(4)  [8]001DC2B0:MALLOC(4)
[9]001DC2BE:MALLOC(16)
reverse_ppbuf CORRUPTED the HEAP - ABORTING!
Here is the corrupt heap!
[1]001DBED8: FREE (876) [2]001DC24E:MALLOC(4)
[3]001DC25C:MALLOC(4)
[4]001DC26A:MALLOC(6) memory_map: CORRUPTED HEAP!
ABORT!
```

Let's dissect the heap to see when we fell short:

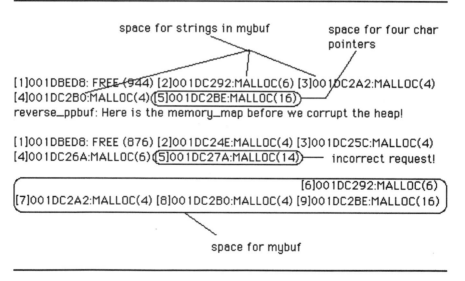

Figure 14.1.   Heap dissection.

It is very easy to see how we should have requested 16 bytes, but the block size on the heap was only 14 bytes. If you are wondering why we received 14 bytes when we only asked for 13, remember the alignment requirements we discussed in the last chapter! Do you see how when we assign the NULL to the fourth pointer in our malloced block of 14 bytes we will write over our end-magic?

/* null terminate the ppbuf - **** Here we corrupt the heap! */
outbuf[count] = NULL;

Here is a picture to show the overwrite clearly:

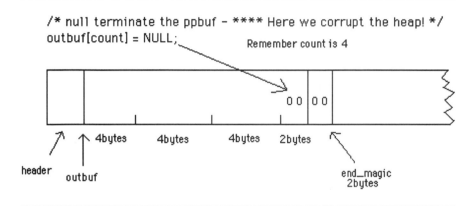

Figure 14.2.   Heap corruption.

14.8.   TRAP THREE: OVERRUNNING ARRAYS

This trap is closely related to the previous trap except we are overrunning the stack ("smashing the stack") instead of the heap. Also the method we use to catch the problem is different. Here is a simple example of the problem:

```
/* bad_array.c */
#include <stdio.h>
#include <stdlib.h>
#include <string.h>

void main()
{
  char test_array[10];

  strcpy(test_array,"longer than ten.");
}
```

Source 14.4.   bad_array.c.

14.9. TRAP THREE DISSECTION

The problem is clear to see only because we are using a two-line program. You overrun an array in a 10,000- to 20,000-line program and watch havoc reign! The compiler allocated 10 bytes on the function stack for the automatic variable in main(); however, I instruct strcpy to copy 16 bytes (actually 17, since strcpy will add the NULL character). The RESULT: SMASH THE STACK!

14.10. TRAP THREE CATCHER:

The method to catch this error is to write a program to scan the source code and detect when an array is being targeted for a copy operation and check how many characters you want to transfer from the source to the target. To accomplish this the program receives tokens (chunks of meaningful data) and a token_type description identifying what the token is from a set of functions in simple_clex.c. The simple_clex routines are in the Code Libraries in Chapter 15. By "simple_clex" I mean a simple C language lexical analyzer. Simply put, a lexical analyzer scans a body of text in order to extract meaningful chunks of data into tokens. Let's study two programs, tokenize_it and terminator.c, to see how we can use the lexical analyzer to catch not only this trap but many other programming problems. I ardently encourage you to get excited about writing "checking" programs to increase the reliability and maintainability of your C programs, which in turn will increase the reliability of the systems you work on!

The program terminator.c is the grammatical analyzer of the tokens returned by get_c_token (the key part of simple_clex). First, let's understand the functioning of get_c_token before we examine how terminator.c uses its output. We get an understanding of the program by examining its input and outputs, which is exactly what the program tokenize_it does for us.

```
/* tokenize_it.c */
#include <stdio.h>
#include <string.h>
#include <stdlib.h>

#include "memory.h"

extern char *get_dynamic_str();
extern char *get_c_token();
```

Source 14.5.   tokenize_it.c.

```
extern char *type_str();
extern int check_heap();

void main()
{
  char  *source=NULL,*token=NULL,*desc=NULL;
  FILE *fp=NULL;
  int last_token, token_type;

  /* get the source file */
  printf("Source file to tokenize: ");
  source = get_dynamic_str();
  if (!source)
    exit(0);

  if ( (fp = fopen(source,"r"))== NULL)
  {
    fprintf(stderr,"unable to open %s.\n",source);
    exit(0);
  }

  while ( (token = get_c_token(fp,&token_type,
  last_token)) != NULL)
  {
    last_token = token_type;
    desc = type_str(token_type);
    if (desc)
      printf("TOKEN %d (%s) is %s.\n",
      token_type,token,desc);
    if (token) free(token); token = NULL;
    if (desc) free(desc); desc = NULL;
    if (!check_heap())
    {
      fprintf(stderr,"HEAP CORRUPTED! ABORT!\n");
      exit(0);
    }

  }
  if (source) free(source); source=NULL;
  memory_map();
  fclose(fp);
}
```

Source 14.5. *Continued.*

Here is a run of tokenize_it on bad_array.c:

Source file to tokenize: bad_array.c
TOKEN 1000 (bad_array.c *) is COMMENT.
TOKEN 303 (include) is COMPILER DIRECTIVE - INCLUDE.
TOKEN 1011 (stdio.h) is INCLUDE FILE.
TOKEN 303 (include) is COMPILER DIRECTIVE - INCLUDE.
TOKEN 1011 (stdlib.h) is INCLUDE FILE.
TOKEN 303 (include) is COMPILER DIRECTIVE - INCLUDE.
TOKEN 1011 (string.h) is INCLUDE FILE.
TOKEN 105 (void) is DATA TYPE - VOID.
TOKEN 1002 (main) is FUNCTION.
TOKEN 1014 (() is OPEN PARENTHESES.
TOKEN 1015 ()) is CLOSE PARENTHESES.
TOKEN 1004 ({) is BEGIN_BLOCK.
TOKEN 101 (char) is DATA TYPE - CHAR.
TOKEN 1010 (test_array) is ARRAY VARIABLE.
TOKEN 1016 (10) is ARRAY DIMENSION ARGUMENT.
TOKEN 1002 (strcpy) is FUNCTION.
TOKEN 1014 (() is OPEN PARENTHESES.
TOKEN 1005 (test_array) is VARIABLE.
TOKEN 1018 (,) is COMMA.
TOKEN 1001 (longer than ten.) is QUOTE.
TOKEN 1015 ()) is CLOSE PARENTHESES.
TOKEN 1003 (}) is END_BLOCK.

[1]00160350: FREE (1014)

It is clear that tokenize_it merely wraps get_c_token in a while loop. The function doing all the work is get_c_token:

while ((token = get_c_token(fp,&token_type,last_token)) != NULL)

Here is a description of the input and output variables:

token—A character string that is returned that is the recognizable token extracted from the source file.

fp—The file pointer to the source file. The function get_c_token reads directly from the file.

token_type—This is a number returned from the program that identifies what the token is. For example, 1000 is a COMMENT. What all the numbers stand for is defined in simple_clex.h.

last_token—This is the number of the last_token returned from get_c_token and is needed to state information inside get_c_token. We will study the workings of get_c_token in detail in the next chapter.

Knowing this, it is easy to see that get_c_token will continually extract tokens from a C source file and return a NULL when there are no more tokens to extract. In summary, feed in a source file, receive out a stream of C tokens. When we examine the tokens extracted from bad_array.c, you get an idea of how effective this C lexical analyzer can be. Every token in the program will be tagged (typed) and returned to your program. The only thing left to do is to grammatically analyze the tokens returned from get_c_token which brings us to parsing and terminator.c.

The program terminator.c is a very simple parser that was written just to parse our example bad_array.c; however, we can use it to understand the principles of parsing in general so that you can write your own parser for any C problem you want to catch! Parsing is normally broken down into two operations: lexical analysis and grammatical analysis. Lexical analysis applies lexical rules to break a text stream into tokens. Grammatical analysis applies grammar rules on the tokens and performs actions associated with each rule. A natural way to understand why these two phases exist is because text can be broken into two parts— the *syntax* of the text and the *semantics* of how the text is organized to portray meaning. Here is a table that reveals the connection between the relationships:

Table 14.1. Parse operations.

Analysis	Object of Analysis	C Example
Lexical analysis	syntax of text	reserved words, compiler directives variables, functions
Grammatical analysis	semantics of text	assignment, looping, arithmetic expression

Those readers familiar with the UNIX operating system may know about the generic parser tools called lex and yacc. Lex and yacc are code generators that produce C programs to perform lexical analysis and grammatical analysis, respectively. Combining the outputs of lex and yacc together produces a generic parser that can parse a text file and perform actions based on grammar rules. In this same vein, you can produce "checking" parsers by using simple_clex and a "grammar rule program (like terminator.c) to check for possible pointer traps and other common C traps! Here is a graphical picture of the parsing process:

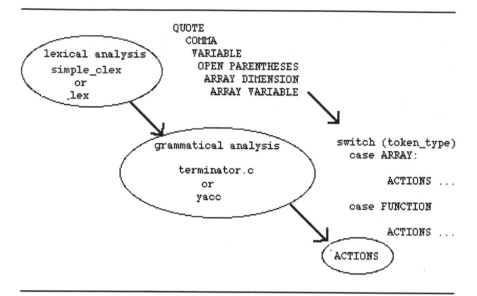

Figure 14.3. The parsing process.

Now let's examine terminator.c:

```
/* terminator.c */
#include <stdio.h>
#include <string.h>
#include <stdlib.h>

#include "gll.h"
#include "memory.h"
#include "simple_clex.h"

extern char *get_dynamic_str();
extern char *get_c_token();
extern char *type_str();
extern int check_heap();

void main()
{
  char *source=NULL,*token=NULL,*desc=NULL,
  *this_array=NULL;
  char *target_array=NULL;
```

Source 14.6. terminator.c.

```
FILE *fp=NULL;

int last_token, token_type,dimension[10],num_dim=0;
int i=0,target_dimension[10],target_ndim,qlen;
int statement_cnt=0;

glptr array_list=NULL,searchptr=NULL;
short copyflag = 0, funcflag = 0;

/* get the source file */
printf("Source file to check for array overrun and
termination: ");
source = get_dynamic_str();
if (!source)
  exit(0);

if ( (fp = fopen(source,"r"))== NULL)
{
  fprintf(stderr,"unable to open %s.\n",source);
  exit(0);
}

for (i = 0; i < 10; i++)
  dimension[i] = 0;

while ( (token = get_c_token(fp,&token_type,
last_token)) != NULL)
{
  last_token = token_type;
  desc = type_str(token_type);
  switch (token_type)
  {
    case ARRAY:
      if (this_array)
      {
        /* store this array in gll before collecting
        next one */
        if (!array_list)
        {
          if (num_dim < 5)
            array_list = initgll(1,6,0,this_array,
              num_dim, dimension[0],
              dimension[1],dimension[2],
              dimension[3],dimension[4]);
```

Source 14.6.   *Continued.*

```
        else
        {
          fprintf(stderr,
          "array_dimensioned over 5.");
          exit(0);
        }
      }
      else
      {
        if (num_dim < 5)
        {
          if (!addgll_node(array_list,
          this_array,num_dim,
            dimension[0],dimension[1],
            dimension[2],dimension[3],
            dimension[4]))
          {
            fprintf(stderr,
            "addgllnode failed!\n");
            exit(0);
          }
        }
        else
        {
          fprintf(stderr,
          "array_dimensioned over 5.");
          exit(0);
        }
      }
      /* get ready for next array entry */
      free(this_array);
      this_array = NULL;
      for (i =0; i < 10; i++)
        dimension[i] = 0;
    }

  this_array = strdup(token);
break;
case ARRAY_DIM_VARIABLE:
  dimension[num_dim] = atoi(token);
  num_dim++;
break;
case FUNCTION:
  funcflag = 1;
```

Source 14.6. *Continued.*

```
      if ( (!strcmp(token,"strcpy")) ||
          (!strcmp(token,"strncpy")) )
          copyflag = 1;
  break;
  case QUOTE:
    if (copyflag && target_array)
    {
      qlen = strlen(token);

      if (target_ndim == 1)
      {
        if (qlen > target_dimension[0])
        {
          printf("**** OVERRUN ATTEMPT! ****\n");
          printf("In strcpy at statement number %d.\n",
              statement_cnt);
          printf("\"%s\" attempted to overrun %s array!\n",
              token,target_array);
          printf("*************************\n");
        }
      }
      else
      {
        /* handle multi-dimension case */
      }
    }

  break;
  case VARIABLE:
    if (copyflag || funcflag)
    {
      if (array_list)
      {
        searchptr = srchgll(array_list,1,'s',
        (double)0,token);
        /* if found */
      }
      else
      {
        /* may only have one array */
        if (this_array)
        {
          if (!strcmp(token,this_array))
```

Source 14.6.   *Continued.*

```
                              {
                                /* MATCH!, this is a target of a
                                function or a copy! */
                                target_array = strdup(this_array);
                                target_ndim = num_dim;
                                for (i=0; i < 10; i++)
                                  target_dimension[i] = dimension[i];
                              }
                          }
                        }
                      }
          break;
          case STATEMENT_END:
            statement_cnt++;
            copyflag = 0; funcflag = 0;
          break;
          default:
          break;
        }

        if (token) free(token); token = NULL;
        if (desc) free(desc); desc = NULL;
        if (!check_heap())
        {
          fprintf(stderr,"HEAP CORRUPTED! ABORT!\n");
          exit(0);
        }

    }
    if (source) free(source); source=NULL;
    memory_map();
    fclose(fp);
}
```

_____

Source 14.6.   _Continued._

Source file to check for array overrun and termination: bad_array.c
**** OVERRUN ATTEMPT! ****
In strcpy at statement number 1.
"longer than ten." attempted to overrun test_array array!
****

[1]001E51F4: FREE (842) [2]001E5548:MALLOC(12) [3]001E555E: FREE (10)
[4]001E5572:MALLOC(12) [5]001E5588: FREE (98)

The program terminator.c follows a very simple method: Recognize a pattern and perform an action. The following patterns are recognized and actions performed:

1. If ARRAY token, then store the array name and array dimensions.
2. If a FUNCTION, set a flag if it is a strcpy() or strncpy().
3. If a VARIABLE and a strcpy, the variable is a target. The code should count and make sure that only the first variable is the target. This is left as an exercise.
4. If QUOTE and a strcpy and we have a target array, check for an OVERRUN! In our case we catch the quote before it would overrun the array.

It is extremely evident that this is not a robust parser and that it would take significant bullet-proofing and expanding to bring it up to real utility. You can take on this challenge as an exercise. We will examine simple_clex in more detail in the next chapter.

14.11. TRAP FOUR: NOT FREEING ALL MEMORY

This trap is commonly referred to as a "memory leak" and is solely a result of just rushing the code or being downright lazy! There are two specific areas where forgetting to free a malloced variable is costly:

1. Inside a loop
2. When exiting out of a function on an error condition (i.e., using multiple exit points)

14.12. TRAP FOUR DISSECTION

Let's examine the first case by removing a critical free out of the program tokenize_it.c and watch how much memory we waste: Here is the main loop, and we will remove the freeing of the variable "token":

```
while ( (token = get_c_token(fp,&token_type,
last_token)) != NULL)
{
 last_token = token_type;
 desc = type_str(token_type);
 if (desc)
   printf("TOKEN %d (%s) is %s.\n",
   token_type,token,desc);

   /* *** REMOVE THE FOLLOWING FREE by commenting it
   out. *** */
```

```
/* *** if (token) free(token); token = NULL;
*** */

if (desc) free(desc); desc = NULL;
if (!check_heap())
{
  fprintf(stderr,"HEAP CORRUPTED! ABORT!\n");
  exit(0);
}


}
```

Here is a look at the memory_map() without freeing token:

```
... (most of the beginning output removed) ...
TOKEN 1016 (10) is ARRAY DIMENSION ARGUMENT.
TOKEN 1002 (strcpy) is FUNCTION.
TOKEN 1014 (() is OPEN PARENTHESES.
TOKEN 1005 (test_array) is VARIABLE.
TOKEN 1018 (,) is COMMA.
TOKEN 1001 (longer than ten.) is QUOTE.
TOKEN 1015 ()) is CLOSE PARENTHESES.
TOKEN 1003 (}) is END_BLOCK.
```

```
[1]001DE4AC: FREE (196) [2]001DE57A:MALLOC(22)
[3]001DE59A:MALLOC(22)
[4]001DE5BA:MALLOC(22)  [5]001DE5DA:MALLOC(22)
[6]001DE5FA:MALLOC(22)
[7]001DE61A:MALLOC(22)  [8]001DE63A:MALLOC(22)
[9]001DE65A:MALLOC(22)
[10]001DE67A:MALLOC(22)  [11]001DE69A:MALLOC(22)
[12]001DE6BA:MALLOC(22)
[13]001DE6DA:MALLOC(22)  [14]001DE6FA:MALLOC(22)
[15]001DE71A:MALLOC(22)
[16]001DE73A:MALLOC(22)  [17]001DE75A:MALLOC(22)
[18]001DE77A:MALLOC(22)
[19]001DE79A:MALLOC(22) [20]001DE7BA:MALLOC(22)
[21]001DE7DA:MALLOC(22)
[22]001DE7FA:MALLOC(22)  [23]001DE81A:MALLOC(22)
[24]001DE83A:MALLOC(22)
[25]001DE85A:MALLOC(22) [26]001DE87A: FREE (40)
```

For a small program like bad_array.c we wasted 528 bytes! If we were parsing a 10,000 line program, it would be easy to see how we could run out of heap space! Remember how the heap looked when we freed everything:

[1]00160350: FREE (1014)

This not only shows how the heap should look when a program completes but also reveals how the dbg_free() routine effectively coalesces small blocks into large blocks. Have you noticed what our memory map does not show us? It does not show us the wasting of our 10 bytes for our header and trailer in our memory blocks. Once you add in the extra 10 bytes for every block on the heap, you see we actually wasted 24 blocks * 32 bytes a block = 768 bytes! The total memory break down is

196 + 10 + (24 * 32) + 40 + 10 = 1024 bytes which is the size of our heap!

The second case is when memory is not freed inside a function which occurs most often when the programmer uses multiple exit points. Here is an example:

```
/* BAD_multiple_exit.c */
#include <stdio.h>
#include <stdlib.h>
#include <string.h>
#include <ctype.h>

#include "memory.h"
extern char *strdup();
extern void memory_map();

char *int2str(int number)
{
  int stat=0;
  char xfer[80];
  char *outbuf;

  if ( (stat = sprintf(xfer,"%d",number) == EOF) )
  {
    fprintf(stderr,
    "int2str: FATAL - sprintf failed on %d.\n",number);
    return(NULL);
  }

  outbuf = strdup(xfer);
  return(outbuf);
}
```

Source 14.7.   BAD_multiple_exit.c.

```c
int work_func(int num1, int num2, int num3)
{
  char *str1=NULL, *str2=NULL, *str3=NULL;

  str1 = int2str(num1);
  str2 = int2str(num2);
  str3 = int2str(num3);

  if (num1 > num2)
  {
    fprintf(stderr,"workfunc Error: num1 <%d> greater
    than num2 <%d>.\n", num1,num2);
    return(0);
  }
  else if (num2 > num3)
  {
    fprintf(stderr,"workfunc Error: num1 <%d> greater
    than num2 <%d>.\n",num2,num3);
    return(0);
  }
  else if (num3 > 1000)
  {
    fprintf(stderr,"workfunc Error: num3 <%d> greater
    than 1000.\n",num3);
    return(0);
  }

  printf("Number:%s%s%s\n",str1,str2,str3);
  if (str1) free(str1); str1 = NULL;
  if (str2) free(str2); str2 = NULL;
  if (str3) free(str3); str3 = NULL;
  return(1);
}

void main()
{
  int i=0;
  int test1[5] = {100, 10, 30, 80, 500 };
  int test2[5] = { 99, 50,300, 90, 200 };
  int test3[5] = {101,100,200,300,1100 };

  for (i=0; i < 5; i++)
  {
```

Source 14.7. *Continued.*

```
    if (!work_func(test1[i],test2[i],test3[i]))
      printf("try %d, work_func failed!\n",i+1);
    else
      printf("try %d, work_func succeeded.\n",i+1);
  }
  memory_map();
}
```

Source 14.7. *Continued.*

Here is a run of the program:

workfunc Error: num1 <100> greater than num2 <99>.
try 1, work_func failed!
Number:1050100
try 2, work_func succeeded.
workfunc Error: num1 <300> greater than num2 <200>.
try 3, work_func failed!
Number:8090300
try 4, work_func succeeded.
workfunc Error: num1 <500> greater than num2 <200>.
try 5, work_func failed!
[1]0015CCA8: FREE (886) [2]0015D028:MALLOC(6)
[3]0015D038:MALLOC(4)
[4]0015D046:MALLOC(4) [5]0015D054:MALLOC(4)
[6]0015D062:MALLOC(4)
[7]0015D070:MALLOC(4) [8]0015D07E:MALLOC(4)
[9]0015D08C:MALLOC(4)
[10]0015D09A:MALLOC(4)

The above program is designed only to illustrate how easy it is to forget to free variables when you have multiple exit points in a function. Some people argue that you should only have one entry and one exit point; however, you reduce code nesting by allowing multiple exit points, which are much less dangerous than multiple entry points.

14.13. TRAP FOUR SOLUTION

The solution is self-explanatory—FREE ALL THE MEMORY YOU AL-LOCATE. To this I will add a method to make your life easier if you want to use multiple exit points like I do. Normally, you just have to free everything before each return and your code would look like this:

```c
int work_func(int num1, int num2, int num3)
{
  char *str1=NULL, *str2=NULL, *str3=NULL;

  str1 = int2str(num1);
  str2 = int2str(num2);
  str3 = int2str(num3);

  if (num1 > num2)
  {
    fprintf(stderr,"workfunc Error: num1 <%d> greater
    than num2 <%d>.\n",num1,num2);
    if (str1) free(str1); str1 = NULL;
    if (str2) free(str2); str2 = NULL;
    if (str3) free(str3); str3 = NULL;
    return(0);
  }
  else if (num2 > num3)
  {
    fprintf(stderr,"workfunc Error: num1 <%d> greater
    than num2 <%d>.\n",num2,num3);
    if (str1) free(str1); str1 = NULL;
    if (str2) free(str2); str2 = NULL;
    if (str3) free(str3); str3 = NULL;

    return(0);
  }
  else if (num3 > 1000)
  {
    fprintf(stderr,"workfunc Error: num3 <%d> greater
    than 1000.\n",num3);
    if (str1) free(str1); str1 = NULL;
    if (str2) free(str2); str2 = NULL;
    if (str3) free(str3); str3 = NULL;

    return(0);
  }

  printf("Number:%s%s%s\n",str1,str2,str3);
  if (str1) free(str1); str1 = NULL;
  if (str2) free(str2); str2 = NULL;
  if (str3) free(str3); str3 = NULL;
  return(1);
}
```

Here is the run with the above changes:

```
workfunc Error: num1 <100> greater than num2 <99>.
try 1, work_func failed!
Number:1050100
try 2, work_func succeeded.
workfunc Error: num1 <300> greater than num2 <200>.
try 3, work_func failed!
Number:8090300
try 4, work_func succeeded.
workfunc Error: num1 <500> greater than num2 <200>.
try 5, work_func failed!
[1]000F87D8: FREE (1014)
```

The run is good because we freed all our memory, but we had to do a lot of typing, which is slow and boring. Here is one solution to the problem:

14.14. THE MULTI_FREE SOLUTION

The function multi_free will make it easy for us to free many arguments with one line of code. Here is the code:

```c
/* BETTER_multiple_exit.c */
#include <stdio.h>
#include <stdlib.h>
#include <string.h>
#include <ctype.h>
#include <stdarg.h>

#include "memory.h"
extern char *strdup();
extern void memory_map();

void multi_free(char **first, ...)
{
  char **next;
  va_list args;

  if (first)
  {
    if (*first) free(*first);
    if (*first) *first = NULL;
```

Source 14.8. BETTER_multiple_exit.c.

```
      va_start (args, first);
      while (next = va_arg(args, char **))
      {
        if (*next) free(*next);
        if (*next) *next = NULL;
      }
    }
}

int work_func(int num1, int num2, int num3)
{
    char *str1=NULL, *str2=NULL, *str3=NULL;

    str1 = int2str(num1);
    str2 = int2str(num2);
    str3 = int2str(num3);

    if (num1 > num2)
    {
      fprintf(stderr,"workfunc Error: num1 <%d> greater
      than num2 <%d>.\n",num1,num2);
      multi_free(&str1,&str2,&str3,NULL);
      return(0);
    }
    else if (num2 > num3)
    {
      fprintf(stderr,"workfunc Error: num1 <%d> greater
      than num2 <%d>.\n",num2,num3);
      multi_free(&str1,&str2,&str3,NULL);
      return(0);
    }
    else if (num3 > 1000)
    {
      fprintf(stderr,"workfunc Error: num3 <%d> greater
      than 1000.\n",num3);
      multi_free(&str1,&str2,&str3,NULL);
      return(0);
    }

    printf("Number:%s%s%s\n",str1,str2,str3);
    multi_free(&str1,&str2,&str3,NULL);
    return(1);
}
```

Source 14.8.   *Continued.*

The program run will be the same as if we typed out all the frees, but we save our fingers a lot of work. Again, you may not appreciate this until you have knocked out a 5,000 or 10,000-line program!

14.15. TRAP FIVE: INCORRECT OPERATOR PRECEDENCE

Operator precedence is a subtle and nasty error that is avoided only by slow and cautious programming. This makes good sense in the same way that you need to slow down when approaching tight curves. Here is an example of how NOT to do it:

```c
/* BAD_precedence.c */
#include <stdio.h>
#include <stdlib.h>
#include <string.h>
#include <ctype.h>

#define MINNUMS 5
#include "memory.h"

extern char *get_dynamic_str();

/* fill array returns the number of entries or 0 on
error. */
int fill_array(int **numbers)
{
  char *response=NULL;
  int num=-1,i=0,maxsize=MINNUMS;
  int *temp = NULL;

  *numbers = (int *) malloc(sizeof(int) * MINNUMS);
  if (!(*numbers))
  {
    fprintf(stderr,
    "fill_array: FATAL - malloc failed!\n");
    return(0);
  }

  do {
    printf("Enter integer or -1 to stop: ");
    response = get_dynamic_str();
```

Source 14.9.   BAD_precedence.c.

```c
      if (response)
        num = atoi(response);
      else
        return(0);

      if (num != -1)
      {
        if (i == maxsize)
        {
          /* realloc */
          temp = (int *) realloc(*numbers,
              sizeof(int) * (maxsize + MINNUMS));

          if (!temp)
          {
            fprintf(stderr,"fill_array: FATAL - unable to
            get more space!\n");
            return(i);
          }
          else
            *numbers = temp;
        }

        /* fill the array - THIS IS WRONG */
        *numbers[i] = num;
        /**** HERE IS THE CORRECT WAY **** */
        /* (*numbers)[i] = num; */
        i++;
      }
  } while (num != -1);
  return(i);
}

void main()
{
  int *my_numbers=NULL;
  int my_count=0,i=0;

  my_count = fill_array(&my_numbers);

  for (i=0; i < my_count; i++)
    printf("%d.\n",my_numbers[i]);
}
```

Source 14.9. *Continued.*

Please do not run the above code before commenting out the wrong way and uncommenting the right way! If you decide to run it "just to see what happens," it is *at your own peril!*

14.16. TRAP FIVE DISSECTION

Here are the two expressions:

*numbers[i]

or,

(*numbers)[i]

Because of the precedence rules, the first expression is the same as *(numbers[i]). The explicit parentheses should help you in understanding the dereferencing. It is very important for you to understand the difference between these two expressions because the first one leads to nasty program bugs!

First, we need to understand the context of the expressions. Numbers is an array that we want to be dynamically initialized, so we pass in a pointer to the array or a pointer pointer (int **numbers). Since you know that indexing is nothing more than pointer arithmetic (Chapter 5), the question we need to answer is what pointer do I want to add i to?

Here is a diagram that will help us visualize the problem:

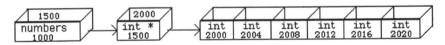

```
facts:  1) The integers take 4 bytes of storage.

        2) numbers is an integer pointer pointer.

        3) To access the int *, I use *numbers.

        4) *numbers is address 2000.

        5) *( numbers[2]) is *(*( numbers +(2*sizeof(int))).

           *(*(1500 + (8))) = *(*(1508)) which is NOT WHAT WE WANT.

        6) (* numbers )[2] is *(2000 + (2*sizeof(int))).

           *(2000 + (8))) = *(2008) which is 3rd array element!
```

Figure 14.4.   Operator precedence with containers.

The key difference between the two expressions is when the indexing takes place. When you say *(numbers[i]), this translates to "(add i to the pointer at numbers and then dereference it) and then dereference it again." But (*numbers)[i] says, "(dereference numbers) and then add i to the dereferenced pointer and dereference that new pointer." The order of operations is critical here because numbers is a pointer pointer and not an integer array pointer! You do not want to do pointer arithmetic (index) on the value of the pointer pointer! You want to do pointer arithmetic (index) the value of the array pointer! If you understand the above discussion, you will understand why *(numbers[0]) and (*numbers)[0] are the same.

14.17. TRAP FIVE SOLUTION

Until you have built checking parsers to handle each trap we have discussed, the best solution to incorrect operator precedence is the two-pronged attack of caution and knowledge. Take caution and move slowly when approaching code with a lot of operators. Second, know the correct operator precedence as shown in the following table:

Table 14.2.   Operator precedence.

Operators
( ) [] -> .
! ~ ++ — + – * & (type) sizeof
* / %
+ –
<< >>
< <= > >=
== !=
&
^
|
&&
||
?:
= += –= *= /= %= &= ^= |= <<= >>=
,

14.18. TRAP SIX: DANGLING POINTERS

A dangling pointer is literally "a pointer left hanging." This description looks at a pointer from the perspective of the pointer's purpose, which is to "point to something." If a pointer is not pointing to its intended target, it is not only dangling but dangerous! Although this problem takes many forms, these are the two most common errors:

1. Assigning multiple pointers to a single object, and when one of the pointers frees the object, the others are left dangling. This often happens with abstract data types.
2. Having a global pointer point to a local function variable, and when the function returns, the function variable is popped off the stack. The global pointer is now "dangling in space." Another variation on this is for a function to return the address of one of its local variables, which will bring the same disastrous results.

Let's look at examples of both cases:

```
/* dangling1.c */
#include <stdio.h>
#include <string.h>
#include <stdlib.h>
#include <ctype.h>

#include "memory.h"

extern char *get_dynamic_str();

void main()
{
  int i=0;
  char  *string1=NULL,*string2=NULL,*string3=NULL;
  char *stringp=NULL;

  printf("Enter first string: ");
  fflush(stdout);
  string1 = get_dynamic_str();

  stringp = string1;
  printf("stringp (%p) before dangling is %s.\n",
  stringp,stringp);
```

Source 14.10.   dangling1.c.

```
    printf("Enter second string: ");
    fflush(stdout);
    string2 = get_dynamic_str();
    free(string1);

    printf("Enter third string: ");
    fflush(stdout);
    string3 = get_dynamic_str();
    memory_map();
    free(string2);
    free(string3);

    printf("stringp (%p) after dangling points to %s.\n",
    stringp, stringp);
    memory_map();
}
```

Source 14.10. *Continued.*

Here is a run of the first example:

Enter first string: aaaaa
stringp (001DF7EA) before dangling is aaaaa.
Enter second string: bbbbb
Enter third string: ccccc
[1]001DF41C: FREE (914) [2]001DF7B8:MALLOC(40)
[3]001DF7EA:MALLOC(40)
stringp (001DF7EA) after dangling points to ccccc.
[1]001DF41C: FREE (1014)

Here is the second example:

```
/* dangling2.c */
#include <stdlib.h>
#include <string.h>
#include <ctype.h>
#include <stdio.h>

char *bad_initialize()
{
    char buffer[128];
```

Source 14.11. dangling2.c.

```
  printf("Enter string: ");
  fflush(stdout);
  gets(buffer);

  return(buffer);
}

void main()
{
  char *names[5];
  int i;

  for (i=0; i < 5; i++)
    names[i] = bad_initialize();

  for (i=0; i < 5; i++)
    printf("name[%d] is %s.\n",i,names[i]);
}
```

Source 14.11.   *Continued.*

Here is a run of the second example:

Enter string: jill
Enter string: john
Enter string: jacky
Enter string: mick
Enter string: mike
name[0] is mike.
name[1] is mike.
name[2] is mike.
name[3] is mike.
name[4] is mike.

The first example is easier to catch because it takes an explicit free on the programmer's part. In other words, *"You have to willfully shoot yourself in the foot!"* The second example is more subtle because the results are dependent on the operation of the application stack and not on your code. This translates into *"shooting yourself because you didn't know the gun was loaded!"*

14.19. TRAP SIX SOLUTION

It is fairly straightforward to write a parser to track the pointers malloced into and other pointers that point to the same malloced block to catch against danglers. This is left to you as an exercise; however, you may not have to write a parser if you follow two rules:

1. Avoid having multiple pointers that point to a single object. If this is impossible, proceed with caution.
2. As a general rule, when returning a pointer from a function, it is best to allocate memory from the heap using malloc() or strdup(). It should be rare that you use the address operator (&) to return an address from a function.

14.20. OTHER TRAPS

There are too many traps to cover all of them in excruciating detail so I will present short descriptions of some other common traps. Some of these traps were provided by fellow members of Prodigy®:

1. Indexing past array bounds:

```
int myarray[10];
int i;
for (i=0; i <= 10; i++)
    myarray[i] = 1000;
```

The above example tries to index eleven elements in an array of only ten!

—John George (RMTR39A)

2. Overrunning a string by gets():

```
char buffer[30];
gets(buffer);
```

A string overrun will occur using gets() if the size of the input data is greater than the size of the string minus 1 (in the above example, if the gets returns a string greater than 29). Since I believe in the art of defensive programming, I use fgets even when getting from stdin, since a maximum length parameter is used that will prevent the string overrun—however, then an fflush may be required, which may be done unconditionally or as a result of a strlen test.

—Bill Fehn (KPNS72A)

3. Forgetting to use the address operator on scanf():

```
int myint;
printf("enter an integer: ");
scanf("%d",myint);
```

Since scanf expects a pointer, you need scanf("%d",&myint);

—Bill Fehn (KPNS72A)

4. Having a function prototype for functions that return pointers:
   For example, forgetting to include alloc.h when using farmalloc() (on DOS machines). Without doing this, the compiler assumes it's returning an integer and not a far pointer.

—Michael Hohenshilt (RBPX70E)

5. The dangers of cut and paste():
   In editing code, I deleted a block and cut and pasted new code in its place. I deleted okay, but the insertion was at the wrong place, so that the free statement was not always executed when the pointer was malloc()'ed. That error would cause the damndest problems, including massive mysterious crashes.

—John George (RMTR39A)

6. Cannot initialize a pointer to a string:

```
char *ptr = "This is a string";
   char carray[] = "This is a string";
```

the sizeof(carray) == 17, but the sizeof(ptr) is NOT 17! The sizeof(ptr) only equals the size of a pointer (either 2 or 4 bytes depending on the operating system or memory model).

—Alan Richey (JFXV08A)

AUTHOR'S NOTE: This is implementation dependent, and some compilers will initialize the ptr correctly. Some compilers will initialize the string and store the pointer in ptr.

7. Don't assign to a pointer without mallocing space, in other words, using an uninitialized pointer:

```
struct person {
char name[20];
int age;
char sex;
} client[2], *ptr2client[100];
```

```
strcpy(ptr2client[0]->name,"John Smith");
ptr2client[0]->age = 30;
ptr2client[0]->sex = 'M';
```

In the above example you are using the pointer before initializing it to a valid memory location by malloc()ing the space. Prior to the assignment, malloc the space for the structure:

ptr2client[0] = (struct person *) malloc(sizeof(struct person));

8. Using == instead of strcmp:

This may especially afflict Pascal programmers who are used to comparing strings; however, strings in C are just NULL-terminated character arrays!

```
char buf1[] = "Jack";
char buf2[] = "Joe";
if (buf1 == buf2)
    printf("strings are equal!\n");
```

The above program compares the addresses of the start of the strings, which are definitely not going to be equal! Should have used if (!strcmp(buf1,buf2)). This is very similar to the simpler error of using = instead of ==, which also affects programmers new to C. Most C programmers have been stung by these incorrect assumptions.

9. Common free() problems:

The function free() probably causes the most heartache of any C Library function and was the primary motivation I had to create debug_memory.c in order to gain some control over free(). Here are several free()problems that can all be avoided by using debug_memory.c.

a. Freeing non-malloced pointers:

```
char *ptr;
char *non_mallocedptr;
ptr = (char *) malloc(20);
non_mallocedptr = ptr + 10;
free(non_mallocedptr);
```

This would corrupt the heap, so dbg_free() will not let this happen.

b. Not resetting to NULL after freeing can lead to a double free.

if (ptr) free(ptr);

However, just because the ptr has been freed does not mean it does not still contain an address. If you have a test that decides when to use a pointer like

if (ptr)
{
    /* do action */
}

The test would be passed because you did not set the pointer to NULL after freeing it. I recommend combining the free protection, free() function call, and resetting to NULL on one line (or using multi-free).

if (ptr) free(ptr); ptr = NULL;

c. Freeing a NULL pointer—if after you freed a pointer and set it to NULL you did not protect your free. The function dbg_free() will return with a warning, but you should always protect your free with an if statement: if (ptr) free(ptr);

d. Freeing a pointer's data and later trying to use it. You can use it until it gets reassigned but you should never use data once it has been freed!

10. Not mallocing enough space for the NULL terminator. Just as when you declare arrays you need to insure they are large enough to accommodate the NULL terminator, the same rule applies to malloc(). Inside a function, remember it is strlen() + 1. Examine the strdup() function for an example of this.

11. NULL pointer assignment. Before you dereference a pointer it must have a valid lvalue (address) stored; otherwise you will be attempting to access an invalid address. A common error is to have the pointer initialized to NULL (a 0) and then try to use the pointer before you assigned a valid address to it (with either malloc or the & operator).

int *int_ptr = NULL;
int myint;
myint = *int_ptr; /* NULL pointer assignment! */

What you are asking the computer to do is access memory location 0 and return the integer there! Memory location 0 is usually reserved for system use and outside of your program's legal address space.

CHAPTER QUESTIONS

1. Why is using strcpy() a solution to forgetting a NULL terminator?
2. How does using debug_memory.c insure against heap corruption?
3. What is the purpose of the routine get_c_token(), and how does it assist in catching pointer traps?
4. What are two operations of a parser?
5. What are two common areas where forgetting to free is costly?
6. How does the multi_free() function save typing?
7. Which has a higher precedence, ! or &&?

CHAPTER EXERCISES

1. Rewrite free_ppbuf() to not use the ppbuf NULL termination as an end condition in the for loop.
2. Write a parser using get_c_token to catch functions that do not free allocated memory.
3. Write a parser to catch dangling pointers.

Code Libraries

OBJECTIVE: A repertoire of source code for study and to enhance your applications.

15.1.   PPBUF UTILITIES

Here is the complete set of ppbuf utilities. I have used these routines extensively for fast text processing. They are also useful for study because of their use of pointer pointers.

```
/* ppbuf_utils */

#include <stdio.h>
#include <string.h>
#include <stdlib.h>
#include <ctype.h>

extern char *strdup();

/* #define DEBUGPP */

/*   **************************************************
   FUNCTION NAME: file2ppbuf
   PURPOSE: read a text file into a character pointer
     pointer buffer.
   INPUT: filename - a character string of the file to
     open.
```

```c
   OUTPUT: a character pointer pointer which points to
      the null-terminated ppbuf.
   NOTE: this function MALLOCs memory.
   AUTHOR: MCD
*************************************************** */
char **file2ppbuf(char *filename)
{
  FILE *fp;

  char str[512];
  char **buf=NULL;

  int linechunk=100;
  int cnt=0, len=0;

  if (!filename)
  {
    fprintf(stderr,
    "file2ppbuf:FATAL - filename is NULL!\n");
    return(NULL);
  }

  if ((fp = fopen(filename,"r"))==NULL)
  {
    fprintf(stderr,
    "file2ppbuf: FATAL - cannot open %s!\n",filename);
    return(NULL);
  }

  buf = (char **) malloc(sizeof(char *) * linechunk);
  if (!buf)
  {
    fprintf(stderr,
    "file2ppbuf: FATAL - malloc failed!\n");
    return(NULL);
  }

  cnt = 0;
  while (!feof(fp))
  {
    if (fgets (str,500,fp))
    {
      len = strlen(str);
      buf[cnt] = (char *) malloc(sizeof(char) * len + 1);
      strcpy(buf[cnt],str);
```

```
        cnt++;
        if (cnt >= linechunk)
        {
          /* realloc in quantities of 100 */
          buf = (char **) realloc(buf,sizeof(char *) *
          (cnt + 100));
          if (!buf)
          {
            fprintf(stderr,
            "file2ppbuf: FATAL - realloc failed!\n");
            return(NULL);
          }

          linechunk += 100;
        }
      }
    }

  buf[cnt] = NULL;

  fclose(fp);
  return(buf);
}

/*    ************************************************
  FUNCTION NAME: free_ppbuf
  PURPOSE: free each string and the array of pointers
    that make up a ppbuf.
  INPUT: inbuf - a character pointer pointer buffer to
                 be freed.
         count - the number of lines in the ppbuf. If 0
                 it will expecd the ppbuf to be null-
                 terminated.
  OUTPUT: none.
  AUTHOR: MCD
*************************************************   */
void free_ppbuf(char **inbuf, int count)
{
  int i;

  if (inbuf)
  {
    if (count>0)
    {
      for (i = 0; i < count; i++)
        if (inbuf[i]) free(inbuf[i]);
```

```
      free(inbuf);
    }
    else
    {
      for (i = 0; inbuf[i]; i++)
        count++;
      for (i = 0; i<count; i++)
        if (inbuf[i]) free(inbuf[i]);
      free(inbuf);
    }
  }
}


/*   **************************************************
  FUNCTION NAME: expandppbuf
  PURPOSE: increase the number of strings a ppbuf can
    hold by num_lines.
  INPUT: inbuf - the pointer pointer buf to expand. If
                 inbuf in NULL the ppbuf will be
                 created, else realloced.
         num_lines - an integer which is the number of
                 lines to expand the buffer.
  OUTPUT: a character pointer pointer to the ppbuf.
    NULL on failure.
  NOTE: this function MALLOCs memory.
  AUTHOR: MCD
**************************************************   */
char **expandppbuf(char **inbuf, int num_lines)
{
  char **outbuf=NULL;
  int cur_cnt=0;

  if (!inbuf)
  {
    outbuf = (char **) malloc(sizeof(char *) *
    (num_lines + 1));
    if (!outbuf)
    {
      fprintf(stderr,
      "expandppbuf: FATAL - malloc failed!\n");
      return(NULL);
    }
    outbuf[num_lines] = NULL;
  }
  else
  {
```

```
   for (cur_cnt=0; inbuf[cur_cnt]; cur_cnt++);

   outbuf = (char **) realloc(inbuf, sizeof(char *) *
   (cur_cnt + (num_lines+1)));
   if (!outbuf)
   {
     fprintf(stderr,
     "expandppbuf: FATAL - realloc failed!\n");
     return(NULL);
   }
 }

  return(outbuf);
}

/*  ***************************************************
  FUNCTION NAME: dumpppbuf
  PURPOSE: prints out a ppbuf to a file or stdout.
  INPUT: ppbuf - a pointer pointer to the string array
                 to be printed.
         filename - the filename of the output file. If
                 NULL, dumps to stdout.
         num_lines - the number of lines in the ppbuf,
                 if 0 assumes null-termination.
         addnewline - an integer flag on whether
                 newlines should be appended to the
                 end of each line.
  OUTPUT: an integer as an error status.
  AUTHOR: MCD
***************************************************  */
int dumpppbuf(char **ppbuf, char *filename,
int num_lines, int addnewline)
{
  int i=0;
  FILE *fp=NULL;

  if (!ppbuf)
  {
    fprintf(stderr,
    "dumpppbuf: FATAL - ppbuf cannot be NULL!\n");
    return(0);
  }

  if (filename)
  {
    if ( (fp = fopen(filename,"w")) == NULL)
```

```
      {
        fprintf(stderr,
        "dumpppbuf: FATAL - Unable to open %s!\n",filename);
        return(0);
      }
    }
    else
      fp = stdout;

    if (num_lines > 0)
    {
      for (i = 0; i < num_lines; i++)
      {
        if (ppbuf[i])
        {
          if (addnewline)
            fprintf(fp,"%s\n",ppbuf[i]);
          else
            fprintf(fp,"%s",ppbuf[i]);
        }
      }
    }
    else
    {
      for (i=0; ppbuf[i]; i++)
      {
        if (addnewline)
          fprintf(fp,"%s\n",ppbuf[i]);
        else
          fprintf(fp,"%s",ppbuf[i]);
      }
    }

    if (fp != stdout)
      fclose(fp);

    return(1);
  }

/*  ***********************************************
    FUNCTION NAME: dupppbuf
    PURPOSE: creates a duplicate copy of a ppbuf.
    INPUT: ppbuf -  pointer pointer to string array to
                    duplicate.
           count -  an integer for the number of lines in
                    the ppbuf. If 0 the function assumes
                    null-termination.
```

```
    OUTPUT: a pointer pointer to the allocated copy.
    NOTE: this function MALLOCs memory.
    AUTHOR: MCD
************************************************  */
char **dupppbuf(char **ppbuf, int count)
{
  char **outbuf=NULL;
  int i=0, outcount=0;

  if (ppbuf)
  {
    if (count > 0)
    {
      outcount = count;
      outbuf = (char **) malloc(sizeof(char *) * (count
      + 1));
      if (!outbuf)
      {
        fprintf(stderr,
        "dupppbuf: FATAL - malloc failed!\n");
        return(NULL);
      }

      for (i=0; i < count; i++)
        outbuf[i] = strdup(ppbuf[i]);

    }
    else
    {
      for (i = 0; ppbuf[i]; i++)
        outcount++;

      outbuf = (char **) malloc(sizeof(char *) *
      outcount + 1);
      if (!outbuf)
      {
        fprintf(stderr,
        "dupppbuf: FATAL - malloc failed!\n");
        return(NULL);
      }

      for (i = 0; ppbuf[i]; i++)
        outbuf[i] = strdup(ppbuf[i]);
    }

    outcount++;
    outbuf[outcount] = NULL;
```

```
  }
  return(outbuf);
}

/*  **********************************************
    FUNCTION NAME: count_lines
    PURPOSE: count the number of lines in a NULL-
      terminated ppbuf.
    INPUT: inbuf - the pointer pointer to the string
                    array in the heap to be counted.
    OUTPUT: an integer which is the number of lines in
      the ppbuf.
    AUTHOR: MCD
************************************************** */
int count_lines(char **inbuf)
{
  int i=0;

  if (inbuf)
  {
    for (i=0; inbuf[i]; i++)
      ;
  }
  return(i);
}

/*  **********************************************
    FUNCTION NAME: strip_trailing_whitespace
    PURPOSE: the end of many text files will have
      blank lines at the end that will spoil an
      analysis function. This routine will strip
      the useless whitespace from the bottom of a
      ppbuf.
    INPUT: inbuf - the pointer pointer to the string
                    array to strip whitespace from.
    OUTPUT: none.
    AUTHOR: MCD
************************************************** */
void strip_trailing_whitespace(char **inbuf)
{
  int i=0,j=0,end=0;
  int valid_char=0,len=0;

  if (!inbuf)
  {
    fprintf(stderr,
    "strip_trailing_whitespace: FATAL - inbuf is NULL!\n");
```

```
        return;
    }

    for (i=0;inbuf[i]; i++)
        ;

    end = i-1;

    /* strip until you hit a valid char */
    for (i=end; i >=0; i—)
    {
        len = strlen(inbuf[i]);
        for(j=0; j < len; j++)
        {
            if ( (isalnum(inbuf[i][j])) ||
                    (ispunct(inbuf[i][j])) )
                valid_char = 1;

            if (valid_char) break;
        }
        if (!valid_char)
        {
            /* this line in the buffer does not have a valid
            character, free the line and set the pointer te
            NULL */
            free(inbuf[i]);
            inbuf[i] = NULL;
        }
        else
            break;
    } /* end of for */
}

/*   *************************************************
  FUNCTION NAME: appendppbuf
  PURPOSE: append one ppbuf to the bottom of another
     ppbuf.
  INPUT: appendee - a pointer pointer to the string
                    array to be appended TO.
         appendee_cnt - an integer which is the number
                    of lines in the appendee ppbuf. if
                    0, assumes a NULL-termination.
         appender - a pointer pointer to the string
                    array to APPEND.
         appendee_cnt - an integer which is the number
                    of lines in the appendee ppbuf.
                    if 0, assumes a NULL-termination.
```

```
   OUTPUT: an integer as an error status. 1 on success,
     else 0.
   AUTHOR: MCD
*************************************************** */
int appendppbuf(char **appendee, int appendee_cnt, char
**appender, int appender_cnt)
{
  int i=0,j=0;

  if (!appendee && !appender)
  {
    fprintf(stderr,
    "appendppbuf: FATAL - ppbuf arguments may not be NULL!\n");

    return(0);
  }

  if (appendee_cnt)
  {
    /* appendee_cnt is the end of the buffer */
    j=appendee_cnt;
    if (appender_cnt)
    {
      /* appender cnt is the length of buffer to append */
      for (i=0; i < appender_cnt; i++,j++)
        appendee[j] = strdup(appender[i]);
    }
    else
    {
      /* append the appender until you hit a NULL */
      for (i=0; appender[i]; i++,j++)
        appendee[j] = strdup(appender[i]);
    }
  }
  else
  {
    /* we must find te end of the appendee buffer */
    for (j=0; appendee[j]; j++)
      ;

    if (appender_cnt)
    {
      /* appender cnt is the length of buffer to append */
      for (i=0; i < appender_cnt; i++,j++)
        appendee[j] = strdup(appender[i]);
```

```
    }
    else
    {
      /* append the appender until you hit a NULL */
      for (i=0; appender[i]; i++,j++)
        appendee[j] = strdup(appender[i]);
    }
  }

  return(1);
}

/*  **************************************************
    FUNCTION NAME: dupnlines
    PURPOSE: duplicate a specific number of lines out of
      a ppbuf.
    INPUT: buf - the pointer pointer to the string array
                 to duplicate lines from.
           from - an integer which is the index of the
                  string to start duplicating.
           numlines - an integer which is the number of
                      lines to duplicate.
    OUTPUT: a pointer pointer to the smaller, duplicated
      ppbuf.
    NOTE: this function MALLOCs memory.
    AUTHOR: MCD
************************************************** */
char **dupnlines(char **buf, int from, int numlines)
{
  /* from is the nth line, so that is from - 1 for c
  arrays. */
  int i=0, cnt = 0;
  char **dupbuf=NULL;

  /* error check input parameters */
  if (!buf)
  {
    fprintf(stderr,
    "dupnlines: FATAL - input buffer NULL!\n");
    return(NULL);
  }

  if ( (from < 1) || (numlines < 1) )
  {
    fprintf(stderr,
    "dupnlines: FATAL - from or numlines less than 1!\n");
```

```
    return(NULL);
  }

  dupbuf = (char **) malloc(sizeof(char *) * numlines +
  1);
  if (!dupbuf)
  {
    fprintf(stderr,
    "dupnlines: FATAL - malloc failed!\n");
    return(NULL);
  }

  from--; /* decrement one to account for c arrays. */
  for (i = from; cnt < numlines; i++, cnt++)
  {
    if (buf[i])
      dupbuf[cnt] = strdup(buf[i]);
    else
    {
      fprintf(stderr,
      "dupnlines: Warning - numlines exceeded input buffer!\n");
      dupbuf[cnt] = NULL;
      return(dupbuf);
    }
  }

  dupbuf[cnt] = NULL;
  return(dupbuf);
}
```

Points to note about the ppbuf_utils:

1. In file2ppbuf(), you may have noticed that I am using a static character array (char str[512];) . There is no good reason to use this, and in fact, it violates my principle of "think dynamic." This function was written before get_dynamic_str() and should be rewritten to use the new more dynamic routine. I have left this to you as an exercise.

2. file2ppbuf() is straightforward. The file is read a line at a time and copied into a malloced ppbuf. The malloced ppbuf is then returned to the caller.

3. free_ppbuf() allows you to specify the number of lines in the ppbuf (count) in case the ppbuf is not NULL-terminated. I recommend all your ppbufs be NULL-terminated. This convention allows ppbufs to be manipulated as easily as strings. free_ppbuf() first frees all the rows of character strings and then the array of pointers.

4. expandppbuf() is a "realloc for ppbufs," which allows you either to create or expand a ppbuf. If the ppbuf argument is NULL, the ppbuf is malloced instead of realloced.

5. dumpppbuf() dumps a ppbuf either to a file or stdout. Again, if num_lines is 0, it expects the ppbuf to be NULL-terminated. The flag addnewline determines whether a newline is added to the end of the string or not. If you create a ppbuf of an address list and you want to dump it to a file, you would set addnewline to 1 and dumpppbuf() would attach the newline character (\n) to the end of every string.

6. dupppbuf() is similar to strdup(), which means that it makes a malloced copy of a ppbuf.

7. count_lines() returns the number of lines in a NULL-terminated ppbuf.

8. If you use file2ppbuf() to extract a ppbuf from a file, there may be unwanted white space (like extra newlines) at the end of the ppbuf. If you don't want your parser or analysis function to bother with trailing whitespace, strip_trailing_whitespace() will find trailing lines of whitespace, free them, and reset the NULL to terminate the ppbuf.

9. appendppbuf() appends one ppbuf to another. If appendee_cnt or appender_cnt is 0, it assumes the ppbufs are NULL-terminated.

10. dupnlines() will create a new ppbuf, which is an extract of a larger ppbuf (sort of a substr for ppbufs).

15.2.   QUICKSORT()—TO SORT PPBUFS

The quick sort is probably the most well known and widely used sorting algorithm in computer science because of its fast average case behavior. Here I will provide a version of quick sort that uses the *string stack* instead of recursion. This version of quick sort is then used to allow sorting of ppbufs.

Here is sorting code added to ppbuf_utils.h:

```
#include "string_stack.h"

extern ppstackp init_ppstack();
extern int mpush(ppstackp thestack, ...);
extern char **mpop();

/*  **************************************************
    FUNCTION NAME: swap
    PURPOSE: swap the rvalues of two variables.
    INPUT: a - a pointer pointer which holds the address
               of the variable in the calling function.
```

```
            b - a pointer pointer which holds the address
                of the variable in the calling function.
    OUTPUT: none.
    AUTHOR: MCD
*************************************************  */
void swap(char **a, char **b)
{
  char *temp;

  temp = *a; *a = *b; *b = temp;
}


/*    ***************************************************
    FUNCTION NAME: split
    PURPOSE: splits a ppbuf (string array) by choosing a
      "split point" and dividing the list into two lists
      one less than the split point and the other
      greater.
    INPUT: buf - the string array to split.
           first - an integer which is the start of the
                   array.
           last - an integer which is the end of the
                  array to split.
    OUTPUT: the index of the value of split point.
    AUTHOR: MCD
*************************************************  */
int split(char **buf, int first, int last)
{
  char *x;
  int unknown;
  int splitPoint;
  x = buf[first];
  splitPoint = first;

  for (unknown = first + 1; unknown <= last; unknown++)
  {
    if ( (strcmp(buf[unknown],x)) < 0)
    {
      splitPoint++;
      swap(&(buf[splitPoint]), &(buf[unknown]));
    }
  }

  swap (&(buf[first]), &(buf[splitPoint]));

  return(splitPoint);
}
```

```
/*   ***********************************************
   FUNCTION NAME: Quicksort
   PURPOSE: sort an array of strings.
   METHOD: the quick sort method is to continually split
      the list recursively until the entire list is
      sorted. Instead of using recursion this routine
      simulates the recursion with a stack. The stack
      requires less memory than recursion.
   INPUT: buf - a string array to sort.
          buf_cnt - the number of strings in the array.
   OUTPUT: an integer as an error status. 1 on success
      else 0.
   AUTHOR: MCD
/*   ***********************************************
int Quicksort(char **buf, int buf_cnt)
{
  ppstackp qstack=NULL;

  int first, last, splitPoint;

  char **sargs, *lasts, *splits;

  static char dup_buf[100];

  qstack = init_ppstack();
  if (!qstack)
  {
    fprintf(stderr,
    "Quicksort: FATAL - could not initialize stack!\n");
    return(0);
  }

  first = 0;
  last = buf_cnt - 1;

  sprintf(dup_buf,"%d",last);
  lasts = strdup(dup_buf);
  mpush(qstack,lasts,"0",NULL);
  if (lasts) free(lasts);
  while (qstack->stack_qty > 0)
  {
    sargs = mpop(qstack,2);
    first = atoi(sargs[0]);
    last = atoi(sargs[1]);
    sprintf(dup_buf,"%d",last);
    lasts = strdup(dup_buf);
    free_ppbuf(sargs,0);
```

```c
      while (first < last)
      {
        splitPoint = split(buf,first,last);
        sprintf(dup_buf,"%d",splitPoint+1));
        splits = strdup(dup_buf);
        mpush(qstack,lasts,splits,NULL);
        if (lasts) free(lasts);
        if (splits) free(splits);
        last = splitPoint - 1;
        sprintf(dup_buf,"%d",last);
        lasts = strdup(dup_buf);
      }
      if (lasts) free(lasts);
    }

  return(1);
}


/*    **************************************************
   FUNCTION NAME: sortppbuf
   PURPOSE: a wrap routine for Quicksort.
   INPUT: inbuf - the ppbuf to be sorted.
          inbuf_cnt - an integer which is the number of
                    lines in the ppbuf. If this number is
                    0, the ppbuf is assumed to be null-
                    terminated.
   OUTPUT: an integer as an error status. 1 on success,
     else 0.
   AUTHOR: MCD
*************************************************** */
int sortppbuf(char **inbuf, int inbuf_cnt)
{
  /* This function will implement a modified quick sort
  technique. The algorithm is quick sort with a stack
  from Baase, pg. 61. */

  int i=0;

  if (!inbuf)
  {
    fprintf(stderr,
    "sortppbuf: FATAL - argument may not be NULL!\n");
    return(0);
  }

  if (!inbuf_cnt)
  {
```

```
    for (i=0; inbuf[i]; i++);
    inbuf_cnt = i;
  }

  if (!Quicksort(inbuf,inbuf_cnt))
  {
    fprintf(stderr,
    "sortppbuf: FATAL - Unable to quicksort the ppbuf!\n");
    return(0);
  }

  return(1);
}
```

Since ppbuf_utils.c is growing into a library, here is a header file for it:

```
/* ppbuf_utils.h */

#ifndef _PPBUF_UTILS
#define _PPBUF_UTILS

extern char **file2ppbuf(char *filename);
extern int count_lines(char **inbuf);
extern void strip_trailing_whitespace(char **inbuf);
extern void free_ppbuf(char **inbuf, int count);
extern char **expandppbuf(char **inbuf, int numlines);
extern int dumpppbuf(char **ppbuf, char *filename, int
numlines,
int addnewline);
extern char **dupnlines(char **buf, int from, int
numlines);
extern char **dupppbuf(char **ppbuf, int count);
extern int appendppbuf(char **appendee, int
appendee_cnt,
char **appender,int appender_cnt);
extern int sortppbuf(char **inbuf, int inbuf_cnt);

#endif
```

Here is a program that will sort a text file:

```
/* qsort.c */
#include <stdio.h>
#include <string.h>
#include <stdlib.h>
```

```c
#include <ctype.h>
#include "ppbuf_utils.h"

#include <console.h>

int main(int argc,char *argv[])
{
char *source=NULL;
char **sbuf=NULL;

char newname[80];
int i;

argc = ccommand(&argv);

if (argc<3)
{
   fprintf(stderr,"USAGE: qsort -f source file\n");
   exit(1);
}
else
{
   for (i = 1; i < argc; i+=2)
  {
      if (argv[i][0] != '-')
      {
      fprintf(stderr,
      "qsort: FATAL - command qualifier must start with a '-'!\n");
      exit(1);
      }

      switch (argv[i][1]) {
      case 'f':
      source = argv[i+1];
      break;
      default:
      fprintf(stderr,
      "qsort: FATAL - command line format incorrect! Retry.\n");
      exit(1);
         }
  }
}
 if ( (sbuf = file2ppbuf(source)) == NULL)
 {
     fprintf(stderr,
     "qsort: FATAL - unable to buffer %s!\n",source);
```

```
  exit(0);
}

 if (!sortppbuf(sbuf,0))
{
  fprintf(stderr,"qsort: FATAL - unable to merge sort
  the file!\n");
  exit(0);
}

 strcpy(newname,source);
 strcat(newname,"_sorted");
 if (!dumpppbuf(sbuf,newname,0,0))
{
   fprintf(stderr,"qsort: FATAL - unable to dump the
   buffer to disk!\n");
   exit(0);
}
 printf("qsort: SUCCESS!\n");
}
```

Here is the data the program was run on (sortme.dat):

```
zebra
yankee
michael
panda
bear
bottle
junk
nickel
bumble
apple
cobweb
cradle
diaper
dog
eagle
xylophone
verily
warm
union
tiger
snake
rooster
quick
```

```
papa
octopus
noodle
monkey
laugh
kite
juliet
indian
howdy
george
franklin
easy
difficult
camera
bottle
aging
```

Here is the file the program produced (sortme.dat_sorted):

```
aging
apple
bear
bottle
bottle
bumble
camera
cobweb
cradle
diaper
difficult
dog
eagle
easy
franklin
george
howdy
indian
juliet
junk
kite
laugh
michael
monkey
nickel
noodle
octopus
```

```
panda
papa
quick
rooster
snake
tiger
union
verily
warm
xylophone
yankee
zebra
```

Notes on sortppbuf():

1. Before we discuss the details of the quicksort algorithm and how we modified the algorithm to work on ppbufs while using the string-stack, you need to understand the basic functioning of the algorithm. The quick sort is "quick" because it moves a key more than one space like the bubble sort. To perform these large key moves, the quicksort takes a divide and conquer approach. It defines the problem in terms of smaller instances of the same problem and then recursively solves the smaller instances. Here is how quicksort defines the problem in terms of a smaller problem: "Given a list of keys to sort, choose a key X and divide the list into two smaller lists, one of all keys smaller than X and the other of keys larger than X. Sort each new list with the same strategy until the entire list is sorted."

   In our version, instead of using recursion, we are pushing the indexes of the sublists onto a stack, and when all the indexes are popped off, the list is sorted. If we used a numeric stack instead of a string stack, this would be faster than a recursive quicksort. Since I wanted my stack to be able to store numbers and strings, I forfeited my speed gains for flexibility.

2. The function swap() is swapping two character strings, which is why character pointer pointers are passed in. It should be clear that the pointer pointer holds the address of the character pointer we want to modify, and the only way to modify the character pointer is by using its address (which is a char pointer pointer on the application stack).

3. The split() function divides the input list into two lists and returns the split point. Notice the call to swap copies the addresses of the char pointers to the stack. What would have happened if I said &buf[splitPoint]? Would the swap still work? The answer is yes

because [] has a higher precedence than &; however, in general it is easier and better coding practice to make your intentions very clear by using parentheses. By using parentheses you don't have to worry about the precedence rules and a software maintainer will appreciate you making the program clear so he doesn't have to dig out his textbooks to look up the operator precedence.

4. In quicksort(), the numerous sprintf calls are necessary because the string-stack only stores character strings. This makes it necessary to convert back and forth between strings and integers. It is left as an exercise for you to create functions that easily push and pop integers, floats, and doubles to and from the string-stack.

    The sort uses the stack to store the indexes of the upper half of the list that it just split. It then works on the lower half, splits it, and stores the upper half of that list—this continues until last == first. Then the algorithm pops a set of indexes off the stack and starts splitting again. The algorithm ends when it has split all the sublists that it pushed on the stack.

5. The function sortppbuf is straightforward.

6. The program qsort.c accepts a file name from the command line, reads the file into a ppbuf, sorts the ppbuf, and dumps the sorted ppbuf to a file.

    Here is one last very useful ppbuf utility:

```
#define MINTOKS 4

/*    **************************************************
   FUNCTION NAME: toks_from_str
   PURPOSE: break a single text line into a ppbuf. You
      passed in the delimiters used to separate the
      string into tokens.
   INPUT: line - the string to be "tokenized."
           delimiters - a string which is the delimiters
               used to extract a token from the string.
               This delimiter string is passed to the
               standard function strtok().
           count - a pointer to an integer which holds
               the address of an integer from the calling
               routine. This will hold the number of
               tokens in the ppbuf returned.
   OUTPUT: a character pointer pointer of the allocated
      token array.
   NOTE: this function MALLOCs memory.
   AUTHOR: MCD
**************************************************    */
```

```c
char **toks_from_str(char *line, char *delimiters,
int *count)
{

  char *temp;
  char *out_temp;
  char **outbuf;

  int numtoks = MINTOKS, cnt = 0;

  if (!line || !delimiters)
  {
    fprintf(stderr,
    "toks_from_str: input arguments cannot be NULL!\n");
    *count = 0;
    return(NULL);
  }

  /* malloc space for ppbuf */
  outbuf = (char **) malloc(sizeof(char *) * (MINTOKS +
  1));
  if (!outbuf)
  {
    fprintf(stderr,
    "toks_from_str: FATAL - malloc failed!\n");
    *count = 0;
    return(NULL);
  }

  temp = strdup(line);
  outbuf[cnt] = strdup(strtok(temp,delimiters));
  cnt++;

  while ( (out_temp = strtok(NULL,delimiters)) != NULL)
  {
    outbuf[cnt] = strdup(out_temp);
    cnt++;
    if (cnt >= numtoks)
    {
      outbuf = (char **) realloc(outbuf,sizeof(char *)
      * (numtoks + MINTOKS + 1));
      if (!outbuf)
      {
        fprintf(stderr,
        "toks_from_str: FATAL - realloc failed!\n");
        *count = 0;
        return(NULL);
```

```
        }
        numtoks += MINTOKS;
      } /* if we need to realloc */
    } /* while strtok does not return NULL */

    *count = cnt;
    outbuf[cnt] = NULL;
    if (temp) free(temp); temp = NULL;
    return(outbuf);
}
```

The above routine is very useful for rapidly creating a text parser on just about any formatted text file. The procedure you would use is to pull the text file into a ppbuf, then feed each line of the ppbuf into toks_from_str, which will let you access the individual tokens in your text file. Once you complete processing (by possibly creating other ppbufs with expandppbuf), you can dump any ppbufs you create to a file using dumpppbuf(). I have used the above model many times for a fast parsing solution! I hope you get as much use out of the routines as I have.

15.3.   PPBLOCK_UTILS

Another new twist on the ppbuf concept is to embed the ppbuf within a structure to allow you more easily to keep track of the memory management. The new structure is declared in ppblock.h and functions to manipulate the structure are in ppblock_utils.c.

Here is ppblock.h:

```
/* ppblock.h */

#define BLOCKSIZE 100

typedef struct ppblock ppblock;
typedef ppblock *ppblockp;
struct ppblock {
  char *name;
  char **ppbuf;
  int allocated;
  int used;
};
```

Here are the ppblock_utils:

```
/* ppblock_utils.c */
#include <stdio.h>
```

```c
#include <stdlib.h>
#include <ctype.h>
#include <string.h>
#include "ppblock.h"
char *strdup();

/*   **************************************************
FUNCTION NAME: create_block
PURPOSE: allocates space and initializes a ppblock
structure.
INPUT: block_name - a character string which is the
name of the structure. This is
       not necessary but my be helpful when dealing with
many ppblock structures.
OUTPUT: a pointer to the allocated ppblock structure.
AUTHOR: MCD
****************************************************   */
ppblockp create_block(char *block_name)
{
  ppblockp outblock;

  /* malloc space for the block */
  outblock = (ppblockp) malloc(sizeof(ppblock));
  if (!outblock)
  {
    fprintf(stderr,
    "create_block: FATAL - malloc failed!\n");
    return(NULL);
  }

  if (!block_name)
    outblock->name = NULL;
  else
    outblock->name = strdup(block_name);

  /* malloc BLOCKSIZE+1 lines for ppbuf */
  outblock->ppbuf = (char **) malloc(sizeof(char *) *
  (BLOCKSIZE));
  if (!outblock->ppbuf)
  {
    fprintf(stderr,
    "create_block: FATAL - malloc failed!\n");
    return(NULL);
  }

  outblock->allocated = BLOCKSIZE;
  outblock->used = 0;
```

```c
    return(outblock);
}

/*  **************************************************
   FUNCTION NAME: add2block
   PURPOSE: adds a string to a ppblock, reallocing when
      necessary.
   INPUT:  inblock - a pointer to the ppblock structure
                       to add to.
           string - the string to add to the ppblock.
   OUTPUT: an integer which is an error status. 1 on
      success, else 0.
   AUTHOR: MCD
************************************************** */

int add2block(ppblockp inblock, char *string)
{
   char **temp=NULL;
   if (!string || !inblock)
   {
      fprintf(stderr,
      "add2block: FATAL - parameters may not be NULL!\n");
      return(0);
   }

   if (inblock->used >= inblock->allocated)
   {
      temp = realloc(inblock->ppbuf,
                  sizeof(char *) * (inblock->allocated +
                  BLOCKSIZE));
      if (!temp)
      {
         fprintf(stderr,"add2block: FATAL - unable to add line,
         realloc failed!\n");
         return(0);
      }

      inblock->ppbuf = temp;
      inblock->allocated += BLOCKSIZE;
   }

   inblock->ppbuf[inblock->used] = strdup(string);
   inblock->used++;
   inblock->ppbuf[inblock->used] = NULL;
   return(1);
}
```

```
/*  **************************************************
   FUNCTION NAME: addbuf2block
   PURPOSE: add a ppbuf to a ppblock structure.
   INPUT: inblock - a pointer to the ppblock to add to.
          ppbuf - the ppbuf to add to the ppblock.
          length - an integer which is the number of
                     lines in the ppbuf. If 0 the ppbuf
                     is assumed to be NULL-terminated.
   OUTPUT: an integer as an error status. 1 on success,
     else 0.
   AUTHOR: MCD
*************************************************** */
int addbuf2block(ppblockp inblock, char **ppbuf, int
length)
{
  char **temp=NULL;
  int i=0,size=0;

  if (!ppbuf || !inblock)
  {
    fprintf(stderr,
    "add2block: FATAL - parameters may not be NULL!\n");
    return(0);
  }

  if (!length)
  {
    for (i=0; ppbuf[i]; i++)
      ;
    length = i;
  }
  if (length>BLOCKSIZE)
    size=length;
  else
    size=BLOCKSIZE;

  if ( (inblock->used+length) >= inblock->allocated)
  {
    temp = realloc(inblock->ppbuf,
        sizeof(char *) * (inblock->allocated + size));
    if (!temp)
    {
      fprintf(stderr,"add2block: FATAL - unable to add line,
      realloc failed!\n");
      return(0);
    }
```

```
    inblock->ppbuf = temp;
    inblock->allocated += size;
  }

  for (i=0; ppbuf[i]; i++)
  {
    inblock->ppbuf[inblock->used] = strdup(ppbuf[i]);
    inblock->used++;
  }

  inblock->ppbuf[inblock->used] = NULL;
  return(1);
}
```

Points to note about ppblock_utils.c:

1. The ppblock structure is designed to allow a programmer to "grow" a ppbuf easily by keeping track of the sizes (used and allocated) inside a structure. The used and allocated sizes are needed when trying to determine if reallocation is necessary.
2. The create_block() function initializes and returns a ppblock structure. It is a good example of initializing a structure for subsequent use.
3. The add2block() routine reveals the use of the allocated and used size fields in the ppblock structure.

   if (inblock->used >= inblock->allocated)
   {
       /* time to realloc */
   }

   This approach is much more logical than using global variables, especially when creating several ppbufs simultaneously.
4. The addbuf2block() function is identical to add2block with the exception of adding a ppbuf instead of one string.

15.4.   SIMPLE_CLEX AND SOFTWARE VALIDATION

Programmers are faced with the hardest of tasks—to fill the enormous deficit of software needed to fill the demand for quicker and more robust information processing, yet at the same time make these systems reliable. We face this challenge with an ever-steeper learning curve as new machines and new operating systems are introduced every month. We can't just say, "It's impossible", because more and more businesses and people are depending on computers. We can't have software-controlled radiation machines killing people because of a bug in the code! One solution to this problem is to build software tools to validate the products before we ship them. Naturally, your deadlines may have to be pushed back to write the validation tools, but those tools must be seen as a necessary part of the software building process!

As discussed in Chapter 14, here is a C lexical analyzer to break down C source files into tokens. The uses for this tool are only bound by your imagination. If you improve upon the tool, please send me a copy.

```
/* simple_clex.h */

#ifndef _SIMPLEC
#define _SIMPLEC

#define TOKSIZE 20
#define COMMENT_SIZE 80
#define ALPHA 1
#define DIGIT 2
#define PUNCT 3
#define SPACE 4

/* TOKEN TYPES */
#define KEY_WORD_OFFSET 0
#define DATA_TYPE_OFFSET 100
#define TYPE_MODIFIER_OFFSET 200
#define COMPILER_DIRECTIVE_OFFSET 300
#define KW_BREAK 1
#define KW_ELSE 2
#define KW_SWITCH 3
#define KW_CASE 4
#define KW_TYPEDEF 5
#define KW_RETURN 6
#define KW_CONTINUE 7
#define KW_FOR 8
#define KW_DEFAULT 9
#define KW_GOTO 10
#define KW_SIZEOF 11
#define KW_DO 12
#define KW_IF 13
#define KW_WHILE 14

#define DT_CHAR 101
#define DT_INT 102
#define DT_FLOAT 103
#define DT_DOUBLE 104
#define DT_VOID 105
#define DT_STRUCT 106
```

```
#define DT_UNION 107
#define DT_ENUM 108
#define DT_FILE 109

#define TM_SIGNED 201
#define TM_UNSIGNED 202
#define TM_SHORT 203
#define TM_LONG 204
#define TM_EXTERN 205
#define TM_AUTO 206
#define TM_REGISTER 207
#define TM_CONST 208
#define TM_VOLATILE 209
#define TM_STATIC 210

#define CD_DEFINE 301
#define CD_ERROR 302
#define CD_INCLUDE 303
#define CD_IF 304
#define CD_IFDEF 305
#define CD_IFNDEF 306
#define CD_ELSE 307
#define CD_ELIF 308
#define CD_ENDIF 309

#define COMMENT 1000
#define QUOTE 1001
#define FUNCTION 1002
#define END_BLOCK 1003
#define BEGIN_BLOCK 1004
#define VARIABLE 1005
#define STATEMENT_END 1006
#define POINTER_VARIABLE 1007
#define DATA 1008
#define ELLIPSE 1009
#define ARRAY 1010
#define INCLUDE_FILE 1011
#define DEFINED_WORD 1012
#define FUNCTION_PTR 1013
#define OPEN_PARENTHESES 1014
#define CLOSE_PARENTHESES 1015
#define ARRAY_DIM_VARIABLE 1016
#define POINTER_ARRAY_VARIABLE 1017
#define COMMA 1018
#define EQUAL_SIGN 1019
#define PLUS_SIGN 1020
```

```
#define MINUS_SIGN 1021
#define QUESTION_MARK 1022
#define MODULUS_OPERATOR 1023
#define LESS_THAN 1024
#define GREATER_THAN 1025
#define NEGATION_OPERATOR 1026
#define OR_OPERATOR 1027
#define AMPERSAND 1028
#define DEF_SUBSTITUTION 1029

static char *keywords =
"break|else|switch|case|typedef|return|continue|for
|default|goto|sizeof|do|if|while|";

static short int kw_length[14] =
{
  5,4,6,4,7,6,8,3,7,4,6,2,2,5,
};

static char *data_types =
"char|int|float|double|void|struct|union|enum|FILE|";

static short int dt_length[9] =
{
  4,3,5,6,4,6,5,4,4,
};

static char *type_modifiers =
"signed|unsigned|short|long|extern|auto|register|const
|volatile|static|";

static short int tm_length[10] =
{
  6,8,5,4,6,4,8,5,8,6,
};

static char *compiler_directives =
"define|error|include|if|ifdef|ifndef|else|elif
|endif|";

static short int cd_length[9] =
{
  6,5,7,2,5,6,4,4,5,
};

#endif
```

```
/* Simple_clex.c
   This will be a simple C Lexical analyzer. The method
   this procedure will use is "gobble, flag (type) and
   analyze."
   The data this procedure will recognize is:
   1)   alphanumeric -
        variables
        data
        functions
        keywords (looping, conditional, data storage,
          math, I/O)
        data types
        compiler directives
   2)   punctuation -
        parentheses
        braces
        colon
        semi-colon
        mathematical operators
        relational operators
        bitwise operators
        structure operators
        brackets
        period
        double quotes
        single quotes
        pound sign
        comma
        comments
   3) white space - ignore */

#include <stdio.h>
#include <stdlib.h>
#include <string.h>
#include <ctype.h>
#include "simple_clex.h"
#include "memory.h"

/* #define DEBUGLEX */
/* #define DEBUG_KW_IDX */

/*   **************************************************
   FUNCTION NAME: calculate_index
   PURPOSE: determine whether the input token is part of
     a list of keywords, if so determine its index in
     the list.
```

```
    INPUT:    in_token - a character string which is the
                    token to search for.
              inbuf - a string which holds the delimited
                    list of words (see keywords, data
                    types and type modifiers in
                    simple_clex.h).
              charcnt_array - an array of word lengths used
                    to determine the position of the word
                    in the list.
              index_offset - since the function can be used
                    with several lists of words, an index
                    offset separates the groups.
    OUTPUT: an integer which is the token NUMBER of the
        input token as in simple_clex.h
    AUTHOR: MCD
************************************************** */
int calculate_index(char *in_token, char *inbuf, char
                    *inptr, short int *charcnt_array,
                    int index_offset)
{
    int kw_tot=0, i=0;
    int idx=0, out_type=0;
    short int keyword_length=0;
    short int token_length=0;

#ifdef DEBUG_KW_IDX
    printf("As pointers, inbuf = %p,
    inptr = %p\n",inbuf,inptr);
    printf("As integers, inbuf = %d,
    inptr = %d\n",inbuf, inptr);
#endif
    /* calculate the index of cptr into the keyword
    string. */
    idx = (int) abs( (int) (inbuf - inptr) );

#ifdef DEBUG_KW_IDX
    printf("idx is %d\n",idx);
#endif

    for (i=0; kw_tot <= idx; i++)
        kw_tot += (charcnt_array[i] + 1);

    /* check if this token is actually the keyword or
        just a "piece" of one. */
    token_length = strlen(in_token);
    keyword_length = charcnt_array[i-1];
```

```
    if (token_length == keyword_length)
      out_type = i + index_offset;
    else
      out_type = VARIABLE;

    return(out_type);
}


/*    **************************************************
   FUNCTION NAME: add2buffer
   PURPOSE: adds a character to a buffer (a string).
   INPUT: buffer - a pointer pointer which holds the
                   address of the character string in
                   the   calling routine.
          Char - the character to add to the buffer.
          bufcnt - an integer pointer which will hold
                   the new size of the buffer.
          buffer_size - an integer which holds the space
                   in the buffer to determine when we
                   need to realloc.
          comment_flag - a flag to determine our realloc
                   size. On the assumption that
                   comments are normally longer than
                   other tokens, we realloc more space
                   for comments.
   OUTPUT: an integer as an error status. 1 on success
      else 0.
   AUTHOR: MCD
**************************************************   */
int add2buffer(char **buffer, char Char, int *bufcnt,
            int *buffer_size, short int comment_flag)
{
   /* This routine will add a character to the token
   buffer.
   If the buffer needs expansion, it will be expanded. */

   if (*bufcnt == *buffer_size)
   {
     /* expand the buffer */
     if (comment_flag)
     {
       *buffer = (char *) realloc(*buffer, *buffer_size
       + COMMENT_SIZE + 1);
       if (!*buffer)
       {
         fprintf(stderr,
         "add2buffer: FATAL - malloc failed!\n");
```

```
        return(0);
      }

      (*buffer_size) += COMMENT_SIZE + 1;
    }
    else
    {
      *buffer = (char *) realloc(*buffer, *buffer_size
      + TOKSIZE + 1);
      if (!*buffer)
      {
        fprintf(stderr,
        "add2buffer: FATAL - malloc failed!\n");
        return(0);
      }

      (*buffer_size) += TOKSIZE + 1;
    }
  } /* end of if need buffer expansion */

  (*buffer)[*bufcnt] = Char;
  (*bufcnt)++;
  (*buffer)[*bufcnt] = '\0';

  return(1);
}

/*   **************************************************
  FUNCTION NAME: flag_order
  PURPOSE: calculate the order of a character type
    inside the current buffer. The primary use for the
    routine is to be able to judge when whitespace
    separates two valid tokens.
  INPUT: type_flag - the type of the character to be
              calculated.
         alpha_flag - an integer which is the last
              index of an alpha character in the buffer.
         digit_flag - an integer which is the last
              index of a digit in the buffer.
         punct_flag - an integer which is the last
              index of a punctuation mark in the buffer.
         space_flag - an integer which is the last
              index af a space in the buffer.
  OUTPUT: an integer which is the index of the current
    type character in the buffer.
  AUTHOR: MCD
  ************************************************** */
```

```c
short int flag_order(short int type_flag, short int
alpha_flag, short int digit_flag, short int punct_flag,
          short int space_flag)
{
  short int out_order=0;
  short int highest=0;

  /* find the highest number flag and set this one
     higher */
  if ( (alpha_flag > highest) && (type_flag != ALPHA) )
    highest = alpha_flag;
  if ( (digit_flag > highest) && (type_flag != DIGIT) )
    highest = digit_flag;
  if ( (punct_flag > highest) && (type_flag != PUNCT) )
    highest = punct_flag;
  if ( (space_flag > highest) && (type_flag != SPACE) )
    highest = space_flag;

  switch (type_flag) {
  case ALPHA:
    if (alpha_flag > highest)
      out_order = alpha_flag;
    else
      out_order = highest + 1;
    break;
  case DIGIT:
    if (digit_flag > highest)
      out_order = digit_flag;
    else
      out_order = highest + 1;
    break;
  case PUNCT:
    if (punct_flag > highest)
      out_order = punct_flag;
    else
      out_order = highest + 1;
    break;
  case SPACE:
    if (space_flag > highest)
      out_order = space_flag;
    else
      out_order = highest + 1;
    break;
  }

  return(out_order);
}
```

```
#define buffer_it(the_type) \
    if (!add2buffer(&out_buf, ch, &cnt, &buf_size, \
    Commentstart)) \
    { \
      fprintf(stderr, \
      "get_c_token: FATAL - add2buffer failed!\n"); \
      return(NULL); \
    } \
    done = 1; \
    out_type = the_type

#define output_buffer \
    done = 1; \
    ungetc(ch,fp); \
    if (Asterisk) \
      out_type = POINTER_VARIABLE; \
    else if ( (Digit) && (!Alpha) ) \
      out_type = DATA; \
    else \
      out_type = VARIABLE

#define buffer1 \
  if (!add2buffer(&out_buf, ch, &cnt, \
  &buf_size,Commentstart)) \
  { \
    fprintf(stderr, \
    "get_c_token: FATAL - add2buffer failed!\n"); \
    return(NULL); \
  }

/*    ************************************************
  FUNCTION NAME: get_c_token
  PURPOSE: extract a valid C language token from a
    file.
  METHOD: gobbles up characters until it can identify a
    token. Uses a large case statement to differentiate
    characters.
  INPUT: fp - the file to read from.
          token_type - an integer pointer which holds
              the address of an integer in the calling
              program. Will be the token type of the
              character string. Token types are listed
              in simple_clex.h.
          last_token - an integer which is the last
              token put out by the function. Needed in
              certain cases where state information is
              necessary to determine the next token.
```

```
   OUTPUT: a character pointer to the extracted token.
   NOTE: this function MALLOCs memory.
   AUTHOR: MCD
*************************************************  */
char *get_c_token(FILE *fp, int *token_type, int
last_token)
{
  char ch, *out_buf=NULL;
  char *cptr=NULL;

  int cnt=0, buf_size=20;
  int out_type = -1;

  /* flags */
  short int characters_buffered=0, done=0, Alpha=0,
  Digit=0;
  short int Punct=0, Space=0;
  short int Singlequote=0, Poundsign=0;
  short int Commentstart=0, Commentend=0;
  short int Includestart=0, Includeend=0;
  short int Definestart = 0, Extendline = 0;
  short int Backslash=0, Asterisk=0, Startquote=0,
  Endquote=0;

  /* counters */
  short int dots=0;

  /* If end of file, fall to end of routine and return
  NULL */
  if (!feof(fp))
  {
    out_buf = (char *) malloc(sizeof(char) * (TOKSIZE +
    1));
    if (!out_buf)
    {
      fprintf(stderr,
      "get_c_token: FATAL - malloc failed!\n");
      return(NULL);
    }
  }

  /* loop, reading characters until end-of-file */
  while ( (!done) && ((ch = getc(fp)) != EOF) )
  {
    if (isalpha(ch))
    {
```

```
/* if not inside a comment or quote or a #defined
substitution */
if ( (!Commentstart) && (!Startquote) &&
     (!Includestart) &&
     (last_token != CD_DEFINE) )
{
  /* to evaluate variable (space) variable we
     need to check the order of the space flag */
  if (characters_buffered)
  {
    /* if the space flagi is greater than one
       than there is space between two variables.
       (probably a typedef) */
    if (Space > 1)
    {
      output_buffer;
    }
    else
    {
      /* letters - store in buffer and set flag. */
      buffer1

      if (!Alpha)
        Alpha = flag_order(ALPHA, Alpha, Digit,
        Punct, Space);

      characters_buffered = 1;
    }
  }
  else
  {
    buffer1

    if (!Alpha)
      Alpha = flag_order(ALPHA, Alpha, Digit,
      Punct, Space);

    characters_buffered = 1;
  }
} /* in comment or quote or def_substitution */
else
{
  buffer1

  characters_buffered = 1;
  if (last_token == CD_DEFINE)
```

```
            Definestart = 1;
      } /* end of if Commentend */
} /* end of isalpha */
else if (isdigit(ch))
{
   /* if not inside a comment or quote or a #defined
   substitution */
   if ( (!Commentstart) && (!Startquote) &&
         (!Includestart) &&
         (last_token != CD_DEFINE) )
   {
     /* to evaluate variable (space) variable we
       need to check the order of the space flag */

     if (characters_buffered)
     {
       /* if the space flagi is greater than one
         than there is space between two variables.
         (probably a typedef) */
       if (Space > 1)
       {
         output_buffer;
       }
       else
       {
         /* digits - store in buffer and set flag. */
         if (!Digit)
           Digit = flag_order(DIGIT, Alpha, Digit,
           Punct, Space);

         buffer1

         Digit = 1;
         characters_buffered = 1;
       }
     }
     else
     {
       /* digits - store in buffer and set flag */
       if (!Digit)
       Digit = flag_order(DIGIT, Alpha, Digit,
       Punct, Space);

       buffer1

       Digit = 1;
       characters_buffered = 1;
```

```
        }
      }
      else
      {
        buffer1

        characters_buffered = 1;
      } /* end of if Commentend */
    }
    else if (ispunct(ch))
    {
      /* if not inside a comment or quote */
      if ( (!Commentstart) && (!Startquote) &&
           (!Includestart) && (!Definestart) )
      {
        /* since everything is evaluated at
           punctuation, do not store the punctuation
           order */
        /* switch on the possible punctuation types */
        switch (ch) {
          case '[':
            if (characters_buffered)
            {
              done = 1;
              if (Asterisk)
              out_type = POINTER_ARRAY_VARIABLE;
            else
              out_type = ARRAY;
            }
          break;
          case ']':
            if (characters_buffered)
            {
              done = 1;
              out_type = ARRAY_DIM_VARIABLE;
            }
          break;
          case '\'':
            if (characters_buffered)
            {
              output_buffer;
            }
            else
            {
              Singlequote = 1;
            }
            break;
```

```
case ')':
  if (characters_buffered)
  {
    done = 1;
    ungetc(ch,fp);
    /* check for keywords, i.e. void all by
       itself */
    if (strlen(out_buf) > 1)
    {
      /* check if data type */
      if ( (cptr = strstr(data_types,
      out_buf) )!= NULL)
      {
        /* a data type, calculate an index */
        out_type = calculate_index(out_buf,
              data_types, cptr, dt_length,
              DATA_TYPE_OFFSET);
      }
      else
      {
        /* not a keyword, some type of
        variable */
        if (Asterisk)
              out_type = POINTER_VARIABLE;
        else if ( (Digit) && (!Alpha) )
              out_type = DATA;
        else
              out_type = VARIABLE;
      }
    }
    else /* out_buf > 1 */
    {
      /* not a keyword, some type of
      variable */
      if (Asterisk)
        out_type = POINTER_VARIABLE;
      else if ( (Digit) && (!Alpha) )
        out_type = DATA;
      else
        out_type = VARIABLE;
    }
  }
  else
  {
    /* add to buffer as CLOSE_PARENTHESES
    token */
    buffer_it(CLOSE_PARENTHESES);
```

```
      }
      break;
    case '/':
      if (characters_buffered)
      {
        output_buffer;
      }
      else
      {
        /* either a divide or comment */
        Backslash = 1;
      }
      break;
    case '+':
      if (characters_buffered)
      {
        output_buffer;
      }
      else
      {
        /* mathematical operator */
        /* add to buffer as PLUS_SIGN token */
        buffer_it(PLUS_SIGN);
      }
      break;
    case '-':
      if (characters_buffered)
      {
        output_buffer;
      }
      else
      {
        /* mathematical operator */
        /* add to buffer as MINUS_SIGN token */
        buffer_it(MINUS_SIGN);
      }
      break;
    case '=':
      if (characters_buffered)
      {
        output_buffer;
      }
      else
      {
        /* assignment operator or relational
        operator (if 2) */
        /* add to buffer as EQUAL_SIGN token */
```

```
                buffer_it(EQUAL_SIGN);
            }
          break;
          case '?':
            if (characters_buffered)
            {
              output_buffer;
            }
            else
            {
              /* conditional operator */
              /* add to buffer as QUESTION_MARK token */
              buffer_it(QUESTION_MARK);
            }
            break;
          case '%':
            if (characters_buffered)
            {
              output_buffer;
            }
            else
            {
              /* MODULUS operator */
              /* add to buffer as MODULUS_OPERATOR
              token */
              buffer_it(MODULUS_OPERATOR);
            }
            break;
          case '*':
            if (characters_buffered)
            {
              output_buffer;
            }
            else
            {
              /* either an operator, a Commentstart or
              a pointer */
              Asterisk = 1;
              if (Backslash)
              {
                Commentstart = 1;
                out_type = COMMENT;
#ifdef DEBUGLEX
                printf("Starting comment.\n");
#endif
              }
```

```
    }
    break;
case '<':
  if (characters_buffered)
  {
    output_buffer;
  }
  else
  {
    /* relational operator or include file */
    if (last_token == CD_INCLUDE)
    {
      Includestart = 1;
      out_type = INCLUDE_FILE;
    }
    else
    {
      /* LESS_THAN token */
      /* add to buffer as LESS_THAN token */
      buffer_it(LESS_THAN);
    } /* if not include file */
  }
  break;
case '>':
  if (characters_buffered)
  {
    output_buffer;
  }
  else
  {
    /* Relational operator */
    /* add to buffer as GREATER_THAN token */
    buffer_it(GREATER_THAN);
  }
  break;
case '!':
  if (characters_buffered)
  {
    output_buffer;
  }
  else
  {
    /* Relational operator */
    /* add to buffer as NEGATION_OPERATOR
    token */
    buffer_it(NEGATION_OPERATOR);
```

```
          }
        break;
  case '|':
    if (characters_buffered)
    {
      output_buffer;
    }
    else
    {
      /* Relational operator */
      /* add to buffer as OR_OPERATOR token */
      buffer_it(OR_OPERATOR);
    }
    break;
  case '&':
    if (characters_buffered)
    {
      output_buffer;
    }
    else
    {
      /* Relational operator or address
      operator */
      /* add to buffer as AMPERSAND token */
      buffer_it(AMPERSAND);
    }
    break;
  case '~':
    if (characters_buffered)
    {
      output_buffer;
    }
    else
    {
      /* bitwise operator */
    }
    break;
  case '^':
    if (characters_buffered)
    {
      output_buffer;
    }
    else
    {
      /* bitwise operator */
    }
```

```
              break;
          case '\"':
            if (characters_buffered)
            {
              output_buffer;
            }
            else
            {
              if (!Singlequote)
              {
#ifdef DEBUGLEX
                printf("Starting quote.\n");
#endif
                /* Startquote */
                Startquote = 1;
                out_type = QUOTE;
              }
            }
            break;
          case ',':
            if (characters_buffered)
            {
              output_buffer;
            } /* else pass out the comma */
            else
            {
              /* add to buffer as COMMA token */
              buffer_it(COMMA);
            }
            break;
          case '(':
            if (characters_buffered)
            {
              done = 1;
              ungetc(ch,fp);
              if (strlen(out_buf) > 1)
              {
                /* check if keyword or function or
                function ptr */
                if ( (cptr = strstr(keywords,out_buf))
                == NULL)
                {
                /* not a keyword, must be a function */
                  out_type = FUNCTION;
                }
                else
```

```
            {
            /* determine which keyword */
            out_type = calculate_index(out_buf,
            keywords, cptr, kw_length,
            KEY_WORD_OFFSET);
            }
        } /* out_buf > 1 character */
    }
    else
    {
      /* add to buffer as OPEN_PARENTHESES
      token */
      buffer_it(OPEN_PARENTHESES);
    }
    break;
  case ':':
    if (characters_buffered)
    {
      done = 1;
      ungetc(ch,fp);
      if (strlen(out_buf) > 1)
      {
        /* check if keyword or function or
        function ptr */
        if ( (cptr = strstr(keywords,out_buf))
        != NULL)
        {
        /* determine which keyword */
        out_type = calculate_index(out_buf,
        keywords, cptr, kw_length,
        KEY_WORD_OFFSET);
        }
      ] /* out_buf > 1 character */
    } /* else ignore */
    break;
  case ';':
    if (characters_buffered)
    {
      done = 1;
      ungetc(ch,fp);
      if (Asterisk)
        out_type = POINTER_VARIABLE;
      else if ( (Digit) && (!Alpha) )
        out_type = DATA;
      else if ( !(strcmp(out_buf,"return")))
        out_type = KW_RETURN;
```

```
      else
        out_type = VARIABLE;
    }
    else
    {
      /* add to buffer as STATEMENT_END token */
      buffer_it(STATEMENT_END);
    }
    break;
  case '{':
    if (characters_buffered)
    {
      output_buffer;
    }
    else
    {
      /* add to buffer as BEGIN BLOCK token */
      buffer_it(BEGIN_BLOCK);
    }
    break;
  case '}':
    if (characters_buffered)
    {
      output_buffer;
    }
    else
    {
      /* add to buffer as END BLOCK token */
      buffer_it(END_BLOCK);
    }
    break;
  case '#':
    if (characters_buffered)
    {
      output_buffer;
    }
    else
    {
      /* set the flag */
      Poundsign = 1;
    }
    break;
  case '_':
    /* this is a valid variable characer */
    if (!add2buffer(&out_buf, ch, &cnt,
        &buf_size,Commentstart))
```

```
          {
            fprintf(stderr,"get_c_token: FATAL -
              add2buffer       failed!\n");
            return(NULL);
          }
          break;
        case '.':
          /* either a decimal point, ellipse, or dot
          operator */
          dots++;

          buffer1

          if (dots == 3)
            out_type = ELLIPSE;
          break;
        default:
          break;
      } /* end of switch */
    }
    else
    {
      /* buffer all comment and quote characters */
      /* first check for comment, quote or include
        end marker */
      if ( (Commentstart) && (ch == '/') &&
            (out_buf[cnt-1] == '*') )
      {
        Commentstart = 0;
        Commentend = 1;
        done = 1;
      }
      else if ( (Startquote) && (ch == '"') )
      {
        Startquote = 0;
        Endquote = 1;
        done = 1;
      }
      else if ( (Includestart) && (ch == '>') )
      {
        Includestart = 0;
        Includeend = 1;
        done = 1;
      }
      else if ( (Definestart) && (ch == '\\') )
      {
        Extendline = 1;
```

```
      }
      else
      {
        buffer1

        characters_buffered = 1;
      } /* end of if Commendend */
    } /* end of if Commentstart */
  }
  else if (isspace(ch))
  {
    if ( (!Commentstart) && (!Startquote) &&
         (!Includestart) &&
         (!Definestart) )
    {
      Space = flag_order(SPACE,Alpha,Digit,Punct,
          Space);

      if (characters_buffered)
      {
        /* check if a defined word */
        if ( (last_token == CD_IFDEF) || (last_token
          == CD_IFNDEF) )
        {
          done = 1;
          out_type = DEFINED_WORD;
        }
        else
        {
          /* determine type */
          if (strlen(out_buf) > 1)
          {
            /* check if keyword */
            if ( (cptr = strstr(keywords, out_buf))
              != NULL)
            {
              /* a keyword, calculate the index */
              /* determine which keyword */
              out_type = calculate_index(out_buf,
              keywords, cptr, kw_length,
              KEY_WORD_OFFSET);
              done = 1;
            }
            else if ( (cptr = strstr(data_types,
              out_buf)) !=    NULL)
            {
              /* a data type, calculate an index */
```

```
                out_type = calculate_index(out_buf,
                data_types, cptr, dt_length,
                DATA_TYPE_OFFSET);
                done = 1;
              }
            else if ( (cptr = strstr(type_modifiers,
              out_buf)) != NULL)
            {
              /* a type modifier, calculate an index
                 */
              out_type = calculate_index(out_buf,
              type_modifiers, cptr, tm_length,
              TYPE_MODIFIER_OFFSET);
              done = 1;
            }
            else if (Poundsign)
            {
              /* check if a compiler directive */
              if ( (cptr = strstr(compiler_directives,
              out_buf)) != NULL)
              {
              /* a compiler directive, calculate an
              index */
              out_type = calculate_index(out_buf,
              compiler_directives, cptr, cd_length,
              COMPILER_DIRECTIVE_OFFSET);
              done = 1;
              }
            }
          }
        }
      }
    /* else ignore */
    }
  /* else ignore */
}
else if ( (Definestart) && (ch == '\n') )
{
  if (Extendline)
  {
    Extendline = 0;
    /* buffer all comment characters */
    buffer1

    characters_buffered = 1;
  }
  else
  {
```

```
              Definestart = 0;
              done = 1;
              out_type = DEF_SUBSTITUTION;
            }
          }
        else
          {
            /* buffer all comment characters */
            buffer1

            characters_buffered = 1;
          }
      }
    else
      {
        /* error, unknown character */
        fprintf(stderr,"get_c_token: FATAL - unknown
        character, in decimal <%d>\n",ch);
        return(NULL);
      } /* end of if else ladder */
  } /* end of while loop */

  *token_type = out_type;
  if (out_type > 0)
    return(out_buf);
  else
  {
    if (out_buf) free(out_buf); out_buf=NULL;
    return(NULL);
  }
}


/*    **************************************************
  FUNCTION NAME: type_str
  PURPOSE: translate the token_type integer into a
    descriptive string.
  INPUT: type - an integer which is the token type.
  OUTPUT: a character pointer to the allocated string.
  NOTE: this function MALLOCs memory.
  AUTHOR: MCD
  ************************************************** */
char *type_str(int type)
{
  char unknown[80];

  switch (type) {
    case 1:
```

```
      return(strdup("KEYWORD - BREAK"));
      break;
case 2:
      return(strdup("KEYWORD - ELSE"));
      break;
case 3:
      return(strdup("KEYWORD - SWITCH"));
      break;
case 4:
      return(strdup("KEYWORD - CASE"));
      break;
case 5:
      return(strdup("KEYWORD - TYPEDEF"));
      break;
case 6:
      return(strdup("KEYWORD - RETURN"));
      break;
case 7:
      return(strdup("KEYWORD - CONTINUE"));
      break;
case 8:
      return(strdup("KEYWORD - FOR"));
      break;
case 9:
      return(strdup("KEYWORD - DEFAULT"));
      break;
case 10:
      return(strdup("KEYWORD - GOTO"));
      break;
case 11:
      return(strdup("KEYWORD - SIZEOF"));
      break;
case 12:
      return(strdup("KEYWORD - DO"));
      break;
case 13:
      return(strdup("KEYWORD - IF"));
      break;
case 14:
      return(strdup("KEYWORD - WHILE"));
      break;
case 101:
      return(strdup("DATA TYPE - CHAR"));
      break;
case 102:
      return(strdup("DATA TYPE - INT"));
      break;
```

```
case 103:
  return(strdup("DATA TYPE - FLOAT"));
  break;
case 104:
  return(strdup("DATA TYPE - DOUBLE"));
  break;
case 105:
  return(strdup("DATA TYPE - VOID"));
  break;
case 106:
  return(strdup("DATA TYPE - STRUCT"));
  break;
case 107:
  return(strdup("DATA TYPE - UNION"));
  break;
case 108:
  return(strdup("DATA TYPE - ENUM"));
  break;
case 109:
  return(strdup("DATA TYPE - FILE"));
  break;
case 201:
  return(strdup("TYPE MODIFIER - SIGNED"));
  break;
case 202:
  return(strdup("TYPE MODIFIER - UNSIGNED"));
  break;
case 203:
  return(strdup("TYPE MODIFIER - SHORT"));
  break;
case 204:
  return(strdup("TYPE MODIFIER - LONG"));
  break;
case 205:
  return(strdup("TYPE MODIFIER - EXTERN"));
  break;
case 206:
  return(strdup("TYPE MODIFIER - AUTO"));
  break;
case 207:
  return(strdup("TYPE MODIFIER - REGISTER"));
  break;
case 208:
  return(strdup("TYPE MODIFIER - CONST"));
  break;
case 209:
  return(strdup("TYPE MODIFIER - VOLATILE"));
```

```c
      break;
case 210:
  return(strdup("TYPE MODIFIER - STATIC"));
  break;
case 301:
  return(strdup("COMPILER DIRECTIVE - DEFINE"));
  break;
case 302:
  return(strdup("COMPILER DIRECTIVE - ERROR"));
  break;
case 303:
  return(strdup("COMPILER DIRECTIVE - INCLUDE"));
  break;
case 304:
  return(strdup("COMPILER DIRECTIVE - IF"));
  break;
case 305:
  return(strdup("COMPILER DIRECTIVE - IFDEF"));
  break;
case 306:
  return(strdup("COMPILER DIRECTIVE - IFNDEF"));
  break;
case 307:
  return(strdup("COMPILER DIRECTIVE - ELSE"));
  break;
case 308:
  return(strdup("COMPILER DIRECTIVE - ELIF"));
  break;
case 309:
  return(strdup("COMPILER DIRECTIVE - ENDIF"));
  break;
case 1000:
  return(strdup("COMMENT"));
  break;
case 1001:
  return(strdup("QUOTE"));
  break;
case 1002:
  return(strdup("FUNCTION"));
  break;
case 1003:
  return(strdup("END_BLOCK"));
  break;
case 1004:
  return(strdup("BEGIN_BLOCK"));
  break;
case 1005:
```

```
    return(strdup("VARIABLE"));
    break;
case 1006:
  /* STATEMENT END, TOO MANY TO PRINT */
    break;
case 1007:
    return(strdup("POINTER VARIABLE"));
    break;
case 1008:
    return(strdup("DATA"));
    break;
case 1009:
    return(strdup("VARIABLE ARGUMENTS (ELLIPSE)"));
    break;
case 1010:
    return(strdup("ARRAY VARIABLE"));
    break;
case 1011:
    return(strdup("INCLUDE FILE"));
    break;
case 1012:
    return(strdup("DEFINED WORD"));
    break;
case 1013:
    return(strdup("FUNCTION POINTER"));
    break;
case 1014:
    return(strdup("OPEN PARENTHESES"));
    break;
case 1015:
    return(strdup("CLOSE PARENTHESES"));
    break;
case 1016:
    return(strdup("ARRAY DIMENSION ARGUMENT"));
    break;
case 1017:
    return(strdup("POINTER ARRAY VARIABLE"));
    break;
case 1018:
    return(strdup("COMMA"));
    break;
case 1019:
    return(strdup("EQUAL SIGN"));
    break;
default:
    sprintf(unknown,"Unknown type <%d>",type);
    return(strdup(unknown));
```

```
    }
    return(NULL);
}
```

Notes on get_c_token():

1. The three macros, buffer_it, output_buffer, and buffer1, probably reduced the length of the above program by 10 pages. I encourage you to use macros in your programs. Macros are easy to construct as long as you keep in mind the fact that they only perform *text substitution* and not calculation.
2. The method get_c_token uses to identify tokens has three simple parts:
   a. Separate characters into four categories—alpha, digit, punctuation, and space.
   b. Determine whether to buffer the character, and get the next one or evaluate the current contents of the buffer to determine the token type.
   c. Once evaluation is done and we identify the token, the loop terminates and the function returns. Most things get evaluated at punctuation. In general, we evaluate the buffer in two ways:
      (1) Setting flags when we encounter key characters or need to keep track of a "state" (like we are in a comment).
      (2) Matching the buffer against the keyword, data type and type modifier lists in simple_clex.h. A strstr was used because it is quicker than strcmp on a ppbuf.
3. Overall, get_c_token is fairly simple and boils down to a lot of conditions and one long case statement.

CHAPTER QUESTIONS

1. Why is the wrap routine sort_ppbuf() necessary?

CHAPTER EXERCISES

1. Create a function to strip_leading_whitespace() using strip_trailing_ whitespace as a model.
2. The ppblock_utils need more functions to complete their capabilities. Create routines to free, duplicate, and append ppblocks. *HINT*: Incorporate ppbuf_utils into wrap routines. Don't rewrite code that is already there.
3. The get_c_token function does not put out a token for every punctuation mark possible. Add this capability.

Appendix A

A.1. HOW DOES A MEMORY LOCATION STORE A BINARY NUMBER?

Here is a more technical definition of a memory location:

A *memory location* is a microscopic portion of a silicon chip that can store a series of voltages that are interpreted as bits. A *bit* is short for *binary digit*.

JUST WHAT IS A BIT? I hate when computer books assume I know a bit from a buffalo! In order to understand bits, we need to delve into a little bit of electronic theory—but not too much—just enough for you to have a general idea of how the electrical engineers get our computers to store these thingys called bits using voltage.

All electronics is based on controlling and manipulating electricity. Electricity is a form of energy caused by *flowing electrons*. Electrons are able to flow from one atom to another because like charges repel and unlike charges attract. The movement of electrons through a wire is called an *electric current*. The idea of an electric current made me immediately think of river currents. So, the way that I understand electricity is by comparing it to water flowing through a hose. The water represents the electrons and the hose the copper wire. Just as we measure how much water is flowing through the tube in gallons, we measure how much current flows through a wire in *amperes*. You may see ampere abbreviated as "amp." The force pushing the water through the hose is called water pressure, and the force pushing (repelling) and pulling (attracting) electrons through copper wire is called *voltage*. You normally see voltage abbreviated as "volt." Some materials allow electrons to flow easily, while others make it very difficult depending on the structure of the atoms in the material. A material's resistance to electron flow is measured in *ohms*.

We need the above basic understanding of electricity because the ones and zeros of a number stored in memory are not really ones and zeros but high and low voltages. In most implementations, the high voltage represents one, and the low voltage represents zero. Just how high and low voltages are stored brings us to a very brief discussion about semiconductors, transistors, and the flip-flop.

Semiconductors are chemical combinations created to allow electrons to flow under certain conditions. Types of semiconductor material are combined to create a *transistor* that allows electronic engineers to *manipulate the voltages* of electric currents. Finally, by connecting two transistors together in such a way that *whenever one is on, it cuts the other off*, we have a *flip-flop*. A flip-flop can be used as a memory cell because it maintains its state and that state can be read at any time. Furthermore, it maintains its stable state because one and only one transistor can be on. This cell can also "flip-flop" to the other state by sending it a high voltage on one of its input lines. A flip-flop normally has a set line and a reset line. The set line sets the output of the flip-flop to the high voltage or "1" state, and the reset line sets the output to the low voltage or "0" state. From now on, we will condense the whole previous discussion on electrons, voltages, and flip-flops into the understanding that our computer stores binary digits as one of two voltages. Those two distinct voltages are then read as either a 1 or a 0.

The binary digit can only be either a zero or a one. It is amazing to me that all of modern technology breaks down into ones and zeroes. The trick comes in interpreting ones and zeroes in the right way. In order to be able to interpret these ones and zeros you have to understand the binary number system.

A.2.   THE BINARY NUMBER SYSTEM

Before we talk about a foreign number system like the binary number system, let's talk about a number system that you are familiar with: the decimal system. The decimal system is a base 10 numbering system. Numbering systems were devised so as not to have a unique symbol for every object. For example, let's pretend we are cavemen and don't have a decimal numbering system. A caveman named Org wants to sell Borg all his pet dinosaurs. Borg says, "How many do you have?"

Org draws him a picture:

Figure A.1.   A number system example.

Borg says, "That is great, but I will only buy your dinosaurs if we can think of a shorthand way of drawing how many there are. Let's make 9 symbols to stand for 9 dinosaurs, and we should add a symbol to stand for no dinosaurs. If we have more than 9 dinosaurs, we will change the meaning of our symbol to stand for a group of 10 dinosaurs. That will let us use the same symbols over and over. If we have more than 99 we will raise our symbol to mean a group of 10 10-groups of dinosaurs." So, with this example, we can see that *number systems save us from writer's cramp* by only having a fixed number of digits and still allow us to represent large numbers of objects by changing the meaning of digits based on their position. Let's look at Org's dinosaurs using the decimal number system: 18 in base 10.

Base 10 means that there are 10 digits (0 through 9) and that we will group things in tens. Looking at the number this way, we have

1	**group of 10 dinosaurs**
+ 8	**dinosaurs**
18	**dinosaurs**

Or as we wrote in elementary school:

hundreds tens ones
          1   8

Mathematicians talk about groupings of objects in terms of powers. So they write numbers in this format:

$$1 \times 10^1 = 10$$
$$8 \times 10^0 = + 8$$
$$\overline{ 18}$$

A larger number follows the same pattern:

1024 in base 10 is

$$1 \times 10^3 + 0 \times 10^2 + 2 \times 10^1 + 4 \times 100 = 1024$$

So, the two key concepts in numbering systems are

a. The base tells us how many digits (symbols) are in our numbering system and the size we make our groups.
b. The position of the digit represents how large the group is (the power we raise the base to) and the value of the digit represents how many groups we have.

Now we can transfer our knowledge of decimal number systems (base 10) to binary number systems (base 2).

In a base 2 system we only have 2 digits, 0 and 1.

Our groups are always in multiples of 2.

Org perks up and says, "OH! I can write the number of my dinosaurs in base 2."

10010

That's correct!
Here's the breakdown:

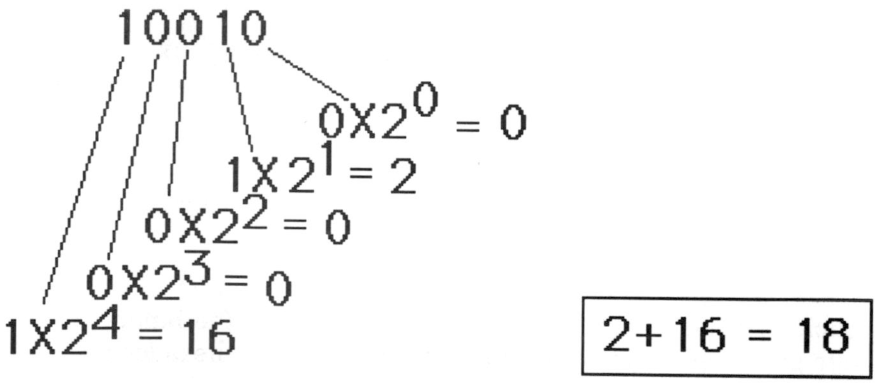

$$10010$$
$$0 \times 2^0 = 0$$
$$1 \times 2^1 = 2$$
$$0 \times 2^2 = 0$$
$$0 \times 2^3 = 0$$
$$1 \times 2^4 = 16$$

$$\boxed{2 + 16 = 18}$$

Figure A.2.   Decimal to binary.

You may have noticed that since the only digits in the base 2 number system are 1 and 0, it is unnecessary even to write out the digit value times the 2 raised to a power.

■ *Rule for converting binary to decimal:* Only add up the powers of 2 where the ones are.

This makes it important to memorize the powers of 2:

1,2,4,8,16,32,64,128,512,1024,2048 ...

Just for fun, let's look at the binary numbers for 0 to 15:

0 = 0000
1 = 0001
2 = 0010
3 = 0011
4 = 0100
5 = 0101
6 = 0110
7 = 0111
8 = 1000
9 = 1001
10 = 1010
11 = 1011
12 = 1100
13 = 1101
14 = 1110
15 = 1111

Another number system that is important in computers is the hexa-decimal system (referred to as "hex"). Hex is a base 16 number system, and it is important because it is a shorthand way of writing binary numbers. It is a shorthand method because it is very easy to convert numbers between hexadecimal and binary, and vice versa.

■ *Rule for converting hex to binary:* Since there are 16 hexadecimal digits (0,1,2,3,4,5,6,7,8,9,A,B,C,D,E,F), each digit can be translated directly into 4 binary digits.

For example, 1A in hexadecimal is 00011010 in binary. To translate numbers from binary to hexadecimal, just break the binary number into groups of 4 and translate each group into one hexadecimal digit. For example, 0101000111100011 is 51E3.

Now that you understand how the computer stores numbers, let's look at how the computer accesses one unique number. Computers use addresses to access specific memory locations.

A.3.   HOW CAN A COMPUTER USE AN ADDRESS TO ACCESS A MEMORY LOCATION?

Computers access a unique memory address by placing the desired memory location's address on the address bus.

A.4.   THE ADDRESS BUS

The number of bits that make up one memory location depends on the number of input pins on the microprocessor and the number of data lines on the computer buses. A computer bus is an electrical conductor (a material that electrons flow through easily, like copper) through which information travels from one place to another. Most microprocessors have a data, address, and control bus. The Intel 8088 and Motorola 6800 microprocessor have 16-bit address buses and 8-bit data buses.

The VAX line of computers from Digital Equipment Corporation have 32-bit addressing and modern microcomputers are moving to 32 bits, just as minicomputers are moving to 64 bits. It is very important to understand the link between the number of data lines on the address bus and the number of memory locations a computer can access. It is simply a question of how many unique memory registers (each assigned one binary number as an address) can be accessed. To calculate the "address space," just know your powers of 2:

$$2^{16} = 65,536 \text{ bytes (64 K)}$$

All 32-bit address buses can access 4 gigabytes (over 4 billion bytes).

Knowing this, we can easily see that an address is just a unique binary number, between 0 and 65,536 (for 16-bit address buses), that is signaled on the address bus to access a unique byte of memory. Remember that the 8088 has an 8-bit data bus—well, that is what a byte is—8 bits. In fact, the 16 bits put on the address bus is called a word. 16 bits = a word. Here is a table of common data sizes and the names associated with those sizes:

Table A.1.   Data sizes.

Bits	Name
8	Byte
16	Word
32	Long Word

APPENDIX QUESTIONS

1. What is voltage and what does it have to do with a memory location's address?
2. How is electricity similar to water?
3. When does a flip-flop change state?

4. How do number systems save us from writer's cramp?
5. Why is the hexadecimal number system useful?
6. Are all addresses the same number of bits long?
7. If a microprocomputer only had an 8-bit address bus, how large could its address space be?
8. Is a half-word equivalent to a byte?

APPENDIX EXERCISES

1. Translate these binary numbers into decimal numbers and hexadecimal numbers:

   a. 0100   b. 0010   c. 1101
   d. 10101010   e. 0010010010 f. 11111111

FURTHER READING

Goldberg, Joel. *Electronic Fundamentals Circuits and Devices*, © 1988, Prentice-Hall, Inc.

Mano, M. Morris. *Computer System Architecture*, © 1982, Prentice-Hall, Inc.

Glossary

abstract data type (ADT)—A specialized representation of data required to perform special operations on the data in an efficient manner. Trees, stacks, and linked lists are examples of abstract data types.

address—A unique location of a memory storage cell. Analogous to a unique number (like a house address) marking a storage container.

address bus—A series of data lines (paths) that connect the cpu with random access memory.

address size—The number of bits that make up an address. This number is dependent on the number of lines in the address bus. See address bus.

address space—The total number of addressable memory locations calculated by 2^n with n being the number of lines on the address bus.

address tag—From the compilers point of view, a symbolic word for an address. Humans see a word, the compiler sees an address. See array name and function name.

aggregate—A collection of data types referred to as a single unit. See structure.

alignment restrictions—Rules that dictate storage requirements for data in a CPU. Determined by the CPU designer usually for performance reasons. See byte addressable.

ampersand (&)—A unary operator that computes the address of its operand.

argument—An expression that appears within the parentheses of a function call. The value of the expression is copied to the application stack for use by the function.

argument passing—The method by which function arguments are copied to the application stack (passed to functions). The two common methods are pass by value and pass by reference.

argument pointer (Dec VAX)—A register that contains the starting address of arguments on the stack. Functions use the argument pointer to access their arguments.

array—An aggregate data type consisting of subscripted members all of the same type.

array index—An offset from the starting address of the array used to retrieve a member of the array. Indexing is accomplished by pointer arithmetic and dereferencing.

array name—An address tag for the start of an array in memory.

asterisk (*)—As a unary operator, used to dereference its operand. See dereference.

background processing—Computer programs that run without interaction with the user. Referred to as daemons in UNIX. See *foreground processing*.

base pointer (BP) (Intel 80 × 86)—A register that contains the starting address of arguments on the stack. Functions use the base pointer to access their arguments.

binary digit (bit)—A number that can only have a value of 0 or 1. Stored in computer random access memory through flip-flops. See flip-flop.

binary search—A technique for rapidly searching a sorted list. The technique continually splits the list in half until it narrows on the solution. The performance of a binary search is $\log_2 n$ for n elements.

bubble sort—The simplest sorting routine whose name describes how the sort is performed. This sort makes n–1 passes through the list of n elements with each pass exchanging the ith element for the next element if the next element (i+1) is less than the ith element. In this manner, the elements with the lowest keys are eventually "bubbled" up to the top. The performance of the bubble sort is on the order of n^2.

byte—8 bits, also the size of a character.

byte-addressable—The ability for a CPU to address each byte in a machine in contrast to machines that have stricter addressing requirements like even bytes or longword boundaries.

cast operator (type)—An operator that forces the conversion of an evaluated expression to a given type. Always used with malloc to convert the void pointer to a pointer of the correct type.

command line—The ability of the main function of a C program to receive a line of text from the operating system upon execution. The text line is broken into tokens and accessed via an array of strings. See token and pointer pointer.

dangling pointer—A pointer trap characterized by a pointer that no longer points to its intended target. This bug can be difficult to track down.

declaration—A statement that gives the data type and storage of a variable.

dereferencing—An operation on a pointer that uses the lvalue of the pointer (which is an address) and extracts the rvalue stored at that address based on the pointer type.

descriptor (DEC VMS)—A structure used to store a string. The structure consists of the starting address and length of the string. This method does not require a NULL terminator like C strings.

expression—One or more operands and operators that can be evaluated to produce a value.

flip-flop—A microscopic electronic device composed of two transistors that has the ability to store a binary digit. See bit.

foreground processing—A program executing interactively with the user or visible to the user.

free list—A linked list of available memory maintained by C's dynamic memory management functions malloc() and free().

function—The primary module from which C programs are constructed. The function definition consists of a return-type, function name, and parameter list.

function call—The invocation of a function. Execution of the current function is suspended, and both the return address and function arguments are pushed on the stack. Execution then jumps to the starting address of the function.

function name—A symbolic word for the address of the starting point of the function. See *address tag* and *function pointer*.

function pointer—A variable that holds the address of a function.

global space—An area of random access memory set aside for global variables prior to program execution.

heap—An area of random access memory set aside for dynamic allocation during program execution. In contrast with global space.

indexing—A high-level operation that allows access of any element in an array through the use of subscripts. At the compiler level, the operation is performed using pointer arithmetic.

indirection—Using the rvalue of a pointer as an address, going to that address, and returning scalar bytes of data.

indirection operator (*)—See *dereference*.

linked list—An abstract data type that allows any number of structures to be created and connected dynamically. A flexible dynamic storage method in contrast to a fixed size array of structures.

lvalue—The address of a variable.

members—The individual elements of a structure that can be accessed separately through the dot or operator. See aggregate and structure.

memory leak—A pointer trap characterized by forgetting to free allocated memory. The analogy comes from thinking of a function as a container. A function that "loses" memory is "leaky."

NULL character—An ASCII NUL (\0).

parameter—A variable that is local to a function whose storage resides on the stack (in most implementations).

pass by reference—Copying the lvalue (address) of the function arguments to the stack.

pass by value—Copying the rvalue (contents) of the function arguments to the stack.

pointer—A memory location that holds an address. In our container analogy, a container that stores the unique number of another container.

pointer pointer—A pointer that holds the address of another pointer.

pointer pointer buffer (ppbuf)—A NULL-terminated dynamic buffer of strings.

portability—The ability to compile a C source file on several different computer platforms without modification.

rvalue—The value stored at a memory location or, in our container analogy, the contents of the container.

scalar— 1. The size in bytes of the object pointed to.

2. The "scaling factor" for pointer arithmetic.

scope—The section of a program where a name has meaning.

sizeof—A compile time operator that computes the size of a data type or collection of data types (structure) and returns size_t bytes. The sizeof operator is often used with malloc and increases the portability of C code.

stack—An abstract data type that stored objects in a last in-first out (LIFO) fashion.

stack variable—A local variable in a function whose storage is on the application stack.

string—A NULL-terminated character array.

structure—A high-level concept to allow aggregation of different data types under one name. Identical to records in Pascal.

system resource—A limited resource like random access memory that needs to be shared among several requestors and therefore managed.

system services—Operating system functions that provide C programs access to system resources.

tokens—A meaningful chunk of data extracted from a text stream. For example, if the text stream is a C program, the token is an element of the C language like a reserved word or data type.

variable—An identifier used as the name of a memory location whose rvalue may change anytime during program execution. In contrast to a constant whose value remains fixed for the duration of the program.

Index